MORE THAN LOVE

Amy Branam Armiento has assembled a wonderful diverse collection of essays on Poe that make clear why Poe and his works are still relevant and loved by his modern readers. The stories of personal encounters to Poe make inspiring and fun reading. Kudos to the editor and to the authors.
—Carole Shaffer-Koros, professor emerita of English/History, Kean University

This collection of essays about Poe's legacy and influence by a variety of contemporary American artists and writers offers a vibrant procession of perspectives on one of America's most pervasively influential and perennially misrepresented literary figures. Whether it is in cenotaphs and cemeteries, in architecture or the plastic arts, queer poetics or suspense cinema, these essays trace Poe's spectral presence through many fields of American cultural production. Whether in or out of academia, readers with an abiding interest in Poe's multi-faceted contemporary reception will find much in this collection to fascinate them.
—Sean Moreland, editor of *The Lovecraftian Poe* and *New Directions in Supernatural Horror Literature*

MERCER UNIVERSITY PRESS

Endowed by

TOM WATSON BROWN
and
THE WATSON-BROWN FOUNDATION, INC.

MORE THAN LOVE

The Enduring Fascination with
Edgar Allan Poe

Amy Branam Armiento,

Editor

MERCER UNIVERSITY PRESS
MACON, GEORGIA

MUP/ P700

© 2024 by Mercer University Press
Published by Mercer University Press
1501 Mercer University Drive
Macon, Georgia 31207

28 27 26 25 24   5 4 3 2 1

Books published by Mercer University Press are printed on acid-free paper that meets the requirements of the American National Standard for Information Sciences—Permanence of Paper for Printed Library Materials.

Printed and bound in the United States.

This book is set in Caslon.

Cover/jacket design by Burt&Burt.

ISBN   978-0-88146-946-2 Print
          978-0-88146-947-9 eBook
Cataloging-in-Publication Data is available from the Library of Congress

CONTENTS

LIST OF ILLUSTRATIONS

ACKNOWLEDGMENTS

I thank José Acosta, Enrica Jang, Andy Duncan, Nicole Halmos, Kevin Knott, John Edward Martin, and the many others who assisted me with recruiting contributors. Poe Baltimore's annual Poe Fest International specifically the *Saturday Visiter* Awards contests, were invaluable resources for locating professionals in the arts.

I also want to acknowledge those people who have to hear me talk *ad infinitum* about any project in which I am involved, including John and Cyndi Branam, Frank Armiento, and my students at Frostburg State University. I appreciate how generous you always are with your time, opinions, and suggestions.

I appreciate the support I received from the staff at Mercer University Press. Without Marc Jolley's idea to create this book, it would not exist. Marsha Luttrell was immensely helpful throughout the publication process.

José Acosta, Tim Beasley, Edward Chimera, Mark Dawidziak, Kalin Thomas, Jamison Odone, Stefanie Rocknak, Chris Semtner, Jason Strutz, and Brian Wilson provided the beautiful images.

I want to express my deepest gratitude to the contributors. Thank you for trusting me with your words, stories, and experiences. I cannot overstate how much I appreciated your grace and flexibility each time I requested changes.

Finally, I want to dedicate this collection to my parents who kept a few books on the shelf behind our piano. When I needed a break from practicing scales, I would spin around and peruse the titles. At some point, *Famous Poems Explained*, which included "The Raven" and "Ulalume," migrated from that shelf to the one in my bedroom, thereby igniting my enduring fascination with Edgar Allan Poe.

MORE THAN LOVE

The Enduring Fascination with Edgar Allan Poe

Edgar Allan Poe Walking High Bridge.
Lithograph by Bernard J. Rosenmeyer.

The Miriam and Ira D. Wallach Division of Art, Prints, and Photographs:
Print Collection in the New York Public Library Digital Collections.

INTRODUCTION

Amy Branam Armiento

Encountering an Edgar Allan Poe statue at the poet's imagined alma mater, Nevermore Academy, in the recent Netflix series *Wednesday* (2022) hardly surprises anyone. Using Poe and Poe metonyms—the word "Nevermore," the raven, and a one-eyed black cat (to name just a few)—has become reliable shorthand, at least in the U.S., for establishing a morbid mood or a Gothic setting. The plotlines that feature bizarre, perplexing murder cases in need of solutions such as those in other Netflix productions from 2022, Scott Cooper's *The Pale Blue Eye* (Netflix, 2022) and Mike Flanagan's series *The Fall of the House of Usher* (Netflix, 2023), pay tribute to the master of the macabre and father of the detective genre. The creators of these recent shows allude to Poe's biography and literary output with confidence, predicting that the audiences will notice and appreciate these references. And they do. Online articles purporting "All the Poe References, Explained," identifying "Poe Easter Eggs You Missed," or revealing "Every Reference to Poe" abound.

Yet the Poe phenomenon is not limited to Netflix, film and television, the 2020s, or the U.S.

Indeed, one might dub him "the ubiquitous Mr. Poe," and someone probably has.

That someone is likely a scholar of Poe studies, a field dedicated to the study of Poe's texts and biography. That someone, like me, may also be a member of the Poe Studies Association, an international organization of approximately 200 members devoted to the study of

Poe's life, works, times, and influence. This vibrant following exceeds the membership of other author organizations, including those dedicated to Mark Twain or Ernest Hemingway. Its members include not only scholars but aficionados from all walks of life. One cannot help but wonder about the reasons for such an expansive fan base.

What draws one to Poe? How is Poe relevant to those with such seemingly diverse interests? Why does Poe persist as a pop culture icon? Why do some creatives emulate Poe? How are others inspired by him? What does Poe mean to poetry? To the short story form? To music? To the visual arts? To U.S. history? To people of all ages and backgrounds? Just what *is* it about Poe?

Poe's impact is felt far and wide, transcending time and place, but this collection focuses on specific instances of his influence on people creating and performing in the U.S. over the last few years. While many nations acknowledge Poe's genius without question, his misfit status in the U.S.' literary canon persists to this day. As one of those Poe scholars ensconced in the so-called hallowed halls of academia (though I have yet to enter a fabled ivory tower), I find myself amazed and delighted by the life Poe has outside the classroom. K-12 educators along with those of us in higher education have quite a bit of power to shape how authors are viewed because we are often the ones to introduce them without interference from external forces. This control does not exist in Poe's case.

It is as if a grassroots movement took shape decades ago to champion his cause. Musicians, filmmakers, illustrators, sculptors, painters, comics artists, history interpreters, performers, impersonators, popular biographers, spiritualists, and countless writers of many genres have felt—and still feel—deep connections to his words and life experiences. And they exhibit those ties in their own creations. Despite Poe's tenuous status in the U.S. literary canon for many, many years, U.S. popular culture ensured his survival.

More importantly, U.S. popular culture conferred celebrity status upon him.

Unlike the numerous essay collections written by professors attempting to explain how Poe has influenced U.S. and world literature, other writers and artists, or even other disciplines such as philosophy and science, this volume turns to those very people in the vocations and avocations. This book features the voices of those who have direct knowledge of Poe's significance for contemporary U.S. culture. They work in professions in which Poe himself had been employed (e.g., poet and short story writer) or represent fields known for engaging Poe and his works (e.g., music and film). Too often, they are not invited to participate directly in answering specific practical questions: When did they first learn about Poe? Who introduced him to them? What were the circumstances? Which stories, poems, or other writings by Poe resonate with them? Why do they feel a connection to him? How do they integrate Poe into their own work?

Although Poe and his writings have served as models for many people, others have reacted against him and them. Adaptations offering subtle revisions or even total overhauls of his texts demonstrate how this towering literary figure may not fit neatly into every time, place, and context. For many of us, our relationships with Poe are complicated. On the one hand, we may identify with his struggle to achieve recognition as an artistic genius. On the other hand, we may feel repulsed by his declaration that "the death of a beautiful woman [...] is, unquestionably, the most poetical topic in the world."[1] Similarly, we may admire his pioneering works in detective fiction yet rightfully denounce his gross mischaracterization of African Americans in the caricatured figure of Jupiter in "The Gold-Bug." By the same token, we may thrill at the ominous presence of the powerful raven while flinching at the mutilation of Pluto in "The Black-Cat." Threads of misogyny, racism, and animal cruelty, among other problematic content, have been acknowledged for decades, and multiple Poe scholars have devised numerous arguments to establish, defend, or equivocate about whether Poe's written works represented his own attitudes and beliefs. Whatever the case may be, the content is present.

---

[1] Edgar Allan Poe, "The Philosophy of Composition," in *The Complete Works of Edgar Allan Poe, Vol. XIV: Essays and Miscellanies*, ed. James A. Harrison (New York: T.Y. Crowell, 1902), 201.

Despite the animal cruelty described in "The Black Cat," Poe was fond of cats. Pluto and Edgar, the two resident black cats at the Poe Museum in Richmond, Virginia, remind patrons of this fact.

Courtesy Christopher P. Semtner

The problems one may have with Poe are not limited to his writings. He does not have an unblemished personal reputation. He married his thirteen-year-old cousin, he was embroiled in public scandals with prominent literary women, he accused others and was accused himself of plagiarism, and he was known to engage in fisticuffs on occasion, especially if that occasion involved alcohol. Although Poe scholars are often quick to blame Rufus Griswold for the blight on Poe's reputation, even without Griswold's notorious Ludwig obituary, Poe had—and continues to have—image problems. The contributors in this volume note ways in which they are drawn to Poe, and some elaborate on how they have had to come to terms with the issues surrounding him and his texts. Some of them clicked with him immediately as if they had met a kindred spirit; others were reluctant, or even hostile, about aligning themselves with him.

To admire Poe is not necessarily to accept him without reservations.

The following chapters offer personal essays in which the writers express how their work intersects with Poe. In some cases, such as those who teach English classes, interpret history, or are employed by a Poe site, the connections are overt. In other instances, the relationship is subtler. For example, as some of the contributors note, to write in a certain genre, such as horror or mystery, means one is *a priori* influenced by Poe—whether or not the writer is aware of or admits the affiliation. In my experience, suggesting to writers that a piece they wrote is reminiscent of another writer is shaky territory, and I am grateful to the writers in this volume who had thought about Poe's role in their careers and agreed to write about how they incorporated something they had learned from him—whether it was a plotline, character, stylistic element, or other facet of his work.

To be sure, readers will appreciate the different ways in which future Poe fans are recruited. Activities that appear unrisky, including bingeing programs on streaming services, sitting in a classroom, watching a film, listening to music, visiting a museum, paying respects at a graveyard, going on a field trip, or merely spotting a particularly alluring book cover on a shelf, may result in a lifelong commitment to a man one has never met. If people think that those living in a "Poe city"—Boston, Baltimore, Richmond, Philadelphia, or New York—are more vulnerable to Poe's allure, their assumption is false. Poe has infiltrated rural, urban, and suburban areas across the U.S. If people believe that readers admire Poe due to his skill at penning horror stories, detective tales, and poems, they have glimpsed only a part of the full picture. His irreverent humor, love poetry, lecture circuit appearances, fantastical settings, and relationships to friends, enemies, and family members also attract readers. The Poe testimonies in this volume span from students in middle school to those who are decades older. Although this volume—like any volume—could not hope to offer comprehensive coverage of the countless ways that Poe's legacy continues, it provides a snapshot of the enduring fascination with Edgar Allan Poe.

1

WORKING THE GRAVEYARD SHIFT

Lu Ann Young Marshall

I became a taphophile at an early age. One of my fondest memories is taking Sunday drives with my father and aunt. We would often visit our family members buried at Loudon Park Cemetery in Baltimore, and after paying our respects to them, we would drive through the cemetery looking at the gravestones, statues, and mausoleums. This tradition continues to this day. I do genealogical research with three of my cousins, and visiting cemeteries is a great way to do research, as the offices often contain burial records for people in that cemetery, including the cause of death, names of parents, and other relevant information.

Considering grave visiting was one of my hobbies, my subsequent love for Poe felt preordained. I met Poe in the sixth grade. We were introduced to "The Tell-Tale Heart" and "The Raven," and I was hooked. Not only did I enjoy the texts, but I was fascinated by Edgar Allan Poe himself. Who was this man who could not only frighten but also enchant me?

Poe was on my radar many times since our initial encounter as he was a frequent subject in English class. We truly connected approximately fifteen years later in 1977 when the University of Maryland School of Law took over Westminster Presbyterian Church and Graveyard. Westminster Preservation Trust, a non-profit organization, was formed and charged with the renovation of the site. I worked with Professor Garrett Power, the law school faculty member in charge of overseeing the renovation on behalf of both the School of Law and Westminster Preservation Trust. I would often go with him through the site as we began raising money. The goal was to create not only a meeting space in the deconsecrated church but also to fix up the graveyard which had fallen into disrepair. Many of the gravestones had fallen over or sunk into the ground, and the catacombs beneath the church were boarded up to keep out trespassers.

During this time, one of the law students was giving tours of the site, and I was asked if I would be interested, as she was about to graduate and move on to her legal career. I jumped at the chance to conduct tours. I would be able to combine my love of cemeteries and history as well as my fascination with Poe!

My first tour was held in what was then the abandoned church, complete with the original pews and the choir loft, along with a non-working organ. I had friends who had been members of this congregation, but like many people, they only went to services on holidays—Easter and Christmas always attracted a large crowd of worshippers. It was rather eerie being in the space alone at first, but after I became more comfortable, I came to enjoy sharing stories about the site, and Poe specifically, with the people visiting the graveyard.

In 1982, the restoration of the building and graveyard was complete and became known as Westminster Hall and Burying Ground. Ironically, the only event that cannot be held in Westminster Hall is a religious ceremony—due to most of the funds used to restore the site coming from government grants, there had to be a separation of church and state. Westminster Hall has become a very popular site for weddings and receptions, conferences, holiday parties, and other non-religious events.

Loving history as I do, I did a lot of research on my own, not only about Edgar Allan Poe, but the other inhabitants of the graveyard. I learned the difference between a graveyard and a cemetery: graveyards surround a church while a cemetery is a burial place that is not affiliated with a church, so the deceased person does not have to be a congregant to be buried there.

The Maryland Historical Society also performed extensive research on the site. The founding fathers and mothers of Baltimore are buried in Westminster. People familiar with Baltimore will recognize many of the names in the graveyard having streets named after them, including Stricker, Ramsay, and Calhoun, to name a few. Thomas Poppleton laid out Baltimore city streets in 1822, using the names of patriots and other famous people buried in Westminster as well as other renowned people.

General Sam Smith, who was responsible for the defense of Baltimore in both the Revolutionary War and the War of 1812, is interred in the Westminster graveyard. By rights, he should be the most famous person buried here. He was a United States senator and representative from Maryland as well as a general in the Maryland militia. He was loved by the citizens of Baltimore, most of whom attended his funeral in 1839. At one point in time, Federal Hill was known as Sam Smith Park.

Premature Burials

Despite Smith's impressive service record at the city, state, and national levels, it is safe to say that most of the visitors to Westminster come because of Edgar Allan Poe. I tell people that the only reason Poe is buried in Baltimore is because he died in Baltimore and his family had a plot in the graveyard. During the antebellum period, when a family member died, that person was typically buried within 12–24 hours, and this was not always for religious reasons. Embalming was not accepted by most people until the time of the Civil War when soldiers were often returned home to be buried with their family.

I have always been fascinated by burial practices. Before embalming became an accepted practice, if someone became ill, lapsed into a coma, or did not appear to be breathing, loved ones would place pennies, or similar objects, on the eyes. If they had to leave the room for whatever reason, when they returned and the pennies were moved, they would know the person had blinked and was still alive. Sometimes, though, the person was buried so quickly, especially in the hot summer months when it was impossible to keep the body fresh, that there was not enough time to wait for movement. People were buried 2–3 feet below ground, and the ground would be very soft for a few weeks. If they became conscious, they could bang on the lid of the coffin or scream to get attention. As someone who is mildly claustrophobic, I am not sure how anyone could recover from this traumatic awakening.

Visitors often ask about Poe's inspiration for his horror stories, which is how many people are introduced to Poe and how they became Poe fans. Many of Edgar Allan Poe's stories are concerned with the topic of premature burial, including the story using this very phrase as its title. While some believe this was a product of his active imagination, these stories had a basis in fact. When someone was retrieved from the grave after being buried prematurely, it was often reported in the local newspapers.[1] People were horrified, yet at the same time, they were fascinated. This same dynamic of attraction and repulsion explains our fascination with modern horror stories and movies. Poe's first horror story, "Berenice," was published in the *Southern Literary Messenger* in 1835. As in many Poe stories, it concerns the death of a beautiful woman as well as the themes of resurrection and obsession—in this case an obsession with a beautiful woman's pearly white teeth that leads to the narrator's horrific assault on her. Not only had he extracted his cousin's teeth, but he had also

---

[1] Taphophobia, the fear of live burial, was a featured topic in many newspapers; some poets and fiction writers of Poe's times took up the subject as well. It is unclear whether actual reports, literary representations, or a combination of these factors inspired Poe's tales. For sources on "The Premature Burial," see W. T. Bandy, "A Source for Poe's "The Premature Burial," *American Literature* 19, no. 2 (1947): 167–168 and Byron K. Brown, "John Snart's Thesaurus of Horror, an Indirect Source of Poe's 'The Premature Burial'?," *ANQ* 8, no. 3 (1995): 11–14. For "Berenice," see Roger Forclaz, "A Source for 'Berenice' and a Note on Poe's Reading," *Poe Newsletter* 1, no. 2 (1968): 25–27.

interred her while she was "yet still breathing—still palpitating—*still alive!*"[2]

The Poes in Westminster: John, Jane, Virginia, Maria, David, Elizabeth, Edgar, and William Henry Leonard

Poe wrote "The Masque of the Red Death" about tuberculosis, or consumption as it was known at that time.[3] The three most important women in Poe's life died from consumption—his mother, Elizabeth "Eliza" Arnold Hopkins Poe, who was a well-known actress; his foster mother, Frances "Fanny" Valentine Allan, wife of wealthy tobacco merchant, John Allan; and his wife, Virginia Eliza Clemm Poe.[4] Virginia is one of many Poes interred at Westminster, including Poe's grandparents, David and Elizabeth Cairnes Poe, his great-grandparents John and Jane McBride Poe, his brother William Henry Leonard Poe, and his aunt/mother-in-law Maria Poe Clemm.

During my tours, I point out that Poe found a loving family when he lived in Baltimore with his Poe relatives. While he lived in Richmond with a foster family that was wealthy and where he could have lived a comfortable life, he did not feel the same level of love and acceptance that he received when he moved in with his Poe

---

[2] Edgar Allan Poe, "Berenice," in *The Collected Works of Edgar Allan Poe*, ed. T. O. Mabbott, vol. 2 (Cambridge: Belknap Press of Harvard University Press, 1978), 218.

[3] Many different diseases have been posited for inspiring the Red Death. For arguments equating the fictitious disease to tuberculosis, see Kenneth Silverman, *Edgar A. Poe: Mournful and Never-ending Remembrance* (New York: HarperPerennial, 1991), 180–181; William Bittner, *Poe: A Biography* (Boston: Little Brown, 1962), 177; and, Sarah Yoon, "Color Symbolisms of Diseases: Edgar Allan Poe's 'The Masque of the Red Death,'" *The Explicator* 79, no. 1–2 (2021): 21–24.

[4] Poe's mother, Elizabeth Arnold Hopkins Poe is buried in the Saint John's Episcopal Churchyard in Richmond, Virginia. Poe's foster mother, Frances Keeling Valentine Allan, is buried in Shockoe Hill Cemetery, which is also located in Richmond, Virginia.

family who were struggling to survive. He lived with his grand-mother Elizabeth Cairnes Poe, his older brother Henry, his young cousin Virginia, and his aunt Maria. He was especially close to his aunt and called her Muddy, an affectionate name he used for her.

I recount the circumstances of Poe's marriage to Virginia. While he prepared to begin a job at the *Southern Literary Messenger* in Richmond, he received a letter from Muddy that explained that his cousin Neilson Poe was going to send Virginia off to school. He replied to Muddy, declaring his love for Virginia whom he called "Sissy."[5] Neilson was married to Virginia's half-sister, Josephine Emily Clemm. On occasion Edgar referred to Neilson as his "bitterest enemy" although he never publicly explained that statement.[6] It may simply have been that Neilson did not provide any assistance that one might have expected from a close family member, especially to his poorer relations. Neilson, at one point in his life, wanted to be a writer, but he abandoned his literary hopes near the end of 1839 and began a law career. When Neilson finally decided to assist his relatives, his actions threatened to destroy Poe's newfound family. In response, Edgar married his first cousin, Virginia, when she was only thirteen and he was twenty-seven. When I tell people this situation, they are shocked by the age difference and the young age of the bride. Due to the high infant mortality rate (as high as 66% in the early 1800s), young girls married as young as twelve and thirteen, and their husbands were often older so they could provide for their families.

People are also disturbed by the fact that Edgar and Virginia were first cousins. I remind people that even today it is illegal in only twenty-four states to marry a first cousin, which means twenty-six states have not passed laws against this practice, including Maryland. Marrying a first cousin means that the family money and position

---

[5] Edgar Allan Poe to Maria Clemm, August 29, 1835, in *The Collected Letters of Edgar Allan Poe*, ed. J.W. Ostrom, B.R. Pollin, and J.A. Savoye (Cambridge: Harvard University Press, 2008), 102.

[6] Ibid.

remain in the family. While the Poe family was basically destitute by the time Edgar Allan Poe was born, they were wealthy at one time. His grandfather, General David Poe, Sr., who served his country in the Revolutionary War as Assistant Deputy Quartermaster General of Baltimore, contributed $40,000 of his own money to the war effort, securing supplies for Washington's Army, and he was never reimbursed. This is how the Poe money disappeared. Today's market value of $40,000 would translate to approximately $1.5 million, a rather tidy sum.

After David Poe's death in 1816, the Marquis de Lafayette, who served as a Major-General in the Continental Army under the command of George Washington, came through Baltimore in 1824 to pay his respects to the Poe family. He discovered that David Poe had died, and Lafayette visited his grave in Westminster. Although no evidence of the wording on David Poe's original headstone remains, after Edgar's death, David Poe's monument was updated to read: *Burial place of David Poe, Sr. Patriot and grandfather of Edgar Allan Poe. Born in Londonderry, Ireland. Died in Baltimore October 17, 1816.*

After visiting his old friend's grave, Lafayette met with David's widow, Elizabeth Cairnes Poe, who was barely subsisting. Due to Lafayette's intervention, Elizabeth began receiving a widow's pension, which supported her family. To show her gratitude, Elizabeth organized a group of women to make uniforms for Lafayette's troops. Although there is no marker for Elizabeth in the graveyard, it is suspected that she is buried next to her husband David.

Evidence found in letters and friends' recorded observations indicates that Virginia and Edgar, David and Elizabeth Cairnes Poe's grandchildren, were a happy couple, even though they were very poor. Virginia is acknowledged as Edgar's muse, as he wrote prolifically while they were together. She would often sit by his side while he wrote. Virginia developed consumption sometime in her teens. She is said to have had a beautiful singing voice, and as she was singing around the time she was twenty years old, she burst a blood vessel in her throat and began hemorrhaging from her mouth. She lingered for years, finally dying at the age of twenty-four.

Virginia Poe died in 1847, while living in the Valentine Cottage in Fordham, New York. Because they could not transport her body to Baltimore due to the fear of disease being spread, she was buried in the Valentine Vault in the Dutch Reform Cemetery. Although many scholars are uncertain about the inspiration, I believe that Poe wrote my favorite work, "Annabel Lee," in her memory. She and Poe would remain apart for nearly four decades until they would be reunited in death under one headstone.

Edgar Allan Poe died two years later, in 1849, at the age of forty. He was discovered unconscious outside a tavern in the area now known as Little Italy. The tavern was being used as a polling place, and as he was found on election day, it was first thought that he was a victim of "cooping."[7] Politicians would round up men, mostly sailors, and put them in the warehouses where Harbor Place now stands. They were packed as tightly as chickens in a coop, thus the phrase "cooping." These men were given drugged liquor and then escorted to a polling place to vote. They returned to the warehouses, changed clothing so they were not easily recognized, plied with another drink, and sent out to vote again. When he was found, Poe was in clothing that was not his own—his pants were too short and were tied with rope, his leather boots were missing, his silver-tipped walking stick was missing, and instead of his usual, elegant black hat, he was wearing an old straw hat. He was taken to Washington Medical College where he was attended by Dr. John Joseph Moran, who later noted in a letter to Poe's Aunt Maria that, during a period of consciousness, Poe held "vacant converse with spectral and imaginary objects on the walls. His face was pale and his whole person drenched in perspiration."[8]

On the tour, I am sure to note that a "tavern" was not just a place

---

[7] For more information on the multiple theories regarding Poe's death, see Mark Dawidziak, *A Mystery of Mysteries: The Death and Life of Edgar Allan Poe* (New York: St. Martin's Press, 2023).

[8] George E. Woodberry, *Edgar Allan Poe* (Cambridge: The Riverside Press, 1885), 344.

to drink; it was a hotel that served food as well. Many visitors believe that Poe suffered from alcohol dependency. When he did drink, he would often have to take to his bed for up to a week to recover. It would have been virtually impossible for Poe to achieve anything as intricate as he did or produce as much work if he had been consistently bed-ridden. Poe likely suffered from manic depression, writing during his manic phase and drinking when he was depressed, which as we know, would only make him more depressed. One can only speculate how his life might have been different had John Allan included him in his will.

Often Poe fans ask me about the many theories on the cause of his death. Possible causes of death include alcoholism, rabies, and a severe beating. The severe beating theory alleges that the brothers of Elmira Royster Shelton (his childhood sweetheart) followed Poe to Baltimore to dissuade him from marrying their sister since they were still concerned about his marrying her for money.[9] This theory is that they beat him severely enough to cause his death. Elmira and Edgar had both been widowed, had reconnected, and were planning to marry at the time of his death. She was concerned about his drinking, and he agreed to never drink again, signing a temperance pledge. If he upheld his end of their bargain, the brothers feared that the marriage would take place.

Poe died quietly before sunrise on October 7, 1849. His final words were reported as "Lord help my poor soul."[10] He was buried in the Poe family plot in Westminster, without fanfare, next to his grandfather, David Poe. Eventually, a headstone was purchased by his cousin, Neilson Poe, and as it was awaiting delivery to the graveyard, a train jumped the track at Camden Station, smashing into the marble yard, destroying Poe's marker.[11] He remained in an unmarked

---

[9] For an extended discussion of this theory, see John Evangelist Walsh, *Midnight Dreary: The Mysterious Death of Edgar Allan Poe* (New York: Griffin, 2000).

[10] Woodberry, 345.

[11] See Jeffrey A. Savoye, "Poe's Lost Tombstone," Edgar Allan Poe Society of Baltimore, November 22, 2018. https://www.eapoe.org/balt/poegravs.htm.

grave from October 1849 until April 1875. That same year the city decided to erect a suitable monument on Poe's gravesite so that people could pay their respects. As his fame grew, people would try to leave flowers and say prayers but were unable to find the exact gravesite. This large marble monument was paid for, in part, by schoolchildren collecting "Pennies for Poe." As people still had difficulty finding him, in November of 1875, it was decided to move him and the monument to the front entrance. Virginia returned to Baltimore about ten years after Poe was moved, in 1855, arriving when the graveyard in New York where she was buried was being repurposed; her bones were rescued before they were discarded. Muddy, Poe's aunt and Virginia's mother, joined Poe upon her death in 1871. Sadly, Maria outlived every one of her children.

After Poe and his monument were moved to the entrance to the graveyard, a headstone was purchased to mark his "original" burial site. This was his second gravesite, as he was moved from his unmarked grave to the other side of his grandfather David Poe in April 1875 where he was laid to rest for a mere six months. The headstone, which was erected in the early twentieth century, reads *Original burial place of Edgar Allan Poe from October 9, 1849. until November 17, 1875. Mrs. Maria Clemm, his mother-in-law, lies upon his right and Virginia Poe, his wife, upon his left, under the Monument erected to him in this cemetery.*

Beginning in 1949, the centennial year of Poe's death, a mysterious visitor began coming into the graveyard on Poe's birthday, January 19, leaving behind a half bottle of Martell Cognac and three red roses (one for each of the Poe family members buried under the monument). The Poe Toaster, as he became known, continued his tribute until 1993. At that time, it was reported that the original Poe Toaster may have died and passed the torch to a younger man. The elusive Poe Toaster ended this tradition in 2009. In 2015, there was a competition to find a new anonymous Poe Toaster, sponsored by the Maryland Historical Society and Westminster Preservation Trust.

People are often surprised to discover that Poe was not an only child. He had two siblings, both of whom were involved with writing during their lifetimes, and one who is buried in the graveyard. Poe's older brother, William Henry Leonard Poe, was born in 1807. He was often referred to as "Henry Poe" or "The Pirate," a nickname he acquired for his sailing expeditions. He was sent to live with his paternal grandparents, David and Elizabeth Cairnes Poe, in Baltimore after his mother's death. Henry died in 1831, at the age of twenty-four, allegedly from consumption; however, cholera and alcohol have been mentioned as possible causes of death. He is buried in the Poe family plot, and a small marker was placed on his grave that bore his initials. Sadly, the headstone is no longer visible. Henry and Edgar maintained a casual acquaintance, often through correspondence, and may have even lived together in Baltimore around 1830 when Edgar prepared to enroll in West Point.

Are the Graveyard and Catacombs Haunted?

One of the questions I am most frequently asked is whether ghosts haunt the graveyard or the catacombs? My reply is always "If I saw or heard anything, you would have another tour guide." I have worked with many groups of ghost hunters over the years and have been told on multiple occasions that I have the "gift" to communicate with those who have died. I tell those people that I will never unwrap that gift!

Ghost hunting groups usually travel with a medium. The mediums usually come up with the same story: a man in a military uniform who yells at them to "go away." One Halloween, one of the mediums I had worked with on numerous occasions came in with a television crew and, upon entering the catacombs, remarked, "Oh, I know you don't like me, but I won't be here long." I assured her that I enjoyed working with her. She then told me that it was "the General" she was speaking to and that "he doesn't like me, but he really likes my daughter." The General she spoke of was General John Swan, who is buried with his wife, Elizabeth Trippe Maxwell Swan.

Being a very curious person, after her television interview, I asked her to speak to the General to see how he felt about me. She went over to his grave, had a short conversation with him, and then—with a Geiger-like instrument in her hand—asked him if he liked me. The little needle started jumping, and she looked at me with excitement in her eyes and exclaimed, "You got an 86!" When I reminded her that this roughly translated to a grade of "B," she informed me that this is a very good score in the spirit world. Having nothing to compare this to, I decided to take her at her word.

This same medium told me that, while the people in the catacombs are fond of me and consider me respectful, they know that when I come into the catacombs, I am bringing a group of people with me. According to her, this is what they do not like! Not only do I consider myself respectful, but also I feel protective of those people interred in the graveyard and catacombs.

Another evening, on a regularly scheduled tour, a young man informed me that he lived with ghosts. While I was conducting the tour, he kept brushing the back of his neck and looking over his shoulder. When we were alone, I asked him if there was a spider or some insect on his neck that was causing his discomfort. He insisted that I could see "the man dressed in a military uniform" who kept poking him on his neck and telling him to "go away." He was skittish the entire time we were in the catacombs, looking over his shoulder until he walked out of the graveyard and visibly relaxed.

Although I do not sense the ghosts, I have had many interesting encounters with the living people in the catacombs. I often give tours for weddings and other social events. At one such wedding, on a Friday night, a man looked over my shoulder with a very odd expression on his face, and his wife crossed her arms over her chest. If someone does something I find interesting, I do not ask them in front of the group; rather, I ask them when I can talk to them alone. It turned out that the man saw an older man on the path behind us—he was dressed in a long-sleeved white shirt, gray vest, dark trousers, with his gray hair tied in a low ponytail. His wife felt the presence rather than saw it and told the "spirit" that she came in peace and meant it no harm.

On the following night, I worked another wedding, and the same thing happened—one of the guests looked over my shoulder with a puzzled look on his face, and when I spoke to him alone, he described the same man down to the gray ponytail. While I did not show either group the slide show that contains pictures of the people being discussed, the man that they described sounded very much like General Sam Smith.

There is one area in the catacombs where I do not go when I am by myself— a very small room in the back, with two gravestones— Elizabeth Gunn and her first husband, William Robb. At the time, if a woman in society was widowed, she either went to live with relatives or remarried. Elizabeth chose to remarry and only outlived her first husband, William Robb, by two years, even though he was twenty-nine years her senior. I was with a ghost hunting group, and their medium said to me, "I know why you don't like it in here." Now I did not think I was behaving strangely (although I am, as I mentioned before, mildly claustrophobic), but she said it was because of the "man in the corner." She said that even if I refused to acknowledge his presence I was aware of it, and that is what affects me and what makes me nervous about entering that space.

None of the ghost hunters or mediums who I have worked with have claimed to contact Poe. I find this strange, as how could anyone prove or disprove someone making spiritual contact with Edgar? Hopefully, he has moved on and is at rest.

While these encounters sometimes give me the heebie-jeebies, I will continue giving tours because I enjoy the people that I meet. I have taken several thousand people through the graveyard and catacombs in the approximately forty-five years I have been doing tours. A fairly large percentage of tourists who visit the graveyard are schoolchildren who are studying Poe. Pre-COVID, we saw large numbers of tourists from abroad, including many from Japan and France. People of all ages come to visit Poe to pay their respects and to learn a bit more about his life and death. Whenever I give a tour on a weekend, especially Saturday, the graveyard is full of people looking for Edgar Allan Poe.

Being a tour guide gives me an opportunity to share information about not only Edgar Allan Poe and his family but also the history of the site, including burial practices, which came to include objects, usually jewelry, given to mourners. For these reasons, I will continue to work with ghost hunters, and I will continue refusing to acknowledge or open my "gift"—despite the possibility that I might meet Poe!

2

POE'S MOVING PICTURES

José Alejandro Acosta

How I Stumbled Across Poe

Poe, the starving artist, the pariah, the unrecognized genius, the brave loner toiling in obscurity. He was born poor, rose swiftly among the elite, and then fell precipitously into poverty again. Highly educated and accomplished but struggling with financial ruin and alcohol to the bitter end. A strange kind of hero for a little Hispanic American boy falling behind in school in the 1970s. An anti-hero?

I grew up in an ostensibly beautiful and prosperous family in a quiet suburb of Washington, DC. Mom and Dad were exiles from the island of Cuba. I was the second of five children. A life of writing did not appear to be in the cards for me. Unlike Poe, I was not gifted in letters at an early age.

Mom suspected my struggles in spelling were not entirely due to a lack of effort. She sent me to summer school at Opus Dei (an orthodox Catholic order) to help improve my reading and writing skills. On the first day, we started by reading some fascinating Poe stories. Was it "The Pit and The Pendulum," "The Tell-Tale Heart," or, perhaps, "The Gold-Bug"? Surprisingly, later that summer I won the impromptu spelling bee in my class of summer school misfits. Perhaps a little inspiration from my new kindred spirit, Mr. Poe.

Whenever we read Poe, the textbook offered a dour photo or woodcut image of the poet scowling and a brief but fascinating biography. His public persona was always the preamble to the stories. "Get ready to read the ravings of a lunatic!" it seemed to indicate. Finally: a fiction that was as interesting and irresistible as science. I may have been a slow reader, but I became a voracious one. Puzzling over every word, trying to solve the secret code.

The Sherlock Holmes stories also fascinated me at that early age. It was years later that I learned that Sir Arthur Conan Doyle recognized Poe as the originator of the detective story—before the word "detective" even existed. So Poe's C. Auguste Dupin and William Legrand actually inspired the creation of Sherlock Holmes. While Sherlock was decidedly British, Poe's gentlemen crime solvers were both French. Poe himself put on French airs, seemingly ashamed of his Irish heritage. Doyle, like Poe, exhibited the dualistic themes of rationalism and supernaturalism in his works and life, which drew me to them both.

I took refuge in Poe. His fiction, verse, biography, and philosophical legacy—often indistinguishable categories—he mixed these genres so subtly in his strange stories, essays, and poems.

My resistance to narrative fiction did not last into my teens. Not only had I encountered Poe's stories, but at the age of twelve, I saw *Star Wars* in a 70mm movie house with one of my few friends, also a Hispanic nerd. Game changer. The bold music, groundbreaking visual effects, and mash-up of genres was like an answer to my prayers. And not long after, a cartoon special appeared on television called *The Hobbit* (1977). I immediately sought out the book and devoured it and started building my personal Tolkien book collection. I still cherish it today.

Perhaps the lies of fiction were useful lies after all. Perhaps "the lie that tells the truth" was worth pursuing. This epiphany prompted my sudden transformation from a science nerd to a fantasy & science fiction nerd. And I began high school with this inner change well underway.

I had made up my mind to become a filmmaker. George Lucas

was my role model. He cultivated his image as a reclusive genius whose incomprehensible masterpiece somehow earned him millions. Scorsese and Coppola were on my radar too. And later the Coen Brothers, Spike Lee, and Robert Rodriguez joined my pantheon of film gods. And Hitchcock was the grandfather of them all.

Dad did not approve of a career as an artist of any kind, despite his avid interest in photography and home movies. The arts were appropriate for a hobby, he admonished, but not as a career. Except maybe for girls who married well. He refused to "subsidize mediocrity," and he made it clear that if I declared a major in art or film I was on my own. Out on the street like a young Edgar Poe abandoned by his foster father John Allan.

Surprisingly, I had managed to earn AP credits in English literature, and I thought at least I had a head start in that major. I also learned at the time (the mid-1980s) that English literature was a common major for those preparing for law school. So I declared a major in English with a minor in anthropology and started college at the University of Maryland under the pretense of an interest in law. I was "considering" law school so that I could become an attorney like my Dad. Or so I said. I'm not normally one to pull off a ruse, but this was a whopper.

Poe in Film

Poe lived during the invention and popularization of photography and, despite his poverty, managed to be one of the most photographed figures of his time. He immediately saw the value of the photographic image to create a public persona. He set out to become the equivalent of a rock star, a reality-TV icon, when the only medium was the periodicals of his day. Poe even wrote articles about the invention of the daguerreotype and speculated on what effect this break-through form of photography would have on the culture, which, long after his death, led to the creation of film.[1]

So it's not surprising that filmmakers have been influenced by Poe from the very beginning. Georges Méliès's early classic *A Trip to the Moon* (1902) was ostensibly based on Jules Verne's 1865 novel *From the Earth to the Moon*, which may have been inspired by Poe's "The Unparalleled Adventure of One Hans Pfaall" (1835) in which the titular character journeys to the moon in a hot-air balloon.[2] Certainly, Poe's humorous tone is captured by Méliès.

Unfortunately, when mentioning Poe-related films, the campy works of Roger Corman usually come to mind first. Throughout the 1960s the legendary low-budget mogul produced at least nine films related to Poe but with little effort at authenticity. The talented Vincent Price always delivered the schlocky material as best he could, but audiences were invited to interpret Poe's masterworks in the most simplistic and obvious way possible. I saw some of these films on TV at an early age and enjoyed them for what they were, but as I aged and read more Poe, I was disappointed in the lack of gravitas, irony, poetry, and attention to detail. These films were so unlike the original stories. If Poe is an unusual amalgam of a hack writer and high artist, Corman could see only the hack.

Poe's influence on Hitchcock is more subtle, perhaps, than Corman's but also more profound. It's quite easy to relate films like Hitchcock's *Psycho* (1960) to Poe's works. The psychotic killer follows an irresistible impulse rather than logical motives. Mental illness is presented as the cause of his evil acts. Or *The Birds* (1963) in which horrifying supernatural events seem to be unwillingly caused by the protagonist. Or *Strangers on a Train* (1951) in which the

---

[1] Murray Ellison, "Poe and the Early Development of Photography," *The Poe Museum*, July 25, 2018, https://poemuseum.org/poe-and-the-early-development-of-photography/.

[2] *A Trip to the Moon*, directed by George Méliès, (1902; Star Film Company) and Jules Verne, *From the Earth to the Moon: A Direct Route in 97 Hours, 20 Minutes* (Belgium: Pierre-Jules Hetzel, 1865). Edgar Allan Poe's story first appeared as "Hans Phaall – A Tale" in the June 1835 issue of the *Southern Literary Messenger*.

protagonist's alter ego acts out his most nefarious desires. But my favorite is the underrated masterpiece *Dial M for Murder* (1954) in which the "perfect crime" comes unraveled due to the courage of the intended victim, Margot Mary Wendice, played by a statuesque yet articulate Grace Kelly. The "perfect crime" must be confessed by her sinister husband in the end.

Most importantly, Hitchcock based his masterpiece *Vertigo* (1958) in part on Poe's "Ligeia," exploring a man's inability to let go of his obsession with a woman whom he had watched die tragically.[3] The protagonist tries impulsively to transform a dark woman into a reincarnation of the light woman—an inversion of Poe's story. Indeed, Poe influenced Hitchcock, who in turn influenced the next generation of filmmakers, and I delved into learning about this line of descent because I desperately wished to follow in that tradition.

In the 1970s and 80s, Spielberg and Lucas knew how to appeal to the popular hunger for good triumphing over evil. Martin Scorsese, on the other hand, wallowed in moral ambiguity. He presented detestable characters who were nevertheless attractive and compelling on some visceral level. Unreliable first-person narrators who were charismatic in spite of, or because of, their flaws. The narrator of *Taxi Driver* (1976) seeks redemption through murder, like a twisted Poe narrator.

Even in one of his earliest films, Scorsese appealed to the character of the double. *Mean Streets* (1973) features close friends whose friendship ends in betrayal and death. It tells the story of a responsible young mafioso named Charlie Cappa (played by Harvey Keitel) and his roguish drunken friend Johnny Boy Civello (played by Robert De Niro). The parallels with Poe's "The Cask of Amontillado" have never been noted to my knowledge. Scorsese's twist on Poe is that the drunken character, Johnny, precipitates the disaster upon himself. The drunk is the betrayer of the ambitious character,

---

[3] For more information on Poe's influence on Hitchcock, see Dennis R. Perry, "Imps of the Perverse: Discovering the Poe/Hitchcock Connection," *Literature/Film Quarterly* 24, no. 4 (1996): 396–397.

Charlie, rather than the other way around. The themes of self-loathing and a subconscious death-wish are perhaps related to Poe's story as well.

Director Miloš Forman created *Amadeus*, which made the rounds in 1984. I was reluctant to watch it at first, having a poor grasp of classical music and German history at the time. This reportedly slow-paced film seemed to emerge from the old-school Hollywood establishment, sweeping the Oscars that year. When I finally saw it on tape, I was surprised and enchanted with the indie-film ethos imbued upon the historical drama. The underlying irony of course was that Mozart's most jealous rival, and perhaps his murderer, Salieri, was in fact his most ardent admirer. Only his fiercest enemy could appreciate the genius of Mozart. The parallels to Poe's relationship with Rufus W. Griswold are irresistible. Poe's death was famously celebrated by his friend, rival, and self-declared literary executor in his infamous obituary. Accusing Poe of drunkenness, drug abuse, insanity, infidelity, and perversion, Griswold inadvertently popularized Poe even more than he already was.[4] There is no such thing as bad press.

Much more recently, director David Fincher's debt to Poe is acknowledged explicitly in *Panic Room* (2002) when the main character, Meg Altman (played by Jodie Foster), mentions reading Poe's novels. We will forgive this common mistake—Poe did not write novels, with the exception of *The Narrative of Arthur Gordon Pym*. But *Panic Room* certainly pays homage to Poe's many claustrophobic short stories, including "The Premature Burial," "The Pit and the Pendulum," "The Masque of the Red Death," and "The Cask of Amontillado."[5] Fincher's previous film, his masterpiece *Fight Club*

---

[4] See Ludwig (Rufus W. Griswold), "The Death of Edgar Allan Poe," *New-York Daily Tribune*, Oct. 9, 1849: 2, https://www.eapoe.org/papers/misc1827/nyt49100.htm.

[5] John Kitterman notes that the film's protagonist Meg Altman is reminded by the panic room of author Edgar Allan Poe, who wrote several short stories related to premature burial. Kitterman highlights one story, "The Premature Burial," as synonymous with *Panic Room*. He says, in both works, "It is in the

(1999), is even more explicitly inspired by Poe. Starring Edward Norton and Brad Pitt, the film has become deeply embedded in American pop culture.

"William Wilson" is Poe's contribution to doppelgänger stories. The narrator claims to see another character who mocks and imitates him, even to the point of having the same name and appearance. As readers, we become aware of the narrator's insanity and inexorably conclude that when Wilson stabs his doppelgänger he is in fact killing himself—or a part of himself. Today, the narrator's mental illness would perhaps be diagnosed as dissociative personality disorder.

Fight Club, too, comes to a searing conclusion when the narrator reveals that his alter-ego is in fact not another character at all but himself. The feeble and pathetic Fortunato-like narrator (unnamed but referred to as Jack by many fans) is the over-confident, homicidal Montresor-like Tyler Durden. The rejected pariah and the worshipped psychotic cult leader, seeming opposites, are in fact the same person. Again, a murder/suicide attempt caps the story. The ego tries to destroy the humble, sensitive, perhaps masochistic aspect of itself. What little humanity he has left is targeted for annihilation.

Charlie Kaufman's brilliant *Adaptation* (2002) can be seen as a parody of *Fight Club* and other doppelgänger films. Nic Cage depicts Charlie struggling to write the film while his shallow "twin brother" Donald has no problem writing and selling a cheesy doppelgänger screenplay. The talented brother is failing due to his pessimism, and the untalented brother succeeds due to his optimism.

Most recently, Poe has appeared on film in Netflix's popular *The Pale Blue Eye* (2022). Like my film, it features Poe himself (played by Harry Melling) as a sympathetic character despite his flaws. The writers did their homework and included many references to Poe's

---

representing or acting out of such fears of being buried alive or being the victim of a home invasion that the protagonist actually calls for that trauma to happen." See John Kitterman, "Home(land) Invasion: Poe, Panic Rooms, and 9/11," *The Journal of American Culture* 26, no. 2 (2003): 238–239.

biography and works. They aptly depict Poe's time as a West Point army cadet, his love of humorous limericks, admiration for Byron, and obsession with solving riddles and codes. The detective Augustus Landor (played by Christian Bale) embodies the philosophy of Poe's sleuths. And like Poe, Landor is driven by the memory of losing a woman close to him. I feel this authentic homage to Poe is in the same spirit as my film.[6]

Edgar Allan Poe's Mystery Theatre
—Some Notes from the Writer

Whenever a writer analyzes their own work, there is a danger of reductionism. I do not ever wish to limit the interpretation of my film to my noted intentions. Art does not work that way. I learned new valid interpretations of the story from the actors and crafters I collaborated with as we made the film. And I continue to learn new meanings from the audiences I interact with. Meaning happens in the audience, not in an isolated writer.

Having said that, I think there is something to be gained by provoking a closer and richer interpretation of my script and film, by sharing some of my heartfelt enthusiasm for the life and works of Poe and how I tried to integrate that within the film.

A major theme of *Mystery Theatre* is the effect of Poe's real-life relationships on his literary works. The main conceit of my story is "what if Poe started a theatre company and depicted his works upon the stage, starring his family, friends, and even his rivals." We tried to be as historically accurate as possible on a very limited budget. Wherever we diverged from accurate biography, we did so to revitalize this theme.

The script is riddled with quotations and references to Poe's works. Some are direct quotes, and some are paraphrased or edited for effect.

---

[6] *Edgar Allan Poe's Mystery Theatre* premiered on public television in October 2014 and became available on Amazon Prime in October 2021.

The first reference is to Poe's "The Purloined Letter." I did not directly quote the story for an embarrassing reason—I could not remember exactly where I had read Poe's philosophy of gaming and intelligence.

We encouraged improvisation, and by a stroke of luck, actor Keith Brooks (*The Walking Dead*), depicting Rufus Griswold, happened to mumble "Purloined Letter" after Poe hands him a note in the opening scene. This scene is followed by the opening credits and then by a poker match in which Poe paraphrases his game theory from "The Purloined Letter":

Scene 2 INT. POKER HALL, FORDHAM NY—NIGHT

The room is frozen with tension as Poe has insulted everyone.

ENGLISH (smiling) So you caught us red handed. All in good sport.

POE No worries. One last hand. All or nothing.

ENGLISH But now you recognize our so-called "marked" cards.

Poe moves the betting pile aside to make room for a new card.

POE Fine. Put a fresh card on the table. A single card face down. You alone look at it. And I will guess if it is red or black. Go ahead. If I guess right, I get everything. If wrong, you and Graham keep it all.

ENGLISH (laughs) You're bluffing.

POE Sir, I am deadly serious.

English opens a new pack of cards. He looks at one and places it face down on the table.

ENGLISH Call it. Red or black?

POE What do you say it is?

ENGLISH What does it matter what I say? It's up to you.

POE But what do you advise me to say?

ENGLISH Hah! It makes no difference. (shrugging) Say Red.

POE Ah! If you were a man of low intelligence, you would say to yourself: Poe will take my advice, so I will lie to him, and he will lose.

ENGLISH Perhaps.

POE But you're smarter than that [however incompetent you may be as a card shark].

ENGLISH Apparently.

POE You shrugged when you said red. So that would lead me to believe the card is red.

ENGLISH I suppose.

POE But you know that I know that. So the card might be black after all.

ENGLISH Now you're stalling.

POE The result then is an exact summation of your opinion of my intelligence.

ENGLISH This trickery won't work.

POE And my answer, a precise summation of my opinion of your intelligence.

ENGLISH Name the color!

POE (as he flips the card) Red. I win.

Poe pulls all the winnings toward himself.

English punches Poe in the face, bloodying his forehead and eye. Griswold clumsily pulls out a knife. Poe gathers himself but Graham and English both pull knives as well.

ENGLISH A gentleman's duel, ah?

Poe stumbles back chuckling to himself as Griswold nervously approaches him with the knife. Poe pulls a sword out of Booth's walking stick.

B. Paul McClain as Edgar Allan Poe demonstrates his philosophy of gaming to Thomas Dunn English played by Tom Thon (left) and Junius Brutus Booth played by Allen O'Reilly (right).

POE Never bring a knife to a sword fight, gentlemen! Ta-ta.

He strikes the knife clean out of Griswold's hand, and it clatters to the floor. Poe escapes, leaving the men flabbergasted.

Another key scene is the first time Poe rehearses with Griswold, who he has cast as the protagonist of one of his plays. By design the audience is not aware of what story they are rehearsing. Some lines are from "William Wilson," but Poe quickly decides the scene is not working and begins to transform the work into "The Cask of Amontillado" by changing the murder weapon from a sword to a trowel. Virginia and Jupiter assist Poe in his playful experiment. I hope this makes the audience aware that even the smallest details of Poe's stories are all carefully designed to create a unified effect.

Scene 22 INT. MYSTERY THEATRE STAGE—DAY

Griswold, directed by Poe, brandishes a sword. Jupiter is fixing a back-stage wall with bricks, mortar, and a TROWEL. Virginia cleans and organizes old props as she observes Poe and Griswold working.

GRISWOLD [AS MONTRESOR] The Montresors were a great and numerous family before our ruin. You are respected, admired, beloved; you are happy, as once I was...And so I thrust my blade into your heart and there end your life! Villain!

POE Yes, yes, you murder him. But something's wrong...

GRISWOLD My performance?

POE We have a character: Montresor, courtesan of Verona.

GRISWOLD Yes.

POE A motive: revenge.

GRISWOLD Yes, revenge.

POE (fondling Griswold's sword) We have the plot, and the weapon: a sword, the symbol of Justice. But it's all wrong...

GRISWOLD What's wrong?

POE (hands the sword to Virginia) The murder weapon. He doesn't mean to kill quickly. He requires more...cruelty.

Virginia offers him a few weapons: mace, spear, bow and arrow, a whip, letter opener. Poe picks up a brick. His eyes wander to Jupiter who's laying bricks.

POE Jupiter! Eureka!

JUPITER What?!

Poe whisks the TROWEL from Jupiter's hand and gives it to Griswold.

GRISWOLD A trowel?

POE Yes: the murder weapon. Along with bricks and mortar. He means to build a dark eternal prison. "And bury him there in his sepulchre, in his tomb there by the sea. In his tomb by the sounding sea." It'll be great.

GRISWOLD I see why Booth quit.

True Poe fans will see that Griswold's lines combine dialogue from "The Cask of Amontillado" with the murder scene in "William Wilson." The idea is that Poe is taking the doppelgänger story and making it more subtle with every iteration—transforming "William Wilson" into "The Cask of Amontillado." This was inspired by Jorge Luis Borges's interpretation of Poe.[7] Actor Keith Brooks capped off the scene by improvising the hilarious concluding line, "I see why Booth quit!" Actor Junius Brutus Booth (the father of John Wilkes Booth) quit Poe's theatre company earlier in our story. While there is no historical evidence that Poe and Booth collaborated, the timing works out. Both were in their heyday in the 1830s. The tension between Poe and Griswold here is a sendup of the tension between

---

[7] For Jorge Luis Borges's discussions of the doppelgänger in "William Wilson," see "La última invención de Hugh Walpole," *Textos recobrados*, 1931–1955, (Buenos Aires: Emecé Editores, 1997–2003), 207–10 and "Sobre 'La literatura fantástica', disertó ayer Jorge Luis Borges," *El País* (Montevideo), 3 Sept. 1949: 4.

director and actor on any set.

"The Cask of Amontillado" is foreshadowed again in the scene where Poe brings John Allan and Griswold down to his foster father's wine cellar to discuss a scene he is working on. Wine cellars often doubled as prisons in wealthy households to punish unruly enslaved people. Historically, the Allan household in which Poe was raised had many enslaved people, so it may not surprise Poe to see iron shackles hanging in that room. In hindsight, this subtle nod to the existence of slavery and cruel corporal punishment in Poe's time is probably understated in the film. The idea was to introduce this theme gradually and devote a separate film to the topic of race, slavery, and Poe's relationship to it—a fertile topic.

Scene 25 INT. JOHN ALLAN'S WINE CELLAR—DAY

John Allan opens the secret passage, hands a lantern to Griswold, and the three head down into the cellar.

JOHN ALLAN (to Poe) You want to rehearse down in the cellar? But I thought you said it was a graveyard?

POE Yes, a necropolis, but a wine cellar also. A catacomb where his ancestors are buried. Casks and caskets!

GRISWOLD Brilliant—I see it. (sees John's disapproval) I mean that's good. I use the wine to lure you down—Fortunato.

JOHN ALLAN But when does the King come in?

POE That's later—it's a double-feature.

JOHN ALLAN A double feature?

GRISWOLD But why the jester?

POE A fool. A fool. His pride is his connoisseurship in wine.

JOHN ALLAN (opening a bottle) For old times' sake?

POE No, no thank you. You know my disposition.

GRISWOLD (hands Poe the lantern) I don't mind if I do.

POE (walking away through the cellar) Montresor lures the fool down to this Hellish place. Surrounded by bodies, ghosts. The chains of his past victims. (he pauses and fondles the shackles of a slave) But the fool can't see it.

As Poe paces through the wine cellar, Griswold and Allan whisper to each other and sip wine.

JOHN ALLAN 1811—it was a very good year.

GRISWOLD Delicious. (in hushed tones) I fear our plan to end Eddy's involvement may have been premature.

JOHN ALLAN You like his writing?

GRISWOLD (loud) Brilliant words. (soft) Could be quite profitable with the right editorial vision. But the weak link is always Eddy himself. If only we could save him from himself.

JOHN ALLAN Take the theatre from him…

Poe stumbles closer to John Allan and Griswold and then walks away again quoting "Cask of Amontillado" to himself.

GRISWOLD I'll do you one better: I—we—take control not only of the theatre, but of everything he's ever written, or will write for time immemorial.

JOHN ALLAN Power of Attorney. I'll have my man draw one up, but how will we ever get him to sign it?

GRISWOLD Vino!

JOHN ALLAN Cheers!

John Allan and Griswold clink wine glasses together.

This provocative scene of Allan and Griswold ridiculing Poe's alcohol dependence illustrates how it was not seen as a disease in that historical period but as a character flaw. While Poe is consumed in his creative process—revealing the double-meanings of the horrific world he saw around him, his enemies scheme to profit from his work. This encapsulates many moments in Poe's life in which publishers, including Griswold, tried to take control of his work.

The scene leads directly to a nightmare sequence that connects Poe's drinking problem to his mother's gruesome death when he was almost three years old.

Scene 26 INT. NIGHTMARE

Eliza lies dead and stiff on a bed. She opens her eyes suddenly and sits up erect. She spits up blood and cries tears of blood.

Scene 27 INT. MYSTERY THEATRE— RESIDENCE—NIGHT

Poe wakes up suddenly and finds himself in bed next to Virginia, who is coughing hard.

POE Ahhh. Virginia?

VIRGINIA Did I wake you?

POE No, just a bad dream.

VIRGINIA Was it her again?

POE Yes, I suppose. I don't know if she would be proud of me— the play. I'm trying…

Virginia coughs hard again. Poe reveals a flask from under a pillow.

POE Take this—it helps with the cough.

Virginia takes a sip of liquor from the flask and winces. Poe tries to drink too.

VIRGINIA Eddy. Not another drop. Remember, you promised.

POE Yes Sissy, I'm sorry. Go to sleep.

VIRGINIA Good night.

POE Good night.

Virginia kisses Poe on the cheek and goes back to sleep. Poe slowly closes the flask and returns it to its hiding place.

Paul McClain's performance here as Poe is among my favorite moments in our film. He dramatizes the extreme difficulty Poe has closing the flask—resisting his impulse to drink.

Poe's wife Virginia and his mother Eliza were both played by actress Carrie Anne Hunt (*Sleepy Hollow*). This was rendered subliminally by photographing Eliza out of focus, distorted, and wearing a long wig. This casting decision implies that Poe experienced some type of Mother complex—constantly striving to revive his mother, a theme suggested by Kenneth Silverman's bestselling Poe biography *Edgar A. Poe: Mournful and Never-ending Remembrance*.

The mystery of Poe's mother that we set up in scene 26 is solved when Poe bares his soul to Griswold in scene 36. Griswold has tricked him into indulging in alcohol ahead of their premiere, and an intoxicated Poe shares his innermost memories. I chose to narrate this scene with Poe's moving poem "A Dream Within a Dream." By using the imagery of the hourglass and pocket watch, we connect the poem to Poe's longing for his mother.

Scene 36 FLASHBACK—POE'S CHILDHOOD

Poor 2-year-old Poe holds the hand of his dying mother Eliza. She coughs into a bloody handkerchief. She kisses his brow which leaves a blood stain behind.

POE V.O. Take this kiss upon thy brow! And, in parting from you now, This much let me avow You are not wrong, who deem That my days have been a dream;

Eliza hands Poe the small painting of herself. He kisses her hands. She caresses his face as she speaks.

ELIZA Always remember me. My little Eddy.

Eliza's hand falls limp, and Poe turns to watch the sands of an hourglass run out in slow motion.

POE V.O. I hold within my hand Grains of the golden sand— How few! yet how they creep Through my fingers to the deep, While I weep—while I weep! O God! can I not grasp them with a tighter clasp?

Poe's little hand tries to revive Eliza's stiff hand. John Allan's large hands come in and grab Poe kicking and screaming away. He grabs the hourglass as he is dragged out.

POE V.O. O God! can I not save One from the pitiless wave? Is all that we see or seem but a dream within a dream? I remember her hands. The hourglass. Her voice. I can't quite remember her face. Only this…image.

The scene is punctuated with a shot of Poe's pocket watch, containing the painting of his mother. This is a reproduction of the authentic painting Eliza Poe left to her son, which he kept in a locket. In our film, we placed it in a watch.

Soon Poe runs off to the theatre to try to salvage the show. As he stumbles out on the stage, he raves a drunken apology, but when he sees Virginia's disappointment off stage, he whispers a line from Shakespeare's *Hamlet*: "Assume a virtue if you have it not."

The first play that Poe's players depicted on stage is, of course, "The Cask of Amontillado." Our version emphasizes the closeness and symmetry of Montresor and Fortunato. As we float out of the catacombs, there is no sign of either character. We are leaving them both behind in eternal darkness.

But upon the cruel conclusion in which Fortunato is buried alive, the stage goes dark. When the lights turn on, we see the same drunken jester chained upon the stage. There is a purposeful misdirection here. We have begun the second play, "Hop Frog: A Tale of Revenge," one of the last works completed by Poe. Now the drunken jester has acquired agency and poses a threat to the King, played by John Allan. We are provoking a question: "Is 'Hop-Frog' a sequel to 'The Cask of Amontillado?'" It certainly turns the tables in favor of the drunken jester.

Our Poe achieves poetic justice as Hop-Frog takes his revenge—the refugee escapes with his true love, Trippetta, played by Virginia. His weakness for drink does not overcome him in the end. At least not in this narrative. We hope so too in real life—that alcohol did not play a role in Poe's untimely death at the age of forty in 1849.

After completing *Poe's Mystery Theatre*, I had the opportunity to visit the Poe Cottage in the Bronx. This is where Poe and Maria Clemm tended to Virginia until she died of tuberculosis in 1847, after a five-year battle with the disease. The tour guide showed us the little guesthouse where Poe toiled away at night, writing his short masterpieces. He directed me to a very narrow winding stairway to Virginia's room. As I worked my way upward, I asked, "Virginia's room was upstairs?" "Yes," answered the guide. "Poe would carry Virginia down this stairway every morning to take her to breakfast and back upstairs every night to put her to bed." At that moment I could almost feel the presence of Eddy and Sissy on the narrow stairway with me. A lump came to my throat and a tear to my eye. The close of Poe's "The Masque of the Red Death" came to my mind:

> And now was acknowledged the presence of the Red Death. He had come like a thief in the night. And one by one dropped the revellers in the blood-bedewed halls of their revel, and died each in the despairing posture of his fall. And the life of the ebony clock went out with that of the last of the gay. And the flames of the tripods expired. And Darkness and Decay and the Red Death held illimitable dominion over all.[8]

We take refuge in Poe. May he take refuge in the arms of his beloved Virginia. May God have mercy on Eddy's poor soul.

---

[8] Edgar Allan Poe, "The Masque of the Red Death," in *The Collected Works of Edgar Allan Poe*, ed. T. O. Mabbott, vol. 2 (Cambridge: Belknap Press of Harvard University Press, 1978), 676–677.

3

CURATING POE:
THE POE MUSEUM AND
ITS AUDIENCES

Christopher P. Semtner

Poe is funny. At least that was my first impression of him upon read-ing "Never Bet the Devil Your Head" in the corrugated steel shed that served as our elementary school library out there in the southern Virginia countryside. While my fifth-grade self completely missed the tale's references to Transcendentalism, I could appreciate the subversiveness of Toby Dammit's surname being one of those words I was forbidden to utter in earshot of an adult. Did the librarian have any idea what she was letting us read? Aside from that, it was a gen-uinely entertaining and twisted story—up until the gruesome end-ing with poor Toby's head getting knocked off by the beam of a cov-ered bridge. That is all it took to get me hooked, and I followed up that work with "Hop-Frog" and "The Cask of Amontillado." In a rural county still seemingly untouched by the twentieth century, this nineteenth-century writer seemed fresh and contemporary.

Fifteen years later, I had just started performing conservation work at the Poe Museum in Richmond when my manager asked if I had any ideas for the booth she was about to set up for an upcom-ing city-wide children's festival. I naturally suggested we perform my old favorite "Never Bet the Devil Your Head" with puppets. We constructed a stage, found appropriate puppets, and developed the right voices for the characters. On performance day, the kids cheered when Toby's head popped off with blood squirting out the stump of his neck, but their parents were less than impressed. We were not invited back the following year. I like to imagine it was because of that puppet show, but it was probably because the city did not repeat the festival. Either way, I hope that show got at least one more kid hooked on Poe. Getting people excited about Poe has driven most of what I have done during my time at the museum.

I came to the museum to conserve an eighteen-foot-long scale model of Richmond as Poe knew it. I spent my first six months breathing through a dust mask to painstakingly dust, repair, and in-paint every inch of the model while visitors watched me through a Plexiglas wall. In the process, I gained new insights into the streets Poe once roamed, but I also picked up the habit of listening to the museum's guests, who spoke freely amongst themselves because they had no idea I could hear them through the plastic. From then on, my work in the museum's exhibits and programs would be guided by the visitors. If the museum was going to grow from a sleepy "mom-and pop" establishment with only about 11,000 visitors a year, it would do so by listening to its multiple audiences and by finding creative solutions to address their needs.

Although eavesdropping on visitors is still a great way to iden-tify the artifacts they find most interesting or which text panels they read aloud to their friends, our audience research soon expanded to polling, surveys, and compiling online reviews. A few of the findings of significance were that the museum's annual visitation consisted of people from all fifty states and about thirty countries. Roughly sev-enty percent of these visitors hailed from outside of Virginia.

The two major types of visitors are the general tourists and the Poe pilgrims. While some of the former visit because they see the museum's interstate highway sign while driving between tourist at-tractions like Colonial Williamsburg and Monticello, most of them come to town to spend time with relatives and need something to entertain, and possibly educate, their children while in Richmond.

Aside from family visits, the other major draws to Richmond are business trips and sporting events, including NASCAR races and the annual marathon. After these general tourists, a not insignificant number of the museum's guests come to Richmond for no other reason than to see the Poe Museum: the Poe pilgrims.

Surveys and reviews have shown how these two groups differ in their expectations of their museum experience. The Poe pilgrims often seek more depth and detail in the museum's exhibits or expect to learn something about Poe that they did not already know or would not find in the standard documentary or biography. They want to examine the most important artifacts, especially ones owned by Poe.

While the general tourists also seek out those important artifacts, they mainly expect to receive the best value for their admission by seeing as many pieces as possible. They long to be overwhelmed with the sheer volume of artifacts. This expectation is something many exhibit designers miss while trying to make clean, simplified spaces highlighting only a few pieces. Given a choice, the general visitor would rather be dazzled by the floor-to-ceiling displays of the Ripley's Believe It or Not! Museum than the sparse white walls of the average contemporary art museum. You have merely to visit examples of each on a Saturday afternoon to see which is empty and which is overflowing with excited visitors.

Particularly relevant is a letter Poe wrote to his employer Thomas White on April 30, 1835, concerning the recent publication in White's magazine of Poe's horrific tale "Berenice." Poe astutely advises White to ignore the critics' opinion of his story and to focus on the subscription numbers.[1] To be successful, a magazine must connect with its audience, and the same is true of a museum. The difference is that the Poe Museum needs to balance this entertainment value with its educational mission.

---

[1] Edgar Allan Poe to Thomas W. White, April 30, 1835, in *The Collected Letters of Edgar Allan Poe*, ed. J. W. Ostrom, B. R. Pollin, and J. A. Savoye (New York: The Gordian Press, 2008), 84–86.

Sculpted in 1884 by Richard Henry Park, the Actors' Monument
to Edgar Allan Poe overlooks the exhibit gallery in the Poe
Museum's Elizabeth Arnold Poe Memorial Building.

Courtesy Christopher P. Semtner

One thing particularly striking about the Poe Museum's visitation is that more than a third of the museum's guests fall into the coveted 18-34 age group that other museums struggle to attract. While other age groups are well-represented among the attendees, it is significant that this group, which is usually deemed uninterested in museums, comes to see Poe, arriving in droves during Spring Break. I have even seen some teenagers celebrate their birthdays with a visit to the Poe Museum!

In summary, the museum attracted at least two major audiences and appealed to a range of age groups and nationalities, but it was not taking full advantage of these assets. In 2003, when the museum's director resigned and its librarian retired, I found myself in the position to steer the museum in a new direction.

Until then, visitors could only experience the museum by following one of the guided tours which began at the top of each hour from ten in the morning until four in the afternoon. This schedule resulted in the loss of many potential guests who were either unable or unwilling to wait until the next start time.

The tour guided visitors through four tastefully decorated galleries with pale yellow or white walls and tan exhibit cases, colors about as far as possible from the Poe "brand." There was little order to the few artifacts on display. An item related to Poe's childhood, for example, might be wedged between one from his final days and another from his sister. There was no continuity from one room to the next, either. A newspaper review from the time complained that the museum was practically empty.[2]

The first phase of remodeling these galleries was the rearrangement of the artifacts and exhibits into chronological order. While this enabled the museum to interpret the narrative of Poe's life, it did not prove entirely sufficient. Over the course of several discussions, my team developed additional interpretive themes to guide the

---

[2] Shannon Proudfoot, "A Fitting Tribute to the Master of Gloom: The Poe Museum Is Short on Artifacts, but the Prevailing Mood Is Spooky and Enthralling," *The Ottawa Citizen*, October 29, 2005, B3.

arrangement of the galleries. We wove the themes "Inspirations for Poe's works," "Poe's literary genres," and "Poe's lasting influence" into the narrative arc of the exhibits.

The museum's color palette also needed to be considered. Dark wall colors and exhibit cases in low lighting not only reduced the amount of harmful light striking the artifacts and made the works on paper stand out better from their surroundings but also set a somber tone significantly more appropriate to Poe's melancholy poetry than pale yellow had been.

With the general layout and color scheme of the museum improved, the percentage of positive reviews increased, and this amounted to a gradual rise in attendance. In response to the increased traffic, the museum converted from an entirely tour-guided format to a partially self-guided experience. This necessitated a variety of new tour options. Among these was the printed tour available in English, Spanish, French, Portuguese, German, Russian, Italian, and Mandarin. An audio tour was available first on mp3 players, then on an iPhone app, and finally on the museum's website, where it can be played on any smartphone.

We continued to remodel the exhibits every few years in response to user feedback. To address criticism of the museum's lack of space, we converted storage rooms into additional exhibit spaces and maximized the use of the existing galleries. We also increased the number of artifacts on display at any given time.

When updated visitation data indicated that local visitors were still underrepresented, we decided to attract more Richmonders by offering a steady slate of must-see changing exhibits and by providing a monthly afterwork concert in the museum's garden. These temporary exhibits enabled us to explore a variety of topics overlooked in the permanent exhibits. Some examples are "Poe Goes to the Movies: Edgar Allan Poe and Cinema," "Poe in Comics," "Poe: Science Fiction Pioneer," "Pandemics and Poe," and "Mesmerized: The Facts in the Case of M. Valdemar." "The Poe Code: Edgar Allan Poe and Cryptography" focused on Poe's interest in ciphers. After learning about the use of secret writing in Poe's tale "The Gold-Bug," visitors practiced solving different types of cyphers and composing some of their own.

For "Investigating History," I attempted to accumulate the most Poe hair since it had been on his head. The exhibit showed what the analysis of Poe's hair could reveal about his lifestyle, environment, and death. University of Virginia professor Stephen Macko collaborated with me on the show and shared the results of his latest stable isotope analysis of Poe's hair.

In "Pandemics and Poe," I examined the ways cholera, yellow fever, and tuberculosis impacted Poe's life and works. In order to demonstrate the variety of ways in which tuberculosis could kill someone, guests spun a "Wheel of Misfortune" to find out how they would die if they contracted tuberculosis in Poe's day. Some possibilities were pulmonary tuberculosis, skeletal tuberculosis, tuberculosis meningitis, or poisoning from a toxic patent medicine "cure."

"CSI: Poe" focused on Poe's attempt to solve the murder of New York cigar store clerk Mary Rogers. Different stations throughout the gallery profiled the suspects and red herrings, analyzed the crime scene, and detailed the timeline. After studying the clues, our guests were asked to vote for the most likely suspect, and we kept a tally posted outside the gallery. No respondents agreed with Poe's solution of an unnamed naval officer; the largest group, thirty-three percent, believed that Rogers's fiancé Daniel Payne was responsible. Two people voted for me.

Sometimes we created installations in which guests could step into the setting of a Poe tale. Among these are "The Pit and the Pendulum," "Hop-Frog," and "The Cask of Amontillado." For the latter, I lined the gallery with simulated stone walls covered with piles of plastic skulls. Missing "stones" revealed interpretive text panels and hidden exhibit cases for related artifacts. The skeletonized remains of poor Fortunato, still wearing his conical cap and bells, were chained to the rear wall of a niche concealed by a simulated stone wall with just enough blocks missing to allow visitors to view the victim. Visitors were encouraged to step behind the wall to have their pictures taken with him. The exhibit's Spanish Inquisitionthemed opening reception featured the museum's staff dressed as inquisitors while treating guests to an Amontillado tasting accompanied by the music of Spanish guitars.

After staging several of these installations, I invited the museum's visitors and social media followers to vote for their favorite Poe stories to showcase in an upcoming exhibit. The four most popular stories by percentage of the vote were "The Tell-Tale Heart" (32%), "The Cask of Amontillado" (19%), "The Black Cat" (2%), and "The Pit and the Pendulum" (1%). The resultant exhibit, "Poe's Greatest Hits," consisted of environments inspired by each work. Visitors crawled underneath the floorboards from "The Tell-Tale Heart," hid behind the basement wall from "The Black Cat," or dodged the pendulum blade from "The Pit and the Pendulum." Guests helped promote the museum by posting selfies taken in the gallery to social media with the appropriate hashtag.

Visual art has also been an important component of the temporary galleries. In addition to displaying works by prominent contemporary artists such as Michael Deas, Richard Corben, and Gris Grimly in various exhibits, we invited local artists to sketch, paint, and photograph the museum's garden for "Painting the Enchanted Garden." The largest art exhibit, "El Cuervo: The Raven, Terror, and Death," featured the works of twenty-four artists from Mexico and forty from the United States in a collaboration between the Universidad Nacional Autonoma de Mexico and the University of Colorado.

Aside from these changing exhibits, another tactic we used to draw more local and repeat visitors was hosting a monthly afterwork concert in the museum's garden. Each Poe-themed event provided live music, an interpretation of a Poe work, exhibits, food, and a cash bar. When we envisioned this drawing young professionals on their way home from work, the event's name immediately presented itself. Since our guests would be coming to the museum instead of visiting their local bar's happy hour, we called it the Unhappy Hour.

The name conjured up Poe's melancholy poetry, and the ad copy practically wrote itself. Among the tag lines were "You'll have a miserable time," "Prepare for Despair," and, my nod to the Partridge Family, "Come on, get unhappy." We held the first Unhappy Hour in 2008 to coincide with the opening of the "Poe in Comics" exhibit, and on June 17, 2009, "What is the Unhappy Hour?" appeared as the question to an answer on the television gameshow *Jeopardy!*[3] Believe it or not, the contestant got it right.

We coordinated Unhappy Hour themes with those of the current temporary exhibits. Among these were "Hop-Frog," "A Descent into the Maelstrom," and "The Murders in the Rue Morgue," which featured a live-action murder mystery. The guests started dropping like flies, and the survivors had to identify the killer before it was too late. For "The Poe Code," we designed a museum-wide scavenger hunt involving encoded messages and riddles.

Many Unhappy Hours included a performance of a Poe work in the garden during the band's break. "Berenice" was especially effective because so few guests had read the story and were completely unprepared to see a box of bloody fake teeth hurled into the crowd. In addition to interpreting Poe's works through readings, art installations, and film, we staged recitations of his poetry in Spanish and in American Sign Language. Other Unhappy Hours provided poetry slams, book signings, and author talks. In recent years, we added the "Curator's Crypt" in which I present rarely seen artifacts from the museum's collection. Although I have not had the chance to resurrect my "Never Bet the Devil Your Head" puppets for an Unhappy Hour, I was able to put on a "Hop-Frog" puppet show.

Unhappy Hour attendance soon swelled to between 200 and 300 people per event. Grants provided funding for the band and actors while local breweries and restaurants donated refreshments. This allowed the event to remain profitable for the first several years.

For a while, we also hosted an annual Poe Death Day. As the tagline says, "We put the 'fun' back in 'funeral.'" The event held on the anniversary of Poe's death would not be nearly as boisterous as the Unhappy Hour. One time, we held a simple wreath-laying

---

[3] *Jeopardy!*, Episode 5718, aired June 17, 2009.

ceremony on Poe's bust, and another year, we recreated the 1875 dedication of Poe's monument with historical interpreters reading the speeches delivered on the occasion by Walt Whitman and others. Guests could view a special exhibit of nineteenth-century mourning artifacts or take a horse-drawn hearse on a tour of neighborhood Poe sites.

Another annual event the museum hosted was Poe's Pumkin Patch, a day of Poe-themed activities for children and families. Even if they left without having read one of Poe's works, each child would at least get to see a shadow puppet show of "The Raven" or make their own raven puppet out of a black paper bag. The other games included scavenger hunts, Pin the Tail on the Black Cat, a black cat piñata, a wheel of misfortune, a costume Poe-rade, and a skull hunt.

One of my favorite programs was the Poe Film Festival, first held in 2004 at the Byrd Theater. The museum brought together horror fans and cinephiles for a day and a half of classic Poe movies. Over the years, we showcased a variety of Poe adaptations from the silents to the latest independent films. Special guests included Vincent Price's daughter Victoria Price and Raul Garcia, director of the animated feature *Extraordinary Tales*.

By far, the museum's largest annual event is the Poe Birthday Bash. While the Poe Museum began celebrating Poe's birthday in the 1920s, the tradition had ended long before I arrived at the museum. In 2002, the museum's director asked me to put something together for the occasion. I brought in the author of a Poe-themed novel to give a book talk, staged a small exhibit, and organized an event that concluded with the cutting of birthday cake. This modest gathering was just the beginning.

It soon evolved into a must-see annual event, and each year our tiny but talented staff committed itself to outdoing whatever we had already done. One year, we held a Poe Showdown in which Poe impersonators delivered competing performances of "The Raven" and "The Tell-Tale Heart" for the audience to judge. Other years, we held a Poe lookalike contest, singing Poes, dancing Poes, a concert by Poe's mother, and a debate between Sarah Helen Whitman, Elmira

Shelton, and Frances Osgood to determine which one Poe loved the most. These gimmicks were interspersed with live music, Poe recitations, dances inspired by Poe's works, film screenings, exhibit openings, museum tours, walking tours of neighborhood Poe sites, trolley tours, and (of course) birthday cake.

By far, our most ambitious Poe Birthday Bash was held in 2010 when the team decided the only way to outdo the previous year's record-setting Poe bicentennial birthday bash was to make it last twenty-four hours. The party began on noon one day and lasted until noon the next, with the first 100 guests receiving Poe mustaches to wear. As young and foolish as we were, we set up air mattresses in one of the offices for us to take turns sleeping between shifts.

The headline gimmick was to be a Poe séance, and *USA Today* hinted that Poe himself might be there. In collaboration with Haunts of Richmond, we arranged for an actress to hold a Victorian-style séance in the garden. The plan was simple. Hidden accomplices would provide lighting and sound effects on cue. Then, at the stroke of midnight, one of our Poe actors, Keith Kaufelt, would rise, illuminated by spotlights, above the Poe Shrine while the audience gasped.

It was an exceptionally frigid night. Keith lay down atop the icy shrine roof, awaiting his cue as the crowd huddled around the "medium," who played her part a little too effectively. The guests were so transfixed on her that when she screamed, "There he is!" and pointed to our glowing Poe impersonator hovering over them, everyone was too startled to turn around to see what she was pointing at.

The Poe Birthday Bash continued to draw enthusiastic visitors from across the country. For the next decade, the event lasted from noon until midnight, concluding with a toast to Poe in the museum's Poe Shrine. Each year, an astonishing number of guests stayed the entire twelve hours to shiver with us in the shrine.

That tradition ended with the COVID-19 pandemic. In 2021, the museum held its first virtual Poe Birthday Bash. In 2022, the event was once again held in-person but continued to feature some virtual components.

As a small museum with a staff typically consisting of one or two full-time employees and five or so part-timers, we are always eager to collaborate with organizations that have the staffing or budget to put on a spectacular show. For Poe's bicentennial in 2009, we convinced the Richmond Symphony and Richmond Shakespeare to host a Poe-themed concert, and the Library of Virginia allowed me to use their remarkable facility to curate the exhibit "Poe: Man, Myth, or Monster?" which examined the three sides of Poe—the historical figure, the myth created by his biographers like Rufus Griswold, and the monster that is the popular image of Poe as the Halloween boogeyman and "Godfather of Goth."

I had a different kind of collaboration with the Friends of Shockoe Hill Cemetery, an organization devoted to restoring and preserving the final resting place of Richmond luminaries such as United States Supreme Court Chief Justice John Marshall and Revolutionary War legend Peter Francisco. Since the cemetery also holds the remains of Poe's foster parents, first love, and last fiancée, the Friends approached me to help them conduct a Poe-themed tour of the site. Finding the average tour too ordinary, I devised a program led by a Poe actor who, in passing the graves of loved ones, encounters actors portraying those people. Haunts of Richmond supplied the actors, and the Enrichmond Foundation provided funding for Poe's Haunted Homecoming. Every performance sold out for three years.

A few years later, I received an urgent call. A group needed a Poe interpreter that evening for a private event. Their actor had dropped out at the last minute, and I must have been the only person available. I knew just enough about Poe to piece together an outfit, to which I added a period-appropriate top hat. I adopted a Tidewater Virginia accent based in part on Poe actor Norman George's well-researched interpretation of Poe's voice. I also consulted historical recordings of Virginians who were born during Poe's lifetime. Without any rehearsal, I donned my fake mustache and spent the evening drifting about the reception quoting Poe's letters and poems. Somehow giving this impromptu performance resulted in recruitment to perform as Poe for other groups, even though I am far from an actor and never bother to memorize lines.

In 2015, I met Ana Ines King, the artistic director of the Latin Ballet of Virginia. She was interested in choreographing a performance interpreting the poetry of Pablo Neruda, Alfonsina Storni, Federico García Lorca, and Edgar Allan Poe, who happens to be very popular in the Spanish-speaking world.

After developing the Poe segment for *Poemas*, Ana and I decided to create an entire show around Poe. *La Pasion de Poe* was such a success that the company toured it through the United States and Mexico. The show consisted of several dancers interpreting the poems "To Helen," "El Dorado," "To One in Paradise," "Annabel Lee," and "The Raven." The lead performer, who portrayed Poe, was the Spanish flamenco dancer Antonio Hidalgo Paz, who flew to the United States for performances.

My job was to open the performance as Poe. Striding across the stage in full costume, I announced,

> True!—nervous—very, very dreadfully nervous I had been and am; but why *will* you say that I am mad? The disease had sharpened my senses—not destroyed—not dulled them. Above all was the sense of hearing acute. I heard all things in the heaven and in the earth. I heard many things in hell. But if I hear any cell phones ringing during the performance, you'll end up under the floorboards![4]

Then followed readings of a few of his poems while some of the performers danced around me. After a few minutes, I stepped aside for the actual dance to begin.

This was fairly easy work until the day Antonio missed his flight from Spain. Ana told me that I would need to fill in for him. When

---

[4] Excepting the last line, which is a parodic addition, these lines open Poe's "The Tell-Tale Heart." See Edgar Allan Poe, "The Tell-Tale Heart," in *The Collected Works of Edgar Allan Poe*, ed. T. O. Mabbott, vol. 3 (Cambridge: Belknap Press of Harvard University Press, 1978), 792.

I explained to her that I could not dance, she assured me that I merely needed to stand in the right spots and emote the part. The real dancers would compensate for my lack of movement as long as I could give them something to react to.

Nobody explained to me the difference between dress shoes and dance shoes. By the time of the climactic scene in which the dancer dressed as an acrobatic raven and the spirits of the dead were pulling Lenore away from Poe into a whirlwind of leaping and spinning bodies, I was slipping and sliding all over the stage. For Poe's dramatic death scene, I merely let gravity take over as I crashed to the floor. The dancers swirled around me, making it look like I had some idea of what I was doing. When the curtain fell, I was certain I would never allow myself to be talked into doing that again. Of course, I did make a couple more appearances as a back-up Poe before the tour ended.

This was far from the last time I would wear the mustache. At the Garth Newel Music Center in Hot Springs, Virginia, I recited "The Tell-Tale Heart," "The Cask of Amontillado," "Hop-Frog," and "Annabel Lee" to musical accompaniment by Jeannette Fang on the piano. Then, at Richmond's Byrd Park Pump House, I performed a selection of Poe's tales for Poe at the Pump House in an abandoned nineteenth-century ruin reminiscent of the House of Usher. The attendees wore hard hats and signed liability waivers to see me perform.

While exhibits and events address the needs of the general visitor and the Poe devotee, the museum's educational programs have the most direct impact on another vital audience—the student visitor. Their ages range from kindergarten through college with most coming from seventh and eighth grade English classes. The most popular program remains the guided tour of the museum. The educators might add a mock-trial of the murderer from "The Tell-Tale Heart," an activity in which the students become the judge, attorneys, and jury in a trial to decide how reliable a witness the narrator of Poe's tale really is. Educators might also opt to send their students on a walking tour of neighborhood Poe sites or to have the class compete in the Poe-lympics, which include Poe-cabulary (determining the meanings of words Poe invented) and the Sad Poetry Reading in which participants see how much sorrow they can evoke while reading one of Poe's melancholy poems.

With annual visitation soaring, the museum increased its staff, allowing me to devote more time to cataloging, researching, preserving, publishing, and presenting the collection, which has also expanded with an influx of important donations and new discoveries. When not holed up in the storage rooms, I continued to study and engage with our audiences by conducting tours for Poe pilgrims, general tourists, students, major donors, and distinguished guests because they make my work relevant. Everything changed on St. Patrick's Day in 2020, when the world's museums closed their doors for what we thought would be two or three weeks.

Well before the COVID-19 pandemic put a temporary halt on the museum's in-person tours, virtual tours and programs had been growing in popularity for several years. For the museum's first virtual tours, I placed a laptop and webcam atop a rolling office chair and pulled the contraption around the museum with me. From these humble beginnings, the museum's virtual programming grew to offer multiple tours and presentations as well as improved technology. The museum also features author interviews, readings of Poe's works, and "Curator's Crypt" videos on YouTube and other social media platforms.[5]

My specialty, exhibits, have also gone online. As I write, the museum is engaged in creating 3-D scans of the artifacts and assembling the scans in a virtual reality version of the museum, and we have uploaded over 4,000 items from the collection into a searchable online database.

---

[5] Visit the Poe Museum's social media accounts to access videos and other information: Poe Museum, YouTube videos, https://www.youtube.com/@PoeMuseum/videos; The Poe Museum, Facebook, https://www.facebook.com/PoeMuseum/videos; The Poe Museum (@poemuseum), Instagram, https://www.instagram.com/poemuseum/; and The Poe Museum (@Poe Museum, X, https://twitter.com/poemuseum.

After fully reopening its facilities and events, the Poe Museum conducted a new survey of fifty-seven randomly chosen general admission guests interviewed at the conclusion of their visits between February 1 and April 4, 2023. All age groups are still strongly represented with the largest portion consisting of people aged thirty to forty-nine at thirty-three percent. The second largest group, at thirty percent, consists of visitors between the ages of eighteen and twenty-nine.

The reasons given for their visits indicated that Poe pilgrims outnumbered the general tourists with the former making up fifty-one percent of respondents and the latter comprising twenty-nine percent. Goth and horror fans made up four percent of the visitors. The stated objectives for their visits revealed an overlapping interest in Poe's biography and his writing. Twenty one percent reported that they came to learn more about both Poe's life and literature. Eighteen percent said they visited solely to learn about Poe's life, and seven percent toured the site for no other reason than to learn about Poe's writing.

After nearly two decades of studies and the rise of a new generation of guests, the Poe artifacts remained the greatest draw. Of those surveyed, eighty percent wanted to see more artifacts, and only four percent preferred fewer historical objects. At the same time, fifty percent wished to read more informational placards while only nineteen percent desired more audio tour options.

When compared with previous surveys, the greatest change was that Virginians now make up forty-seven percent of the guests, with twenty-one percent of total visitors coming from Richmond. It appears that our efforts to attract local audiences have been successful.

These numbers only tell part of the story. Social media and the internet have allowed the museum, the physical footprint of which has not grown in over ninety years, to expand virtually to impact millions of people who may never see the site in person. Over 1.3 million unique visitors a year utilize the museum's website and even more engage with us through social media.

The Facebook page had a respectable 15,000 followers until the end of 2012, when I met two tiny black stray kittens in the museum's garden. Edgar and Pluto soon drew new fans to the museum's social media. Posts about the cats were interspersed with ones about the museum's programming, exhibits, and events. A year of regular posting quadrupled those followers, surpassing those of all other museums in the Greater Richmond Region, including the Virginia Museum of Fine Arts and the Science Museum of Virginia. A decade later, the museum's other social media platforms continue to reach new audiences, and the cats have their own calendar, which can be found in the Poe Museum's gift shop next to the black cat socks, dolls, and T-shirts.

This shop has expanded from a selection of Poe Museum mugs and facsimiles of Poe manuscripts to a vibrant stock of Poe shirts, bobbleheads, dolls, finger puppets, magnets, socks, boxer shorts, pins, shot glasses, flowerpots, books, and more. As frivolous as some of the merchandise seems, the gift shop is often the first place to look to learn if our efforts to get people excited about Poe's works have been successful. Every time a student spends their last wadded up five-dollar bill on a paperback edition of Poe's tales or poems—instead of on a hat or sticker—we know we have made an impact. Before they leave the museum, that budding Poe fan has decided to carry back into the outside world, with its indifference to literature and creativity, a little portal to Poe's imagination.

With any luck, they will stumble across "Never Bet the Devil Your Head" in that book.

4

PSYCHOTIC SIMULATIONS: ACTING POE

Dean Knight

At the age of about ten, which was around the time I started reading the stories of Edgar Allan Poe, my mother took me to the Poe Museum in Richmond, Virginia, my hometown. That visit must have been on the cusp of my entry into middle school when I soon began my involvement in theatre. I was an actor in the Drama Club all three years of middle school while continuing to think of myself as some kind of burgeoning writer. If I ever read Poe for school, I do not specifically remember it.

My only regret in choosing to attend Open High School is that it did not have a theatre program, but this regret was quickly passed over with the idea that I did not really want to pursue acting as a career anyway and thought my destiny was to be a great writer.

I majored in English and American literature at New York University in the heart of one of Poe's many neighborhoods. After I graduated, NYU tore down Poe's last remaining house in Manhattan—I have one of the bricks. I did not think much about him then, though. I may have consigned him to my childhood in search of other writers I was discovering. In high school, I was stunned by Jean Genet's novels then later enraptured by William Faulkner and his world; sometime after college, I discovered Thomas Pynchon and a way of writing about things I had not seen before. Later, I re-encountered Jean-Paul Sartre and his extraordinary multi-faceted explanation of the world through philosophy, drama, and literature.

I tried to be a writer, but it was not working so well. I tried to write Serious Important Literature which, if you deliberately *try* to write it, will not happen. I did not really know that. I thought I was a smart guy and thus should be able to write great, intelligent Literature. It did not happen. Years later, I encountered Pynchon's thoughts on the topic in his personal essay—he wrote of his early writing that "I was operating on the motto 'Make it literary,' a piece of bad advice I made up all by myself and then took."[1]

In my late twenties, several divergent things converged—I started attending local theatre productions; I started spouting/developing "characters" ad hoc in various accents/dialects for no particular reason for my friends and acquaintances; and, by the age of about 30, I realized that it was not happening for me as a writer and that I might need to look to other paths for fulfillment. All of these things came together, along with my day job at a museum, with Haunts of Richmond.

I was asked to go along with a group from my museum to a meeting at a new "haunted museum" that was not a museum at all really but a more sophisticated take on the traditional haunted house. The meeting was not related to my position, but those who went invited me because they knew I liked Halloween and horror and thought I might be interested in this new venture. They were certainly right. The following day I sent an email to the owner, who had included a brief recruitment pitch for actors in his presentation, offering myself, saying that I was not a "real" actor but thought I could do what he needed. I did not hear back right away; I eventually reached out again, knowing it was something like that new path that I needed, and he put me in the schedule as "Prisoner #1"—my first paid acting gig and my first acting role since eighth grade.

It was at Haunts of Richmond that I encountered Poe again,

---

[1] Thomas Pynchon, *Slow Learner* (Boston: Little, Brown & Co., 1984), 4.

since in addition to the walk-through attraction in which we terrified people using theatrical monologues and short scenes based on Richmond history, we started to offer short productions based on Poe's works (we also did "A Christmas Scare-All" based on Dickens wherein I played Marley the first year and the next a murderous Scrooge).

After a year or so of this, I thought that maybe I could be a "real" actor after all. I took this growing confidence, and Poe, into my second theatre audition. My first was for a couple of Shakespeare plays in which my audition was the opening monologue from *Richard III*. Not realizing how cliched a choice this was and basing my performance on the great British actors I had seen in movies and BBC productions, my audition was, only semi-consciously, in an English accent. The director, seeing that I was so new to theatre as to not have an acting resume, kindly, after quickly ascertaining that I was not, in fact, English, asked me to drop the English accent and to let myself shine through more. I was not entirely sure what he wanted but did try to drop the accent. I did not get a part, but I had survived my first audition.

My second audition was a five-minute monologue based on Poe's story "Berenice," which I had learned for Haunts of Richmond and performed there and in the Enchanted Garden of the Poe Museum on a cold and rainy January day as a part of the annual "Birthday Bash." Performed this time for an assembly of local theatre directors with casting needs, it resulted in being cast less than twenty-four hours later in a new play by a local writer set during the 1864 siege of Petersburg, involving the Confederate soldiers in Robert E. Lee's Army of Northern Virginia reading and re-reading Victor Hugo's *Les Misérables* while mired in the trenches around the city. The writer was neither the first nor the last to make use of the punning epithet "Lee's miserables." I found when I read the script that my role was that of a soldier who masturbates while having a particularly salacious scene read aloud to him. I asked how this was going to be done on stage. The director replied, "You can do a lot with a blanket."

This production was at a new theatre called Sycamore Rouge in the old section of Petersburg near where Poe and Virginia had honeymooned at his friend Hiram Haines's hotel. The building still stands, and a few years later, I would again perform that five-minute version of "Berenice"—this time with my wife playing the role of Berenice—in the very room where the two had stayed. There is a photo from the last show I did at that theatre, which was almost the last show anyone ever did at that theatre, showing the cast with me in a Poe Museum T-shirt. Two years later, I started working there.

Those two years were a bumpy road for me—I turned 40, got divorced, took a new job at an institution into whose culture I was not fitting, and got laid off from it. I then sought out two jobs at institutions that I had long been interested in but had been unavailable to me while employed full-time: the Poe Museum and the Standardized Patient Program at Virginia Commonwealth University's School of Medicine. Before being unemployed, I could not contemplate leaving a full-time job to seek part-time work, but now that I no longer had a full-time job, I certainly could.

Four days after being terminated, I was filling out paperwork at the Poe Museum. My new boss, a friend I had made soon after her own arrival at the museum, had offered me a job as soon as I told her my situation, and I accepted immediately—so quickly that she told me to think about it over the weekend. I called her at 9AM Monday morning, and the job was mine. Hired as a tour guide, which I had plenty of experience with in my museum career, I plunged into re-reading Poe, absorbing the exhibits, and writing a script for myself. I was soon in charge of group tours and programs.

I felt my interests merging. I plunged into Poe's poems, although I had never taken a strong interest in poetry before. The poetry appealed to me beyond professional necessity because as an actor I could read the poems aloud, as Poe had intended. "A poem is a composition for the human voice" is a mantra I remembered from the initial literature class I took as an English major and one that certainly applied to Poe's poems.

My main experience in reading poetry aloud had come with

Shakespeare (despite that first audition)—I had played roles in verse onstage, including the Friar in *Much Ado About Nothing*, Albany in *King Lear*, and Clarence in *Richard III*. Like Shakespeare, Poe knew and wrote in iambic pentameter, but he also used other patterns. I pasted oversized sticky notes of stanzas from several of Poe's poems on the walls of my office space at the Poe Museum, complete with scansion marks—anapestic for "Ulalume" and "Annabel Lee" and the quite rare trochaic octameter for "The Raven." I was fascinated by the work behind the magic; I loved the idea of being something like a literary mechanic, understanding how poems are put together and how they should sound, how the syllables should be stressed. I also, as with Shakespeare, got to delve deeper into the works themselves and understand more about how to speak them based on the scansion.

Understanding how poetry works and how to speak metered poetry is vital to effective performance; it is the sort of thing that if it is done without that knowledge an audience member who does not know about scansion or poetry may not know exactly what is wrong but can hear and feel that something is off. An actor speaking Shakespeare's verse without understanding how it works can sound like a wrench banging about inside a metal box.

I made of "The Raven" something of a showcase for meter, as did Poe. Each stanza—each line—of the poem adheres strictly to Poe's carefully devised format, including the deliberate omission of one syllable in every second, fourth, and fifth line.[2] I created a program called "The Raven Poetry Workshop" in which I first introduced Shakespeare's iambic pentameter to the audience then "flipped" it over to trochaic octameter, showing them how Shakespeare used iambs—feet composed of one unstressed and one stressed syllable—and then showing how Poe wrote "The Raven" in trochees—feet of one stressed syllable followed by one unstressed

---

[2] Edgar Allan Poe, "The Raven," in *The Collected Works of Edgar Allan Poe*, ed. T.O. Mabbott, vol. 1 (Cambridge: Belknap Press of Harvard University Press, 1969), 364-369.

syllable. Shakespeare kept to five feet, while Poe used eight; the difference between

A pair of star-crossed lovers take their life[3]

and

And the silken, sad, uncertain rustling of each purple curtain[4]

is dramatic when one pays attention to how the lines scan. I used what I called a "Mr. Robot" voice to over-emphasize for students where the stresses lay in each line such as

a PAIR of STAR-crossed LOVErs TAKE their LIFE

in *Romeo and Juliet*, and this in "The Raven":

AND the **SILK**en **SAD** un**CERT**ain **RUST**ling **OF** each **PUR**ple **CUR**tain

To close out the program, I turned to "Ulalume" to introduce students to a different metric foot, the anapest. "Ulalume" is probably my favorite Poe poem—it is appropriately mysterious and strange; it is set quite probably on Halloween night in an era before Halloween as we know it really existed.

I was born on November 1, at 6:29 AM, in the midst of Samhain: the ancient Celtic end of summer festival that also marks one of the poles of the calendar when the line between the living and the dead is at its thinnest. That line is something that Poe was interested in throughout his career, perhaps most obviously in "The Facts in the Case of M. Valdemar" but perhaps most beautifully in "Ulalume." The Celtic rituals around the end of summer are something that Poe—who had an Irish-American biological father and a Scottish foster father—would have known about and have influenced

---

[3] William Shakespeare, *The Tragedy of Romeo and Juliet*, ed. Barbara A. Mowat and Paul Werstine, The Folger Shakespeare, Prologue, line 6, https://shakespeare.folger.edu/downloads/pdf/romeo-and-juliet_PDF_FolgerShakespeare.pdf.

[4] Poe, "The Raven," 364.

"Ulalume" and would later influence our modern Halloween.

"Ulalume" is indeed a gorgeous poem, a remarkable composition for the human voice but also a way of communing with the ancient Celtic past through the lost Ulalume in a graveyard on what must be Halloween night itself. On a trip to Salem, Massachusetts, some years ago—home of Nathaniel Hawthorne, one of Poe's very few equals among his American contemporaries, and one of the very few he admired and respected—in exploring the lore around the notorious seventeenth-century witch trials (which I was soon to connect with in a direct literary and theatrical manner by portraying Reverend Parris in a production of *The Crucible* at the same Petersburg, Virginia, theatre where I got my acting start), I encountered the concept of Wicca. Having been non-religious my whole life, I was intrigued by this modern form of spirituality that ultimately hearkened back to the earthly concerns of harvesting and the changing seasons. I did not become spiritual, but I did become more connected to the earth, the seasons, and my own Scots-Irish and English roots. "Ulalume" for me is a direct connection to the life of the earth at the time when the veil between the living and the dead is at its very thinnest—which is also when I slipped into this world.

These words in this meter are rhythmic and melodic, as close to a song as possible—Poe, who composed it in response to a request for a poem suitable for a lecture on elocution, subtitled it "A Ballad."[5] Perhaps this is why whenever I spent time with the poem my mind summoned up the Irish-themed and set folk song "The Black Velvet Band."[6] Whatever the reason, after reciting the poem, even just a stanza or two on a tour, that song would come into my head.

---

[5] See Kenneth Silverman, *Edgar A. Poe: Mournful and Never-ending Remembrance* (New York: HarperPerennial, 1992), 335–336.

[6] For the lyrics, see "The Black Velvet Band," Donal O'Shaugnessy Irish Songs, 2011, https://www.irishsongs.com/lyrics.php?Action=view&Song_id=43.

And I cried—"It was surely October
On *this* very night of last year,
That I journeyed—I journeyed down here!—
That I brought a dread burden down here—
On this night, of all nights in the year,
Ah, what demon has tempted me here?
Well I know, now, this dim lake of Auber,
This misty mid region of Weir;—
Well I know, now, this dank tarn of Auber,
This ghoul-haunted woodland of Weir."[7]

Poetry can touch upon strings in the world, in the body, in the mind, or in the heart that connect one song to another. It is as though the math embedded in the poems stretches out into the universe connecting with invisible lines spread throughout the sky; the rhythms of anapestic meter roll all around the planet.

A few months after starting at the Poe Museum, I took an additional job as a Standardized Patient (SP) at Virginia Commonwealth University's School of Medicine. This job employs actors to portray patients with a variety of medical and psychiatric illnesses; we play these roles for medical students as well as nursing students and occasionally dental, pharmacy, and social work students so that they can develop their skills in dealing with patients in a variety of situations before they encounter actual patients.

Around the same time, I inherited the Tell-Tale Heart Mock Trial at the Poe Museum. The program was structured around Poe's great story "The Tell-Tale Heart" and my dramatic reading of it as testimony in a murder trial. I would describe how it would proceed, with four roles cast from the audience: a judge, a jury foreperson, a prosecuting attorney, and a defense attorney. Everyone else was on the jury.

---

[7] Edgar Allan Poe, "Ulalume," in *The Collected Works of Edgar Allan Poe*, ed. T. O. Mabbott, vol. 1 (Cambridge: Belknap Press of Harvard University Press, 1969), 418.

The judge called the court to order and then summoned the defendant—me, in the role of Poe's narrator in the story—to the stand. I read the story in dramatic fashion from behind a podium that served as a sort of "witness box." The end of my "testimony" had me shouting the shocking final words of the story in which I imagined I could hear the still-beating heart of my dismembered victim under the floorboards:

> I felt that I must scream or die!—and now—again!—hark! louder! louder! louder! *louder!*—
>
> "Villains!" I shrieked, "dissemble no more! I admit the deed!—tear up the planks!—here, here!—it is the beating of his hideous heart!"!"[8]

Next, the judge began cross-examination by calling first the prosecuting then the defense attorney to interrogate me on the stand. I had emphasized before the trial began that the job of the jury was *not* to determine whether or not a murder had been committed—that was clear enough already for those of the jury who had already read the story, and the defendant would make it very plain in his testimony for all to hear. The crux of the case was, then, the sanity of the defendant. The prosecutor's job was to prove that I was *sane* and in control of my senses and thus responsible for my actions. The defense attorney's job was to show that I was insane and thus should not be held fully responsible for what I had done.

I used the basic format of the trial that I was given, but it did not include much written direction. I found after doing it a number of times that the lawyers, particularly for younger groups, might benefit from some assistance as to what they might say in cross-examination. So I created prompts for both lawyers with an assortment of sample questions they could use if they chose. I also created a script for the judge, which they were to follow word for word until the end

---

[8] Edgar Allan Poe, "The Tell-Tale Heart," in *The Collected Works of Edgar Allan Poe*, ed. T. O. Mabbott, vol. 3 (Cambridge: Belknap Press of Harvard University Press, 1978), 797.

when they could use their own creativity in sentencing the defendant based on the verdict.

After I started doing the Tell-Tale Heart Mock Trials, I started regularly portraying patients experiencing psychotic episodes for students attending VCU's School of Medicine. I have portrayed a wide variety of cases over the years but have always been more drawn to the psychiatric ones—they are more interesting and challenging as an actor, and I found that I seemed to be more attuned to illnesses of the mind than those of the body. In particular, I became a regular in the psychosis cases at the School of Nursing—which offers a graduate degree for those interested in becoming a Psychiatric Mental Health Nurse Practitioner. In that program, I offered four intense experiences portraying patients with depression, anxiety, mania, and psychosis. I also served a six-month stint as the Client Coordinator at the School of Nursing, overseeing these and other simulations. At the School of Medicine, students in the third year had to do a psychiatric rotation, and they encountered me or one of my fellow SPs as a person described as having "chronic paranoid psychosis."

The psychosis cases include instruction on certain ways to respond to aspects of the Mental Status Exam the students are learning to give and some fairly detailed information about the patient's recent history and paranoid delusions. We have a whole list of phrases to use that express our delusional worldview (e.g., "Some people come from spiders. You can tell by the shape of their ears.") and a jarringly non-linear story to tell that expresses dark concerns about the world proceeding from our delusions. One character I have played many times had his first psychiatric admission at twenty-three due to his going into the streets to proclaim that he was Jesus Christ and continues to be chronically psychotic, though he understands now that he is not Jesus. He is deeply suspicious of the government, particularly Homeland Security, whose agents he believes he can detect due to the way they use their turn signals in traffic. Since he believes that Homeland Security is operating an electric machine that has irradiated all consumable foodstuffs except tuna fish and milk, he has been consuming only those two things for the past two weeks—until the morning of the interview when he has come to understand that the radiation has penetrated the tuna fish as well, leaving him with just milk as a food option. The students are presented with a patient who is not rational or linear and without any insight into his own condition; he can respond to a basic question with a complete *non sequitur* or a tangent that sometimes chillingly reflects a brain not operating on a normal plane.

As I started to play these cases regularly while also portraying "The Tell-Tale Heart" narrator at the Poe Museum, the roles started to feed into each other. With the knowledge and experience gained from portraying patients experiencing psychotic episodes, I could see that Poe had achieved a terrifying realism in the way he was able to portray, in an extraordinarily vivid manner, a character in a short story that delivers a monologue straight from the mind and mouth of someone in the grips of a psychotic episode.

At the museum, giving tours, I emphasized that part of Poe's genius was that he was able to portray mental illness in a sophisticated, specific way that had not really been done before in horror fiction. Poe revolutionized the horror genre by injecting great psychological depth and reality into his stories and his characters, giving us realistic portrayals of characters suffering from specific, recognizable mental illnesses when horror fiction has tended to portray mental illnesses in very reductive, simplistic ways—the generically "insane," babbling "mad scientist" with frizzled white hair. An example from a writer who knows Poe's work well but has not mastered this aspect of it nearly so well is Stephen King. In his 1981 story "The Jaunt", which I read around the same time I was starting to read Poe, it struck me even then as a crude—if vivid and memorable—rendering of mental illness. King uses the phrases "mental spaz," "lunatic," "insane," "crazy," and "mad as a hatter" throughout the story to generically encompass mental states without delving any deeper into the minds he depicts.[9] The final depiction of "insanity"

---

[9] Stephen King, "The Jaunt," in *Skeleton Crew* (New York: Putnam, 1985), 203–226.

is of a boy now with "a snow-white fall of hair and eyes which were incredibly ancient," emitting "choked, lunatic cackles," a garish and illogical conclusion.[10] Compare this to the stunning Soviet film *Come and See* from the same period that depicts a boy acquiring the marks of age before our eyes as he experiences the horrific brutality of the Nazi invasion and occupation of Belarus and we can see a master artist exploring the ravages of war on the psyche and body. This film's handling of mental illness is much more nuanced and in line with what Poe achieved in his depictions.

"The Fall of the House of Usher," certainly one of Poe's greatest achievements in short fiction, is suffused with severe depression amidst its portrayal of grief, guilt, fear, and anxiety in the person of Roderick Usher. "Berenice" features a narrator who, "ill of health and buried in gloom," speaks quite directly about his own affliction, which he calls "monomania"—perhaps a psychiatrist today would class it as an obsessional disorder.[11] The cousin that he marries he describes with great sadness as "roaming carelessly through life, with no thought of the shadows in her path, or the silent flight of the raven-winged hours" and who also succumbs to mental illness, "pervading her mind, her habits, and her character, and, in a manner the most subtle and terrible, disturbing even the very identity of her person!"[12]

In "The Tell-Tale Heart," I knew now that Poe had completely succeeded in his portrayal of someone in the grips of psychosis. That informed my reading of the story on the stand as testimony, and it especially informed my improvisational portrayal of the narrator during the cross-examination from the lawyers. The prosecuting attorney, going first, might ask me one of the following questions that I had suggested:

---

[10] Ibid.

[11] Edgar Allan Poe, "Berenice," in *The Collected Works of Edgar Allan Poe*, ed. T. O. Mabbott, vol. 2 (Cambridge: Belknap Press of Harvard University Press, 1978), 210, 211.

[12] Ibid.

Are you an intelligent person?

Could someone unintelligent or "crazy" have planned this out the way you did?

Why did you feel that the old man had to die?

Do you consider yourself a good person?

Do you understand the difference between right and wrong?

To any one of these questions, I would reply enthusiastically and informatively. *Of course* I was an intelligent person! In fact, I was the most intelligent person on the planet—and certainly not no one who was of lesser intelligence and certainly not a "crazy" person could have planned something like this out. *Of course* I considered myself a good person—and I certainly understood the difference between right and wrong! That, after all, is why I did what I did—I had detected an evil that had hatched itself within the old man, in his eye. That is why he had to die—not because of anything he had done himself—after all, I loved the old man, I had no wish to harm him— but the eye was evil, and I had to eliminate it from the world.

The cleverest prosecutors would steer away from the parts about an evil eye and concentrate on the fact that I had indeed carefully, and with forethought, planned out the murder, to show that I was of sound mind and had methodically, rationally committed murder. I would appreciate the prosecutor's questions as ways to show my brilliance and perfect sanity. In fact, I was *more sane* than anyone else, in a way—and I believed I had an alliance with the forces of good. It was a shame that someone died, but the greater good by far was served by destroying the evil entering this world through the old man's eye.

Much of my improvisation in the cross-examination was influenced by my portrayals of psychotic patients at VCU. Typical of people experiencing psychosis is a fixation upon religion, electricity, machines, governmental structures, and/or the delusion that they are extraordinarily intelligent and on the side of good in the war between good and evil in the world, between God and the devil. This fit in well with Poe's protagonist—I was doing good in the world by using my powers to detect evil and remove it from the world.

The defense attorney's job of showing me to be insane might seem to be the easier one, but it was rendered more difficult by me as the defendant as I would strongly oppose any attempt to portray me as insane, even by my own counsel. The questions I had suggested for this role were

How did you know that the eye was evil?

Have you ever been diagnosed with a mental illness?

How are you able to hear things in heaven and hell?

What makes you so different from other people?

Do you see yourself as superior to other human beings?

My response to question 1: How did I know the eye was evil? *It told me it was evil.* Oh, now, wait a minute. It didn't *talk* to me, eyes can't talk, I know that, I'm not crazy. It *sent me images through the sky into my brain,* showing me the havoc it would wreak upon the world. Buildings collapsing, corpses everywhere, cities in ruins. I knew I had to stop it before it could do these things.

To question 2: A "mental illness"? Oh, now you sound like those doctors, those quacking ducks that don't know anything at all. As I said, a while ago I was feeling a little ill. So I went to a doctor, and he said some things, I don't know, a bunch of *words,* and they gave me some pills. I thought I would try them, and I did—but do you know what they did? *They clouded up my brain.* I couldn't think clearly anymore! So after two days—I threw them in the river. And you know what happened then? My brain cleared up. The fog lifted. I have been thinking better and more clearly every day ever since then. And I don't listen to doctors anymore.

To the remaining questions: God made me different than other people. He chose me to become superior to others—it is through him that I have greater powers such as hearing things in heaven and hell. I am a warrior in God's army on the side of good, fighting evil—which is why I had to kill the old man. I had to stop the evil from growing. You people of limited intelligence, you don't understand at all—I am your intellectual superior, trying to help the world—you all should be giving me a medal rather than putting me on trial!

Most juries found me to be quite mad. I only hope that I was able to bring Poe's brilliant short story to life in a compelling manner that also accurately depicted—in both Poe's words and my own post-testimony cross-examinational contributions influenced by my depictions of patients suffering from psychosis at VCU—"The Tell-Tale Heart" narrator as credibly within the grips of psychosis.

Poe's great contribution to horror literature was to bring psychological depth and reality to the stories and characters portrayed within; he once wrote, in reference to his less-sophisticated German predecessors in horror fiction, "Terror is not of Germany, but of the soul."[13] What Poe knew, and expressed in his greatest stories, is that true horror is not found in imaginary monsters—it is within us.

---

[13] Edgar Allan Poe, "Preface" in *Tales of the Grotesque and Arabesque* (Philadelphia: Lea and Blanchard, 1840), 6, unnumbered.

5

DEDICATED TO THOSE KINGDOMS BY THE SEA: ILLUSTRATING POE

Jamison Odone

Death always looms right behind my eyes. I think about it at such a rate during the average day that I often have to force myself to do one of two things—either stop thinking about it or embrace it and use it to create something inspired by the gloom. I prefer to embrace it—to create based upon that cloudy veil of nothing. That strange, low bell that some of us just hear in our imaginations. I am not alone in this club of broken minds. In fact, I have good company. Some of these members are still around, and some only exist in the place behind my eyes where all this strangeness begins.

In this club, I can guarantee a few things. First, none of us has ever simply walked past a cemetery and thought nothing. It is a section of land with stones pointing towards the sky. We all know the purpose. To most, a glance over into that terrain to see if anything is happening, anybody paying respects, anything at all, is what is done. To us in the club, our minds stray far beyond the constraints of our world above the ground. We see rot. We see a woman in a black veil weeping beside the grave of her child who was taken a century and a half ago. It started with a cough and a pallor. The cough began to yield more clues. A silk handkerchief bespeckled with tiny blood droplets. The days after that were filled with agony and helplessness. Then, her child was gone. Lowered down in a jet-black box detailed by silver filigree and handles. She has never left that place. She forsook the rest of her family. All the while, the child below faded more and more into the actuality of things, rot.

Have you ever thought about that? If not, then you may go now. If so, you are probably a member of the club. Welcome.

Another thing that I can guarantee (about our club members) is that we seek out the recorded, macabre stories that allow us to paint these pictures mentally.

On October 25, 1990, at the age of ten, I was first exposed to Edgar Allan Poe through a visual adaptation. I remember it vividly because it came in the form of a cartoon on a Thursday night. I remember the couch positioned adjacent to the television in the front room of our small, rented house on East Avenue in Burrillville, Rhode Island. Our house sat directly across the street from the Brown Family Funeral Home. This location played no role in my first experience with Poe, but in retrospect, it further set the scene, and I think Poe himself would appreciate the notation of that proximity during the early years of my life.

The television was set to Fox 25 Providence, and *The Simpsons'* inaugural "Treehouse of Horror" episode aired.[1] This episode featured Bart and Lisa telling each other scary stories while sitting up high in their backyard treehouse beneath the moonlight. Lisa began reading to Bart a poem which began "Once upon a midnight dreary..." I recall bursts of purples and lavenders. Deep reds and blues. Yellows. I remember spirits and ghosts, haunting moments that seemed eerie and funny and perfect. The humor crept in as the lovable buffoon Homer Simpson, cast as Poe's grieving lover, was led by the speaker of Poe's "The Raven," which switched from Lisa's

---

[1] *The Simpsons*, season 2, episode 3, "The Raven" in "Treehouse of Horror," directed by David Silverman, written by Edgar Allan Poe and Sam Simon, featuring James Earl Jones, Nancy Cartwright, Yeardley Smith, and Dan Castellanetta, aired October 25, 1990, in broadcast syndications.

child voice to the deep baritone of Darth Vader...or James Earl Jones (depending on where your imagination went). At this moment, I was fully engrossed and entertained. Not once before in my life had poetry had any effect on me but with the right teachers, the right media, the right moment, the right poet—it was the most powerful form of communication and storytelling that I had experienced.

As the reading and animation continued, I recall a specific word: "Plutonian"—the placement and sound of that one word. I know now what the intent of the word is, what the meaning is. But then, as a ten-year-old, I had no clue. It was just a sound to me. A meaningless word. Somehow, even as just a sound in a metered lyric, I saw in my mind what I was supposed to see. He had made the poem thrilling and haunting to those of us with a limited vocabulary.

The narration and animation carried on through the story: the empty study where the writer sits and ponders; the mystery of who is knocking; the awful places the mind drifts in the darkness of things unseen; and the hopelessness of being alone. The fear I felt when my mother was not in the house with me. I had viewed this cartoon alone on a Thursday night in October. It was the perfect combination of something that I wanted to see and something I had never heard before, coming together and altering my life's course in perpetuity. At ten, I devoured that poem both visually and aurally and proceeded to live another twenty-five years.

Another sign that I was a member of the club occurred a few years back when I wrote and illustrated a graphic novel titled *The Man in The Painter's Room.*[2] The story follows Vincent van Gogh in his final days. Vincent died by suicide (a gunshot to the chest) at the age of thirty-seven, and for the most part, his final days were quite regimented and ordinary. My interest in this subject piqued when I happened across an obscure letter from the painter Émile Bernard to the poet Albert Aurier; the description of the great painter's funeral stuck

---

[2] Jamison Odone, *The Man in the Painter's Room* (Toronto: Black Panel Press, Inc., 2021).

74

with me and became something I had to write about.

After Vincent had finally succumbed to his injuries, a local carpenter was hired to build a simple casket. The body of the painter was placed inside this humble structure, which was set inside the room that was dubbed The Painter's Room. The inn where Vincent had been staying in Auvers-sur-Oise, France, was called, the Auberge Ravoux, which is situated near the Oise River—not quite the sea but adjacent to the water. The owners, the Ravoux family, had grown fond of the kind man who spent his days painting in the fields, so they took great care in sending his soul off into eternity with love and respect. Another painter staying at the inn was Tom Hirschig; Vincent and Tom were friends. Their paths had crossed during the final months of Vincent's life, and Tom was enlisted to help with the visual arrangements for the funeral. What he did painted the image in my brain enough to create the initial draft for my book; he hiked to the fields and collected as many yellow flowers as he could to bring back to the inn. I do not know the exact number of flowers he was able to pluck from those hot July fields. What I do know is in that instant of reading about the funeral details of van Gogh's death, I was transported to a scene of beauty. The resting body of an immeasurably troubled soul surrounded by the safety, the covering, the protection of the yellow flowers he loved so dearly in life. These excerpts from Bernard's letter struck me and directed my work:

> On the walls of the room where his body was laid out all his last canvases were hung making a sort of halo for him and the brilliance of the genius that radiated from them made this death even more painful for us artists who were there. The coffin was covered with a simple white cloth and surrounded with masses of flowers, the sunflowers that he loved so much, yellow dahlias, yellow flowers everywhere. It was, you will remember, his favourite colour, the symbol of the light that he dreamed of as being in people's hearts as well as in works of art.
>
> Near him also on the floor in front of his coffin were his easel, his folding stool and his brushes.

[…] At three o'clock his body was moved, friends of his carrying it to the hearse, a number of people in the company were in tears. Theodore [van Gogh] who was devoted to his brother, who had always supported him in his struggle to support himself from his art was sobbing pitifully the whole time…

[…] We reached the cemetery, a small new cemetery strewn with new tombstones. It is on the little hill above the fields that were ripe for harvest under the wide blue sky that he would still have loved…perhaps.

Then he was lowered into the grave…[3]

What does any of this have to do with Edgar Allan Poe? Well, we are in the same club. Any of us who write stories or paint pictures in the space behind our eyes when hearing such tales of life and death are in this club. I feel as though this funeral description is something that would have lingered with Poe. It would have set the story working in his troubled brain, and he would have become obsessed over the written description of Vincent in his casket. If you are still here, still reading these words, you are too. It is a fine feeling to be in your company. Let's proceed.

In late 2014, being fairly tired of the slow pace of traditional publishing, I decided to try something on my own. I have always been inspired by Edward Gorey's Fantod Press, so I let this inspiration guide me. The Fantod Press was Gorey's own independent press whereby he published the books that his traditional publishers found too strange or unmarketable for a general audience. In like fashion, I decided to publish a small, illustrated version of "Annabel Lee."[4] I had scratched out a rough version of the drawings in my notebook in 2009, and there they sat until five years later when I was ready.

---

[3] Émile Bernard to Albert Aurier, August 2, 1890, *van Gogh's Letters: Unabridged and Annotated*, https://www.webexhibits.org/vangogh/letter/21/etc-Bernard-Aurier.htm#:~:text=My%20dear%20Aurier%2C,fact%20that%20he%20killed%20himself.

[4] *Annabel Lee by Edgar Allan Poe*, illus. Jamison Odone (Box Books, Independent, 2014).

"It was many and many a year ago, / In a kingdom by the sea[.]"[5] When I first read these lines, I had to immediately draw each and every last word of Poe's poem. I could not purge the words from my mind. The meter and the tone transformed into vivid pictures in my mind's eye. I have a habit of reading and rereading and rereading. When I fixate on something, I care about it, and if I care about it, I will never let it go. So in 2009, which coincidentally was the bicentennial of Poe's birth, I printed out the words and taped them into my sketchbook so that I could hash out the thumbnail sketches over the next week. I put a crude pen line to paper and drew a rudimentary rough draft of an illustrated version that I would one day return to.

Growing up near the sea in New England has also left lasting visuals in my brain.[6] I have spent countless hours staring off into it. I have always taken these encounters with the sea as an opportunity to clear my mind and think. So my formative years, at times, felt much like a "Kingdom by the sea." It was not a kingdom of money or luxury—but a kingdom of thought. A kingdom of a mind as yet unaffected by the responsibilities that come with aging. The entirety of "Annabel Lee" felt to me like a moment from my youth that happened so simply—in black and white. How brief the poem is makes it more profound. That is why childhood is so profound; it is gone before we can appreciate how brief it will be. Perhaps that is one reason why I have read and reread this poem hundreds of times. The lines "For the moon never beams, without bringing me dreams / Of the beautiful Annabel Lee;" conjure an image of a lunatic gazing up

---

[5] Edgar Allan Poe, "Annabel Lee," in *The Collected Works of Edgar Allan Poe*, ed. T. O. Mabbott, vol. 1 (Cambridge: Belknap Press of Harvard University Press, 1969), 477.

[6] New England also inspired me to create a graphic novel about Ann Putnam's role in the infamous witchcraft trials of the 1690s, which I published under a pseudonym. See Jakob Crane, *Lies in the Dust: A Tale of Remorse from the Salem Witchcraft Trials* (Yarmouth, ME: Islandport Press, 2014). I also composed a book of sonnets based on my hometown, Woonsocket, Rhode Island. See Jamison Odone, *Mill Town Sonnets* (Los Angeles: Bottlecap Press, 2022).

at the expanse of space on a night when he can think of only one good thing in his life, in this case his true love.[7] Like for this man, the moon exists for some artists to bounce our ideas off of. With these lines—and many others in mind, I progressed beyond those initial sketches, creating about fifteen drawings that would be my "Annabel Lee," which I dedicated to "Those kingdoms by the sea."

My work took a Goreyesque path—not only in the approach to publication but in style. I chose black pen with thin, detailed lines. The characters were direct in their likeness, a man visually similar to Edgar and a woman visually similar to Virginia Clemm Poe, his wife. I wanted to draw images that showed love and loss and mystery set against the background of alternating peaceful and chaotic seas. The peace and the tumult play an equal role in this visual metaphor; an artist can tell any number of tales by using the unpredictable behavior of tidal waters, and that is what I intended.

For about ten nights I feverishly drew. The illustrations were tiny, only slightly larger than a standard business card. I made every effort to pack detail and finesse into such small packages, and in some instances, I felt success, others failure. I reached a point when I had the realization that nothing I could make would ever stand up to the actual words of the poem or overtake them in skill. That is a big weight to hold up as an artist—to know that you are working on something that is better than you could ever hope to do. I mostly told my brain to be quiet about that and proceed on. Whiskey helps to dull that noise, as it did with Poe.

It was winter, and I was in New England. Every night was a frozen, snow-covered landscape. I would often look out into the darkness of the backyard from the room where I was working and read these lines quietly aloud:

For the moon never beams, without bringing me dreams
Of the beautiful Annabel Lee;
And the stars never rise, but I feel the bright eyes

---

[7] Poe, "Annabel Lee," 478.

Of the beautiful Annabel Lee:—
And so, all the night-tide, I lie down by the side
Of my darling—my darling—my life and my bride,
In her sepulchre there by the sea—
In her tomb by the sounding sea.[8]

When I work on projects that are about real people (van Gogh) or on projects whereby I use the works of people (Poe), I often take far too much time to mentally set my brain to their imagined situations. I feel like this small courtesy is the least I can do for their posthumous positioning in the advancement of my career. With Poe, it was tough. This poem most likely dealt with the death of his wife. The beautiful words are packed with an eloquent sadness that caused legions of weirdos like me to love the words, the imagery. But I sat there many times, looking out into the frozen night trying to force myself to feel the loneliness that he must have felt after the death of Virginia and while penning this poem. He lived during a time of no instant communication, no scrolling, and little contact with others after sunset. All he had were candles to keep the darkness away—that darkness must have invaded the hearts and minds of everyone who was prone to depression and sadness. It must have invaded Poe on a nightly basis. It must have chased him around his home. The cold of the night air must have been a minute-by-minute reminder of the embrace that was wrapping the body of his late wife. He felt no comfort. A watercolor portrait the only likeness of his wife to gaze upon.[9] The air would never carry the sound of her voice again, so Poe survived with only his memories.

---

[8] Poe, "Annabel Lee," 478.

[9] Although Virginia seems to have sat for daguerreotypes, the only confirmed image of Virginia is a watercolor painting of her corpse; it is sometimes referred to as "the deathbed portrait." See "A Poe Mystery Solved?," The American Museum of Photography, 2011, https://www.photographymuseum.com/virginiapoe.html.

"So that her highborn kinsman came and bore her away from me." *Annabel Lee by Edgar Allan Poe*, illustrated by Jamison Odone (Box Books, Independent, 2014).

I made myself try to feel these things like he would have. I scratched away at my drawings for his poem as he had scratched away at the words. Whiskey was part of my nightly efforts as I am sure it was of his. The liquor likely elevated the emotions as his pen glided across the paper. I could shut my brain off and go to sleep because I did not actually experience what he had. He did not have this luxury, so those dark forces probably guided him off very dark cliffs. As I said, I tried my best to take into consideration that what I was working on was created by a real human being with real emotions. I tried to be an empathetic person as I drew these illustrations for words written by a suffering man.

"Annabel Lee" was first published by the *New-York Daily Tribune* on October 9, 1849. As that edition was hitting the streets, Edgar Allan Poe was being lowered into the ground. He had died two days prior on October 7. I took this fact as a strange bit of inspiration while making the pictures for my edition of the poem. These anomalies have their way of driving an artist. They are the strange surprise twists that are too implausible to be faked. They are the universe giving us what we need to make our brains wonder about oddities and mystery.

Two years after completing my "Annabel Lee," I was offered the role of Guest Juror and Guest Lecturer for the MFA Class of Illustrators at the Maryland Institute College of Art (MICA), in Baltimore, Maryland. This was not the first time I had spoken at MICA, but it was the first time that I had spoken at MICA since dedicating some of my artistic efforts to illustrating Poe. When I arrived in Baltimore the October evening before I was to lecture, the weather was poor. Drizzly, not so good for walking and not so good for remaining dry. I knew where I was going and what I would be speaking about, so I pointed my car in the direction of West Fayette Street. What I recall about the night is mostly visual. I remember how the streetlights through the mist lit everything up in an orange glow. The buildings surrounding me all looked coated in foggy-tangerine shrouds. The people on the streets took on the same atmospheric perspective—there but glowing. Carrying grocery bags and glowing.

When I arrived at the Westminster Hall and Burying Ground, I parked my car on the street and braved the rain. The ground of the small churchyard was muddy. There was no grass, and there was quite a bit of refuse scattered about. The soil looked like it had been heavily trod upon, and the grave markers in the yard looked unimpressive. I had to look through the gates because access had already closed for the day, but before me stood the monument to our club member, Edgar.

What a strange thing being an artist or an author can be. I had spent so much of my mental efforts trying to feel what he must have felt. How odd is that? What sort of connection was I trying to feel with someone who never once in his lifetime had any clue that I would be born one hundred and thirty-one years later? I suppose that is what great works coupled with the lore that we create about our heroes' lives can do to us. For me, art and artists, stories and authors, have always been my connection to history and to the past. Poe's poem, along with the works of many great poets, offers a lesson in history. A beguiling turn of phrase, a line, or a stanza for me to latch onto makes me feel like I know a bit more about life in their times. I process these words in my mind, and I see colors, smell aromas, and hear sounds. The connection that I feel to my predecessors comes through the reading of poetry and the viewing of paintings.

When I lecture in my classes at Frostburg State University, I harp on the fact that visual art is another language. Any language can be learned and is simply a form of communication. What people choose to do with their language and how they communicate is wholly inside each individual to realize and express. Most will confine their language use to the practical purpose of navigating the daily needs of life. A few will awe all of us with their virtuosity.

I hope that I will always remember sitting on my couch as a ten-year-old boy and being introduced to "The Raven" through a cartoon. I hope that I will always remember the orange glows on a rainy night in Baltimore—the night I visited the grave of a great poet. I do not remember much about what I said when I lectured the following evening about drawing the pages for "Annabel Lee," but I am certain it had to do with forging a strange connection with a person whom I had never met. I hope that I will always be able to close my eyes and see pictures when I think of the words "In her sepulchre there by the sea." I hope I will always be able to smell the sharp, salt air evoked by "In her tomb by the sounding sea." If I cannot do these things, then I am probably in mine.

6

"THE WILD COURAGE OF DESPAIR": ON VISITING POE'S QUEER SPACES IN THE YEARS AFTER PULSE

Ian Muneshwar

I moved to Boston in my early twenties, having known I was gay for some years but not yet having dared to enter a bar or club, to be visible. I was lucky, during this time, to meet L—a gentle, rootless boy who would become a close companion. It was L who convinced me to attend my first public event in Boston's queer community. It was an evening called Fascination, a monthly gathering for the kink, fetish, and leather communities. At the time, Fascination was held at a dive bar just south of the Boston Common, a few hundred feet from the place where Edgar Allan Poe was born.

I attended Fascination for the first time on the sort of dour, Bostonian evening that populates so much of Poe's work—it was late into autumn, the leaves well past their peak and now thoroughly glutted into the drainpipes and sewer grates. I got off the T and hurried across the Common alone; L would be waiting for me outside the bar. I was already a bit drunk and more than a bit cold, but I still stopped, after exiting the Common, to study the statue that stood at the center of a red-bricked square. It was Poe, patinaed green and striding purposefully, suitcase in hand. A raven clamored out of the suitcase, a few wingbeats ahead of its author. The wind was too brisk for me to linger, but when I started walking again, I lengthened my strides, ginning myself up to the task of entering that bar with the conviction I saw in the statue's features. A small homage from an aspiring horror writer to a master of the craft.

I would pass Poe's statue on the way to Fascination once a month for the next few years. Most weeks, I thought nothing of it, being preoccupied with thoughts of L and the other friends I had made through those years. But one week early in the summer of 2016, I stopped to face the statue. I stopped that evening because I was afraid to keep walking, afraid to enter the bar.

The night before, the queer community had endured a shattering horror: a man had walked into Pulse, a gay nightclub in Orlando, and murdered forty-nine people inside. It was—until the following year—the deadliest mass shooting in American history.[1] The killer had violated the holiest of queer spaces: the local club, the drag queens' stage, the dance floor. In doing so, he had sent a message to every gay person hurt by the atrocity: You are not safe, and you should be afraid.

As I stood in front of Poe, I considered whether or not I should keep walking, whether or not it would be safer to just stay home tonight. I was furious but terrified—fixed by a paralysis that was, I imagine, exactly what the killer had hoped I would feel.

I first met Poe many years before this night, in the form of Roger Corman's 1960 film *House of Usher*. I saw this adaptation when I was eleven, courtesy of my mother's obsession with silver screen scares. Vincent Price's performance is what my mother would describe as "good, creepy fun"—as Roderick Usher, Price stalks across the set in garish Victorian garb, simultaneously sinister and effete, brooding and hysterical.

---

[1] Alyson Hurt and Ariel Zambelich, "3 Hours in Orlando: Piecing Together an Attack and its Aftermath," *National Public Radio,* June, 26, 2016, https://www.npr.org/2016/06/16/482322488/orlando-shooting-what-happened-update.

What my mother could not have anticipated was that Usher spoke to my still-closeted but burgeoning queer sensibilities with an alarming intimacy. Corman situates Usher as a foil to the film's virile protagonist, Philip Winthrop. Mark Damon plays Winthrop as a square-jawed, assertive Bostonian who charges into the Gothic dereliction of the Ushers' lives to rescue his betrothed—Roderick's sister, Madeline. In his first meeting with Usher, Winthrop strides to the center of the room, hands clenched in fists; he is heterosexual masculinity embodied, so convinced of the purity and necessity of his love for Madeline, so certain that he must overcome anything that stands between him and his desire. Usher, by contrast, skirts the room's edges, waving his long, delicate hands when Winthrop speaks too loudly, confining himself to a chair against the wall while Winthrop remains fixed at the center of the frame. Even before I understood Usher's motives, I identified with his reactions. This was also how I responded when faced with the (often-misplaced) confidence of the other boys my age. Price's wincing, hostile reluctance externalized what I felt so acutely and so often in the presence of my peers.

My attachment to Usher only intensified as this interaction went on. Upon being asked by Winthrop whether it was really "so incredible" that he should want to marry Madeline, Usher drily replies: "If you only knew how incredible. And I suppose this—this vision—includes children?"[2] In my eleven years raised by a Fox News-watching, church-attending family, this was the first time I had ever heard someone seemingly reject the imperative of heterosexuality, the necessity of marriage and the nuclear family. And not only did he reject it, but he did so with such venom and disdain! I sat up a little straighter, watched more closely. At this point in my young life, I did not fully understand why I was filled with a nebulous sense of dread at the idea of a wife and children being a mandatory

---

[2] *House of Usher*, directed by Richard Corman, performances by Vincent Price, Mark Damon, and Myrna Fahey (1960; Los Angeles, CA: Alta Vista Productions).

aspect of my future; all I knew was that Roderick Usher was the only lifeline that had been thrown my way as I floundered, silently, in the tide of heteronormativity.

I would not know until a few years later that Corman's adaptation had not captured the totality and complexity of Usher's queerness. In high school, I finally read "The Fall of the House of Usher." I was surprised to find that the unnamed narrator of Poe's story does not share any of Winthrop's motivations in coming to the estate. He is not betrothed to Madeline; in fact, he is not even aware of Madeline's existence until after he enters the house. It is, instead, his own relationship with Roderick—an intense and inscrutable friendship—that draws him into the Ushers' doomed presence.

Early in his account of Usher, the narrator notes that, in their youth, they had been "boon companions" and "intimate associates."[3] These descriptions did not, at first, strike me as anything out of the ordinary until I reached the passage where the narrator first describes his memory of Usher. He says,

> the character of his face had been at all times remarkable. A cadaverousness of complexion; an eye large, liquid, and luminous beyond comparison; lips somewhat thin and very pallid, but of a surpassingly beautiful curve [...] a finely moulded chin, speaking, in its want of prominence, of a want of moral energy; hair of a more than web-like softness and tenuity [...][4]

The abundant detail of this description serves, in part, to contrast some of the changes the narrator notes in Usher's physicality: to create parallels between Usher's bodily transformation and the ever-deteriorating state of the house. But the attentiveness of the narrator's recollection also reminded me, uncomfortably, of the way I looked at my close male friends. Though the description veers toward occasional sensuality, it is not a wholly flattering portrait. It is

---

[3] Edgar Allan Poe, "The Fall of the House of Usher," in *The Collected Works of Edgar Allan Poe*, ed. T. O. Mabbott, vol. 2 (Cambridge: Belknap Press of Harvard University Press, 1978), 398.

[4] Ibid., 401–402.

a catalogue borne of careful observation and comparison, of reflection on how Usher's physicality seems to mirror the narrator's understanding of his personality. It is a surprisingly intimate inventory of detail for one man to make of another man's body.

The intimacy that the narrator builds with Usher over the course of the story is not physical. It cannot be because Usher is retreating from embodiment, plagued as he is by a "morbid acuteness of the senses" that forces him away from sound, light, and taste alike.[5] The narrator approaches Usher, instead, through creative media. They spend "many solemn hours" alone together, playing the guitar, painting, and reciting poetry.[6] In the tale's climactic moments, as Usher descends into irrationality, the narrator comforts his companion by reading to him from the fictional "'Mad Trist' of Sir Launcelot Canning"—a text that the narrator jokingly calls a "favorite" of Usher's because its "unimaginative prolixity" does not align with their shared literary taste.[7]

This relationship built on shared artistic pursuits also felt, to my high-school-aged self, distressingly familiar. This was how I interacted with my closest male friend, whose features I studied with stolen glances and whose every accidental touch I committed to memory. Any deliberate expression of physical intimacy between us was unimaginable. Instead, we memorized the same Romantic poetry and listened to the same string quartets; we took all of the same classes, watched the same silent films. We fashioned a relationship out of shared references and compatible sensibilities, creating a world entirely separate from the mundane, concrete reality of our peers. For me, for many years, this was substituted for anything approaching the romantic; impossible queer longing sublimated into safe, sexless intellectual intimacy.

That first time I read the ending of "Usher," it felt like a warning. Roderick is destroyed by the murderous return of his ugliest secret:

---

[5] Ibid., 403.
[6] Ibid., 405.
[7] Ibid., 413.

Madeline breaks free of her living burial and kills her brother, leaving him "a victim to the terrors he had anticipated."[8] This phrase haunted me. How long had Usher anticipated his own demise? Was it when he sealed his own sister's tomb that he knew his familial curse would end him? Maybe when he invited the narrator to the house? Or was it earlier still, before the events of the story even began: did he first foresee his destruction when he realized he would have to keep his darkness hidden, entombed? I identified all too well with the prospect of holding a secret that felt impossible to articulate to anyone other than that closest companion but knowing, simultaneously, that the act of articulation would also be one of self-annihilation. Perhaps not an annihilation as literal and dramatic as Usher's but still a destruction of the sexless, anodyne public self I had so carefully crafted: a destruction that would denature the tenderness I shared with my close male friends.

The narrator of Poe's story avoids this end. By fleeing the one space in which he could create his "closer and still closer intimacy" with Roderick, the narrator is able to observe its demise: a fissure splits the house from its roof to its foundations.[9] The House of Usher is not just destroyed, though; it is erased completely, swallowed by a "deep and dank tarn."[10] At fifteen years old, terrified by a secret that I was certain would ruin me, this seemed like the only appropriate conclusion. Every space that could nurture queerness was slated for oblivion. Every deviation from the heteronorm erased.

Years later, as I faced Poe's statue in fear and in grief, that dank tarn felt closer than ever.

11/20/22: As I write this, I'm learning that last night a gunman walked into Club Q, a gay club in Colorado Springs, and opened fire. Five people are dead. Many others are hospitalized in critical condition.

---

[8] Ibid., 417.
[9] Ibid., 404–405.
[10] Ibid., 417.

89

The night after Pulse, I did go to the club. I could tell that Fascination was a different place even before I entered. There was a line of men at the front door, showing IDs and paying the cover. The normally raucous group was so hushed I could hear traffic moving at the far end of the block.

The event was held in the bar's basement, a windowless place with concrete floors and an understocked bar. The single restroom, burrowed into the back wall, had two urinals without a divider and a single stall that did not lock. Someone had raised a portable screen alongside the bar. Vintage porn played from a projector: a man laid out on a locker room bench, his feet in white tube socks hooked over his coach's shoulders.

We undressed silently, slipping out of overcoats and unlacing sneakers, leaning back against the walls so we could take our jeans off, unburden ourselves of respectability. We wore harnesses beneath our button-downs, jockstraps and cockrings beneath the rest. We pulled out pumps and leather jackets, neoprene pup masks, lace and fishnets and unlit cigars. There was nowhere to put the clothes we had shed, so we bunched them into corners and heaped them under stacked chairs. We never worried that anything would be stolen.

That night, I studied the basement with shameful attention: I made a list of possible exits; I inventoried potential hiding places; I imagined different scenarios for survival if a man with a gun appeared in one of the doorways. I loathed myself for this because it felt like submission. I was living by the Pulse shooter's rules, allowing him to shift the gay bar's center of focus away from joy, desire, and community and toward the all-consuming locus of fear. I was Roderick all over again, relentlessly anticipating terror.

Eventually, though, the music came on and cocktails were poured. Eventually, we began to dance and to flirt, and a cute boy coaxed my eyes away from the two unprotected exits and toward the eagerness of his smile, the warmth and prick of his beard. Eventually, it was two in the morning, and the lights came on.

As the evening ended, I ran into Fascination's organizer on the street. I thanked him for another invigorating gathering, and unable or perhaps unwilling to avoid the obvious, I thanked him for not cancelling Fascination tonight, of all nights.

"How could I?" he said to me. "We need this now more than ever before."

11/21/22: It's reported that the Club Q shooter was stopped by some of the patrons, one of whom bludgeoned the shooter with their own gun.[11]

When, as a teenager, I first read "The Masque of the Red Death," I could not have known how Prince Prospero's "gay and magnificent revel" would one day mirror my community's experiences of queer nightlife.[12] Then, my teachers interpreted the short story as a moralizing tale about hedonism and excess, an indictment of Prospero's attempt to evade his duties to his dying kingdom. Entrenched as I was in the internalized heterosexism of the closet, I did not question the notion that there must be some inherent link between immorality and the decadence of Prospero's masquerade. I never asked whether or not there was anything Prospero could do to aid his ailing citizens. I never considered that the masquerade itself might represent the fulfillment of such an obligation. My judgment of the Prince was also informed by how discomfiting I found the descriptions of the ball: I did not need to be out of the closet and in a kink community to imagine what was meant by the masquerade being equipped with "all the appliances of pleasure."[13]

I would encounter "Masque" again later, a few years after Pulse. This second reading was a very different experience from the first. It shocked me how personal this story now felt and how my

---

[11] Dave Phillips, "Army Veteran Went into 'Combat Mode' to Disarm Club Q Shooter," *The New York Times*, Nov. 21, 2022, https://www.nytimes.com/2022/11/21/us/colorado-springs-shooting-club-q-hero.html.

[12] Edgar Allan Poe, "The Masque of the Red Death," in *The Collected Works of Edgar Allan Poe*, ed. T. O. Mabbott, vol. 2 (Cambridge: Belknap Press of Harvard University Press, 1978), 673.

[13] Ibid., 671.

identification had shifted away from the omniscient first-person narrator's judgement of Prospero and toward the masque's attendees themselves.

The Prince's ball is queer in many senses of the word. Queer, certainly, in the sense that it is aesthetically strange, with its tolling clock and color-coordinated chambers that seem to serve no purpose other than to give the guests an atmosphere of otherworldliness. The narrator never explicitly states that Prospero or the attendees are themselves queer. In fact, the narration is so preoccupied with relating the physical space of the masquerade that it is noticeably—and, perhaps, tellingly—absent any descriptions of what happens within these rooms. We know that the ball "was a voluptuous scene" and Prospero's plans for it were "bold and fiery, and his conceptions glowed with barbaric lustre."[14] "Voluptuous" connotes sensuality, carnality, and pleasure, but what does it mean for that description to be tempered by the notion of barbarism? Would the narrator perceive queer sensuality as barbaric? This absence in the story's otherwise abundant descriptions creates a space for the queer imagination to intervene.

In revisiting these details of the masquerade, the aspect of its queerness that I most identified with, and that most clearly recalled my evenings at Fascination, actually had little to do with these intimations of gay sex. I was reminded of bell hooks's articulation of the "essence" of queer selfhood:

> queer not as being about who you're having sex with (that can be a dimension of it); but queer as being about the self that is at odds with everything around it and has to invent, create and find a place to speak and to thrive and to live.[15]

The masquerade is just this: an audacious act of invention that aims to build a space in which the remaining members of a set-upon

---

[14] Ibid., 671, 673.

[15] bell hooks, "Are You Still a Slave? Liberating the Black Female Body," YouTube, uploaded by The New School, 7 May 2014, https://www.youtube.com/watch?v=rJk0hNROvzs&t.

population can survive and, in their survival, find pleasure. Prospero's aims are queer in the sense that they are at odds with heteronormative sensibility. Is it really "barbaric" for the rooms of his cloistered palace to be filled with dancing, music, and fornication? For the ball to "beat feverishly with the heart of life" even while there is so much death and suffering beyond its walls?[16] To the queer eye, this is not barbarism but necessity; it is the preservation of self and the creation of culture in the face of obliteration.

Of course, Prospero and his revelers cannot evade destruction. Many queer readers will see a double image when the stranger enters the ball, "shrouded from head to toe in the habiliments of the grave."[17] First, it is nearly impossible to read of the Red Death and not immediately have AIDS called to mind. Much has been made of the connection between this epidemic and Poe's fictional disease defined by "redness and the horror of blood."[18]

But for the modern queer reader, there is a second horror transposed over the first: the figure of an intruder breaking into our most intimate, celebratory space, covered in blood. During the Pulse massacre, the victims lost so much blood that the Orlando Regional Medical Center depleted its supply entirely and needed to send for more from local hospitals. A surgical resident at ORMC wore sneakers stained with the victims' blood every day he worked until the last living victim was discharged. "I will keep them in my office," he said of the sneakers. "I want to see them in front of me every time I go to work."[19]

---

[16] Poe, "The Masque," 674.

[17] Ibid., 675.

[18] Ibid., 670. For an example of a reading of this Poe tale within the context of the AIDS epidemic as well as additional queer interpretations of Poe's texts, see Paul Christian Jones, *Poe, Queerness, and the End of Time* (New York: Springer, 2022).

[19] Merrit Kennedy, "A Surgeon's Bloodstained Shoes Have Become a Symbol of Defiance," *National Public Radio*, June 17, 2016, https://www.npr.org/sections/thetwo-way/2016/06/17/482532247/a-surgeons-bloodstained-shoes-have-become-a-symbol-of-orlandos-defiance.

12/16/22: Twenty-five people were injured in the Colorado Springs shooting, nineteen by gunfire. Five are dead: Daniel Davis Aston, Kelly Loving, Ashley Paugh, Derrick Rump, Raymond Green Vance. Vance was at the club celebrating his girlfriend's birthday; it was his girlfriend's father who attacked the shooter and beat the shooter with the shooter's own gun.[20] Two others assisted him: a man who later pulled the gun away and a transwoman who stomped on the shooter with her heels.[21]

Perhaps the most humanizing moment for Prospero—and the moment in which my identification shifts wholly away from the narrator and toward the revelers—comes in the story's final moments. Upon seeing the "spectral image" of the Red Death enter, the Prince's emotions vacillate: he is, at first, consumed by anger that someone would break into his space and dress in a mockery of the people dying outside; then, in fear, he runs from the intruder before being pushed by his courage and outrage to confront the Red Death with a dagger.[22] The narrator assesses Prospero's impulse to flee as "momentary cowardice," but I cannot imagine a more sane and relatable reaction.[23] Running from the specter of death is, I know, what I would do in this situation; it was, for so long, the first recourse suggested by the Department of Homeland Security in the event of an active shooter; it was what so many of the patrons of Pulse and Club Q did to try to save their own lives.[24]

---

[20] Phillips.

[21] "Club Q Mass Shooting: Trans Woman Stopped Killer with 'High Heels,'" *news.com.au*, Nov. 23, 2022, https://www.news.com.au/world/north-america/two-patrons-and-a-drag-queen-praised-for-preventing-more-deaths-in-colorado-springs-mass-shooting/news-story/cf3d521ef-bcda4c316bc04ab50ca08dc.

[22] Poe, "The Masque," 675.

[23] Ibid., 676.

[24] "Active Shooter: How to Respond," *U.S. Department of Homeland Security*, accessed December 29, 2022, https://www.dhs.gov/xlibrary/assets/active_shooter_booklet.pdf.

In the case of the Colorado Springs shooting, though, not everyone sought shelter. Like Prospero and the revelers, several patrons of Club Q attacked the shooter. Richard Fierro, the combat veteran who tackled the shooter, said that he does not remember how he overcame his fear in that moment. He did not even remember what was happening when he made the decision to attack: "Was he shooting at the time?" Fierro wondered in an interview. "Was he about to shoot?…I do not know. I just knew I had to take him down."[25] The narrator of "Masque" says that the revelers "threw themselves" at the figure of the Red Death with "the wild courage of despair."[26] It is difficult to imagine the quality of courage that could motivate someone to run toward the bullets discharging from a rifle. To imagine the despair that would obliterate every memory of the moments that were nearly Fierro's last. The type of hopelessness that, as Poe's narrator suggests, creates this "wild courage" seems like it should belong solely to battlefields and war zones. Now, it also belongs to the gay bar.

I initially read the phrase "the wild courage of despair" as meaning that the revelers found courage in their despair. This is a tempting interpretation; I would like to subscribe to the notion that there is strength to be found even in our bleakest emotional states. There are, though, other possible valences of meaning here. Early in the story, the narrator criticizes Prospero and his followers, saying that they felt it was "folly to grieve, or to think" while within the walls of the Prince's abbey.[27] If I am being honest with myself, this numbness to the horrors of the outside world is what I wanted to feel when I attended Fascination the night after Pulse. Yes, I wanted to be with my community, and yes, I wanted to prove to the shooter that our community could survive even this. But I also wanted to drink and dance, to forget, however briefly, that we just endured a wound that might never truly heal. I hoped that I could compartmentalize my

---

[25] Phillips.
[26] Poe, "The Masque," 676.
[27] Ibid., 671.

grief, if only for a night.

Perhaps, in the short story's final moments, the revelers start thinking and grieving. The phrase "the wild courage of despair" does not only suggest that they find courage in their despair but also that they have the courage to finally feel their despair. Maybe it is not courage but grief, loss, and hopelessness that finally motivate the revelers to fling themselves at the Red Death in an attempt to protect the only space in which they might survive. I know that it must take a truly wild courage to give yourself to that kind of despair because all these years later, when I go to the gay bar, I am still trying to stop myself from marking the exits, scanning the crowd, anticipating ruin.

Maybe I should not stop myself anymore.

I went to Fascination last night for the first time in some years. It is now held at a different club, but I still passed Poe's statue on my way. I did not stop because I was already thinking about Pulse and the Red Death, about five dead family in Colorado Springs.

In the wake of this most recent shooting, Fascination's organizers changed their policies: entry into the space required a pat down and a bag check. When I stepped into the club and began to undress, I did not chastise myself for seeking every exit. When I scanned the crowd, I did not dismiss my anxiety as ridiculous or unnecessary. I saw so many others watching the dance floor with nervous eyes, breaking away from their conversations every time the front door opened and a stranger entered. I saw friend groups go out of their way to approach the lone figure standing in the corner, to enfold them into conversation, into revelry.

What is the function of despair? For me, right now, it is this: Despair demands constant anxious attention. It does not admit space for unthinking hope. At the same time, though, it will not let us turn our faces away or slide toward numbness and apathy. Despair is an unresolved state. Working toward its resolution might push us toward hopeless, clear-eyed vigilance or it might even produce that wild courage. I believe we need our despair more now than we ever have before.

7

REFLECTIONS ON "POE RETURNING TO BOSTON"

Stefanie Rocknak

It was a cold spring day when I came across the collection of Poe stories in my parents' small library with the crooked, slanted floor. I was in grammar school, a place in rural Maine where the first-grade teacher would put you in the trash can for pulling out your shoelaces. "Why did you do that?" she asked Trevor, who was standing in the trash, crying. "Because I wanted to." She had a name to match her eyes: Mrs. Pierce. "Don't ever tell me that you did something just because 'you wanted to,'" she snapped and plucked him out of the can.

Just a couple of paragraphs into "The Tell-Tale Heart," Poe starts in about the old man's eye: "I think it was his eye! yes, it was this! One of his eyes resembled that of a vulture—a pale blue eye, with a film over it."[1] That wasn't Mrs. Pierce's eye, but it was pretty close. I had to read more. And more. My six-year-old mind could not help but wonder whether there was something underneath the floor in my house.

---

[1] Edgar Allan Poe, "The Tell-Tale Heart," in *The Collected Works of Edgar Allan Poe*, ed. T. O. Mabbott, vol. 3 (Cambridge: Belknap Press of Harvard University Press, 1978), 792.

I read Poe again in college, as an American Studies major at Colby College. "The Cask of Amontillado" struck me. What was it with Poe and people being walled in? Trapped? I was reading Faulkner at the same time—the last lines of *Light in August* have stayed with me for over thirty years: "My, my. A body does get around. Here we ain't been coming from Alabama but two months, and now it's already Tennessee."[2] Not really. Her body didn't go much of anywhere. She was stuck in the desperate, dulling bigotry of the South, in small-mindedness.

Many of my early sculptures, all wooden human figures, are about this. Their eyes are generally blank and wide, and their limbs are still and unmoving. They are witnesses, or even victims, but never perpetrators. Some of the titles of these early pieces speak for themselves: "The Thousand Yard Stare: Cambodian Prisoner at Phnom Penh," "Woman on a Train," "Woman in Crowd," "Crucifix."[3] They seem to be mired in human depravity, trapped under the floor of a wicked world.

But my Poe sculpture, "Poe Returning to Boston," is not. Years earlier, back in that library in Maine, I am sure I ran across a small book with Poe's poems and a few of his stories. It was my grandmother's when she was a child, published in 1907. Inscribed inside the front cover, in my grandmother's careful handwriting, are the following lines: "Here comes Poe with his raven like Barnaby Rudge / 3/5 of him genius and 2/5 fudge LOWELL." At the time, I had no idea who Lowell was, but somehow, I absorbed those lines and reappropriated James Russell Lowell's graphic insult into Poe's triumphant return home.

So with a giant raven at his side, Poe strides away from his detractors and critics; the Boston "Frogpondians" (e.g. Lowell) represented by the Frog Pond in the Common behind him. He is marching towards his childhood apartment, which used to stand just a few

---

[2] William Faulkner, *Light in August* (New York: Vintage Books, 1972), 204.
[3] To view images of these sculptures, visit https://www.steffrocknak.net/otherwork.

blocks from the sculpture at 62 Carver Street.[4]

When Poe was alive, three railroad stations, just to the west of Poe Square, dispersed and collected thousands of travelers. This included the Boston-to-Providence route, which Poe frequently traveled, especially near the end of his life. My Poe is just off this train, on his way home. His reputation, represented by the oversized raven at his side, bursts from the trunk on a vindicatory flight. Despite his critics' best attempts, his work has prevailed, although he was confined and diminished in so many ways during his lifetime: trapped by poverty, shame, anger, drink, and death.

It is fitting, then, that this sculpture is Poe's actual height (5'8"), which is smallish, while the raven is huge. At night, one light shines on their eternal walk, casting a large shadow of the raven to the right of the statue. It's as if in two dimensions; Poe becomes the raven, which is appropriate. Like it or not, an artist is often annexed by their signature work, especially in the shadow of death.

When sculpting Poe's head, I looked at a number of images to capture his spirit, but I primarily focused on the "Ultima Thule" and "Whitman" daguerreotypes. They were taken a few days apart in 1848, just four days after Poe attempted suicide.[5] I focused on the pronounced asymmetry of Poe's face that we see in the Thule image—which is probably the most well-known image of Poe. But I changed the direction of his hair to reflect the howling Boston wind—the ghosts of his critics. Some features, e.g., the bags under his eyes, are exaggerated so they would show up in the bronze. Although Boston's Poe is determined, he is tired.

The clothes that he returns home in are also based on these images, including the great coat, which "may be the one Mary Gove Nichols describes as having been used to provide warmth for

---

[4] For additional information on Poe's connection to Boston, see Katherine J. Kim, "Poe and Boston," in *Poe and Place*, ed. Philip Edward Phillips (London: Palgrave MacMillan, 2018), 21–41.

[5] Michael J. Deas, *The Portraits and Daguerreotypes of Edgar Allan Poe* (Charlottesville: University of Virginia, 1989), 36–46.

Virginia Poe as she lay dying of tuberculosis in 1847."[6] This precious garment blows hollow in the wind, mimicking the raven's wings; they are one in Poe's expansive grief: "Darkness there and nothing more."[7]

Trailing behind the sculpture are six bronze "pages" that sit flush with the bricks. Each page includes a fragment—chosen in collaboration with scholars—from Poe's writing that is either about Boston or was published in Boston, underlining his connection to the city:

1. "Villains!" I shrieked, "dissemble no more! I admit the deed!—tear up the planks!—here, here!—it is the beating of his hideous heart!"

From "The Tell-Tale Heart," first published in The Pioneer, *a Boston literary magazine, in January 1843.*

2. *All* that we see or seem / Is but a dream within a dream.

From "A Dream within a Dream," first published in The Flag of Our Union, *a Boston newspaper, on March 31, 1849.*

3. The Bostonians are very well in their way. Their hotels are bad. Their pumpkin pies are delicious. Their poetry is not so good. Their common is no common thing—and the duck-pond might answer—if its answer could be heard for the frogs.

From "Editorial Miscellany," Broadway Journal, *a New York literary magazine, November 1, 1845.*

4. I reach'd my home—my home no more— / For all was flown that made it so— / I pass'd from out its mossy door, / In vacant idleness of woe.

From "Tamerlane," included in Poe's first book, Tamerlane and Other Poems by a Bostonian, *printed in Boston by Calvin F.S. Thomas in 1827.*

5. Because I feel that, in the heavens above, / The angels, whispering to one another, / Can find, among their burning terms of love, / None so devotional as that of "mother,"

---

[6] Deas, 42.

[7] Edgar Allan Poe, "The Raven," in *The Collected Works of Edgar Allan Poe,* ed. T. O. Mabbott, vol. 1 (Cambridge: Belknap Press of Harvard University Press, 1969), 365.

From "Sonnet—To My Mother," first published in The Flag of Our Union *on July 7, 1849.*

6. We want characters—*characters*, man—something novel—out of the way. We are wearied with this everlasting sameness. Come, drink! the wine will brighten your wits.

From "Hop-Frog," first published in The Flag of Our Union, *on March 7, 1849.*

In keeping with the Boston theme, a heart sits on the pile of papers that spill out of the back of the trunk. Not only was "The Tell-Tale Heart" published in Boston, but it was the first Poe story that I read years ago in Maine while sitting on that crooked floor. Initially, I had planned to have the heart secured to the ground behind Poe, but this would have been a tripping hazard, so I placed it high up on the papers instead, out of the way of busy feet.

From start to finish, the sculpture, including making the maquette and the extensive planning, took about 1,000 hours of my time (and the time of multiple administrators and assistants, especially Professor Paul Lewis). It was completed under unrelenting deadlines: I had about two months to create the 19" wooden model and about three months to make the life-size clay sculpture. When the clay figure was finished, I carefully cut it up, packed it into a moving van, and drove it from my studio in upstate New York to the foundry in Chelsea, Massachusetts. It was a frigid winter day, and luckily I had friends who helped me make the trip, including someone who drove my car to Boston so I would have a way to get back to New York.

I put the clay sculpture back together again at the foundry, and Poe was inspected one last time by the Boston Art Commission and the Edgar Allan Poe Foundation of Boston. Then he was cut up—again—and turned into wax pieces. I spent about a week cleaning up all the details in the wax, and then they were cast in bronze. The foundry welded him together, applied the patina, and attached him to a giant steel plate, which lies beneath the bricks. At around 5 am, he was trucked into Boston, and the steel plate was bolted to the concrete foundation, just below the surface of the square. The bricks were then carefully wedged between his feet and the plate, so it looks like he is walking on them.

Friends of mine who live in Boston tell me that they visit Poe often, some on their way to and from work. They touch his hand or the tip of the Raven's wing, causing the bronze to turn gold. I am honored that I could give him the homecoming that he never had in his lifetime, that in some small way I could free him from the disrespect that Boston plastered him with when he was alive.

The large wooden sculpture that I completed immediately after finishing Poe depicts an oversized man in a labored run: "Gut Check."[8] But unlike Poe, this figure is not triumphant. If wood could sweat... "Gut Check" is a vignette of depravity lurching through depravity. He is repellent. In some respects, it's about the patriarchy on the run—the parochialism that has suppressed, and continues to suppress, so many women. Maybe making Poe inspired me to stop carving witnesses and to start making the plug-uglies instead.

For instance, in 2019, I finished "The Hollow Man."[9] He is the male capitalist dragon. His torso is a hollow, brightly painted children's block. Smaller antique building blocks comprise his lair; they are his hotels, banks, and high-rises. He takes, he hoards. But he seems to be entirely unaware that he is standing in his underwear. Flies crawl over him, as if he is covered in his own waste.

"The Star Spangled Idiot: An American Nutcracker" was finished in the summer of 2020, before the capitol riots.[10] He represents a perverted form of American patriotism: toxic nationalism. From some angles, the figure is frightening and dangerous—he is overcome with rage. But from other angles, it is clear that he is a toy soldier, playing dress-up. His boots are too big, and his costume is

---

[8] To view images of this sculpture, visit https://www.steffrocknak.net/gutcheck.

[9] To view images of this sculpture, visit https://www.steffrocknak.net/the-hollow-man.

[10] To view images of this sculpture, visit https://www.steffrocknak.net/the-nutcracker.

mismatched. It's as if he is an overgrown child who found Daddy's old army boots and cobbled them together with a gladiator skirt from last year's school play. The "patriotism" emanating from his head is confused and twisted. The "tribal" tattoos on his back and upper shoulders are fueled by his idolization of indigenous courage, although he is overtly racist towards anyone of color. He is being manipulated: his mouth opens and barks when a lever is moved on his back. His arms swing back like a threatening bully but only when pulled by a figure much larger than him. The tattoo on his belly reads: "I Follow The Chosen One."

"The Bad Egg," completed in 2021, consists of three carved wooden figures and four prefabricated nesting eggs.[11] The first, largest figure is a ballet dancer, in full delightful flight over a field of daisies. His progressive goodness is on overt display; he is performing for his audience. But as we move further inside his head, we see that he is angry, stubborn, and not quite as beautiful as we first thought. Still further inside his head, we see him crawling about, depraved and desperate. The daisies have morphed into his female victims trapped below him. The fourth and smallest egg is cracked and solid with rot. Ultimately, despite all his gesticulations, we know that this is a very small man.

In 2022, I finished "Peach Tree Dish," which is modeled after a traditional "rod puppet."[12] The female figure is attached to the control plate with a rod through its head. She hovers over a painted "peach tree dish" and wears a polka dot dress to emphasize how she infantilizes herself. She is a political clown, doing the bidding of what controls her. Strings are permanently attached.

---

[11] To view images of this sculpture, visit https://www.steffrocknak.net/the-bad-egg.

[12] To view images of this sculpture, visit https://www.instagram.com/steffrocknak

Poe Returning to Boston, which is located at
Edgar Allan Poe Square in Boston, Massachusetts.

Courtesy Stefanie Rocknak

It's hard, though, to immerse myself in this toxic soup on a daily basis. How did Poe manage it? I guess, in the end, he didn't. The world ate him up, and we continue to feast on his work—his soul. So a couple of months ago, to pull myself away from Poe's dark vision of the world, I started to work on a small sculpture of a woman reclining in a chair. She is still but not horrified. The chair, which will be painted, embraces her. The wood is a limb of white pine taken from the massive tree that used to stand guard over my childhood home in Maine. My family doesn't live there anymore, but a neighbor, who is the same age as I am, grabbed a piece, and I brought it back to my studio in New York. Growing up, we told lots of stories about that tree—how it had been there for an eternity and how it reached for miles into the sky. Watching us, waiting for me to preserve a small piece of it—calling on me to make my way home.

8

SHAPING THE PHILADELPHIA GOTHIC: FROM POE TO THE NEW MILLENNIUM

Christine Neulieb

Delirium and Delight

I am pretty sure my first encounter with Edgar Allan Poe was in fifth grade when my class went to see a stage adaptation of "The Tell-Tale Heart." Wild, maddening, beating-heart sounds pounded louder and louder beneath the stage as the narrator's tense, thrilling descent into madness held me spellbound. Our teacher later used the story as a way to introduce the concept of the unreliable narrator. Don't just take the madman at his word when he tells you "how healthily—how calmly" he speaks. Question and look deeper. In other words: writers can wink; tease; say one thing and mean another. They can be entirely separate people from the narrators they create. That, I thought, was great fun.

I already wanted to be a writer at ten. I had started scribbling novels in spiral notebooks with the ink of an erasable blue ballpoint pen whose smell I will never forget because I felt so much like myself in those hours when I was writing. I had never found anything else that fit so well. So it was as an aspiring storyteller that Poe's story-telling power made me delirious. His words cast a spell. I wanted to learn how to do the same.

One of the things that appealed to me as a half-baked cookie of a youth was how seamlessly he managed to be entertaining and existential at the same time. He was always, always entertaining—evil eyeballs! getting buried alive! dungeons and haunted mansions!—even when he explored love and loss and the fundamental absurdity of the universe. This was something I would never stop believing: "great" literature was not defined by being brainy *instead of* entertaining. A story, any story, could be both at once.

By the time I started sifting through these ideas consciously, I was an English major at a land grant university in the Midwest. There was a distinguished professor there, of the New Criticism school, who had written the introduction for a 1970 paperback anthology of Poe's stories and poetry. When I met him in 1996, he was a grandfatherly lion with a glorious white mane whose booming, gravelly voice won him the role of God in departmental productions of Milton's *Paradise Lost*. The Leonine Professor was very interested in irony, and he made sure we understood what our earlier school-teachers had mentioned in passing about unreliable narrators: that we knew how to spot the use of irony and understand how it worked, so we could see what writers like Poe were up to and be delighted by it.

There has always been something about Poe that is deeply attractive to adolescents, the Leonine Professor was fond of pointing out. Something about his fiction that's accessible even to teenagers, unlike a lot of nineteenth-century works: an element of the lurid, the sensational, the exaggerated and overwrought. Many scholars of the mid-twentieth century treated him dismissively because of this, as though no one would write about madmen and metempsychosis if they had any grasp of reality at all. But when you read Poe closely, there is almost always the undeniable undercurrent of irony and dark comedy, the flash of metafiction.

I ended up being deeply formed by all the nineteenth-century American Romantics, especially Poe and Hawthorne, who were the most accessible to my teenage mind. I developed a sensibility that leaned toward the baroque, the atmospheric, and the subtly ironic, and I do not think that has changed much. I was so immersed in

107

both the fiction and the critical conversation of early nineteenth-century America during my secondary and post-secondary education that to this day my friends tease me for being a walking anachronism. And for better or worse, I was in my twenties before I read much of anything (with the exception of YA series) published after 1900. When I was a teenager, I wanted to have fun, and part of what I found fun, because I am a colossal weirdo, was Hawthorne and Poe (also Shakespeare).

The range of what I read back then was admittedly limited by the boundaries of the Western canon, and I am grateful that my adult horizons have broadened beyond the deceased white fellows whom my teachers venerated in the 1990s. But what my early teachers did right was to underline the idea of reading nineteenth-century fiction because it was delicious and funny and spooky and insightful, not because it was somehow good for me like broccoli. I was never shamed for enjoying Gothic fiction as such, which is fortunate, because I had an incredibly short attention span for books that I disliked, and I do not know that I would have found a way to stick with the art of writing otherwise. Whenever I was told "read this boring book because it's good for you," I ignored it. Physically, neurologically, I could not force my eyes to stay on the page unless there was some genuine pleasure involved. I would receive a diagnosis of ADHD much later, when I was in my 30s; at the time, I just thought of myself as a principled hedonist.

In other words, I read what I liked. In my free time, I was reading an ocean of Christopher Pike, Tamora Pierce, and Lurlene McDaniel at the same time as I was reading Poe and Hawthorne, Shakespeare and Homer. I loved Shakespeare because it was wall-to-wall dick jokes, drama, and people dying all over the stage in addition to clever wordplay and insight into human nature that pierced like a hidden rapier and then withdrew into the shadows again. And Homer—Homer was delightfully full of monsters. I liked the *Odyssey* much better than the *Iliad* as a student; to this day, I have not once made it through every word of the *Iliad*'s endless catalogues of ships and soldiers. Besides, the *Odyssey* has the unforgettable scene with the dog, which truly fucked me up in the best way and which I still re-read from time to time as a reminder that it's possible to grab a reader's heartstrings and yank them mercilessly and make them beg for more.

I digress. The point is, when I was a young neurodivergent student of literature, it was at the intersection of the lurid and the philosophical that I found what could capture my flighty attention, hold it, and inspire me to engage with it and build on it. When I grew up, those were the kinds of books I wanted to write and the kinds of books I wanted to publish.

Sometimes Mimi Dies at the End

A third memorable encounter with Poe happened when I was in my early twenties, sharing a rickety rental house with six other similarly aged humans. (No, it was not a large house.) It had been passed down from generation to generation of students and young professionals who were hard-up for cash. It was falling apart in a myriad of ways, neglected by its alcohol-dependent owner; once, the living room ceiling collapsed while we were all out of town for the holidays.

Rather suddenly, when I was about twenty-four, the landlord vanished from his house down the block. No one in the neighborhood had heard from him; no one seemed to know where he was. We left rent checks in his mailbox, and they remained uncashed. It was a vast and sinister mystery until he returned, a month or two later—having been to rehab, apparently. He brought a girlfriend home, also from rehab, and announced that it was the last year he would be renting out our house. He planned to renovate it and move in with his girlfriend. We young denizens were de-homed.

This was tragic for us. We loved that house, little though the actual decaying structure deserved it. We decided to hold a wake for it before moving out. Guests were invited to wear black mourning apparel, and during the party, we had a spirited dramatic reading from—what else?—"The Fall of the House of Usher." We read from that same old tattered paperback anthology that had the introduction written by the Leonine Professor.

> With the first glimpse of the building, a sense of insufferable gloom pervaded my spirit. I say insufferable; for the feeling was unrelieved by any of that half-pleasurable, because poetic, sentiment, with which the mind usually receives even the sternest natural images of the desolate or terrible. I looked upon the scene before me—upon the mere house, and the simple landscape features of the domain—upon the bleak walls—upon the vacant eye-like windows—upon a few rank sedges—and upon a few white trunks of decayed trees—with an utter depression of soul which I can compare to no earthly sensation more properly than to the after-dream of the reveller upon opium—the bitter lapse into everyday life—the hideous dropping off of the veil.[1]

Of course there was a certain irony to this reading. Our house was decrepit but not accursed; it was well loved and full of youthful energy and laughter. Still, the decrepitness had its own haunting quality as an ever-present physical reminder of our shared precarious financial situation as young adults in the 2000s. The reality was that *this place* was all we could afford, and when we were turned out, many of us faced limited options. In hindsight, the situation illustrates for me an important reason why Gothic fiction has always appealed to its readers, from nineteenth-century Romanticism right up to contemporary horror: the fragile economic position of the artist in a capitalist economy.

The opera *La Bohème* was written in the 1890s about the fabled life of Bohemians in Paris in the 1830s, which across the pond was the beginning of Poe's full-time writing career. The bohemian artist is a heroic figure of the Romantic sort, free in ways ordinary men can never know, idealized and yet doomed—so precarious is their situation that it may prove fatal, as it does for Mimi in the opera.

---

[1] In order to protect the identity of this professor, I will cite a different anthology for this tale: Edgar Allan Poe, "The Fall of the House of Usher," in *The Collected Works of Edgar Allan Poe*, ed. T. O. Mabbott, vol. 2 (Cambridge: Belknap Press of Harvard University Press, 1978), 397.

Stories like *La Bohème*, written about people akin to Edgar Allan Poe, depict the new industrial economy of the nineteenth century as a devouring beast that often leaves individual creatives out in the cold, burning their manuscripts to keep warm.[2] It demands sometimes unimaginable sacrifices from those who opt out of its profit-driven system. Poe famously struggled with financial precarity, only ever eking out a meager living from his writing. In the first decade of the twenty-first century, my liberal-arts-major friends and I were given a university education that taught us to prize knowledge and art for their own sakes yet saddled us with so much debt that we could hope to make a living from those things even less than Poe. So we related to him on that level, as we did to all the bohemians who have lived in the wake of the Industrial Revolution, as immortalized by Henri Murger and Giacomo Puccini and, a hundred years later, Jonathan Larson.[3] It felt natural to read "Usher" upon the fall of our beloved home, which had been a refuge of cheap rent and convivial community. We were not despairing, back then, not abandoned by society—not yet. But the edge was closer than any of us liked to think about, and some of us were to flirt more closely with it in years to come.

The Gothic, in whatever form—like bohemianism—tends to reflect a society in which creatives face economic marginalization and feel salty about it. I have read with amusement a recent spate of news articles suggesting that surges in goth subculture are harbingers of recession. Beware the goths! An omen of terrible things to come! I'm not sure a correlation like this could ever be statistically

---

[2] In Poe's specific case, his financial circumstances became so dire during the winter of 1846, two years after the publication of "The Raven," that he is reported to have had to resort to covering his wife with his "old military cloak" while she "shiver[ed] in the hectic fever of consumption." When Poe fell ill that same winter, newspapers ran notices to solicit donations for the family. For more details on these instances, see Kenneth Silverman, *Edgar A. Poe: Mournful and Never-ending Remembrance* (New York: HarperPerennial, 1991), 323–326.

[3] In 1996, Jonathan Larson's *Rent*, inspired by *La Bohème*, opened in New York City.

significant, considering the diaphanous and shifting nature of cultural trends. But it does resonate with my understanding of who my audience is and why. I was never a part of American Goth subculture as such. (Not that it wouldn't have been a decent fit in either my teens or twenties; I just had an odd upbringing in which I was mostly too isolated from my peers to be properly a part of any subculture. But that's a subject for a different essay.) My personal aesthetic was Gothic in the sense that I tried to memorize Poe's "The Raven" because it felt cool and darkly Romantic, not in the sense that I was familiar with the merchandise at Hot Topic. It was Gothic in the sense that, of course, I was the one who would suggest reading "The Fall of the House of Usher" at a house party. Yet from my experience interacting with the audiences of contemporary Gothic fiction, I think the sense of economic and existential precariousness is common to both fashion-focused Goth subcultures and to Gothicism more generally.

Growing up in the 1990s, coming of age at the turn of the millennium, there was a veneer of prosperity, a public sense (especially in the conservative Midwest, where I lived) that the Cold War was over, Western democracy had won, and now we could go on in peace and freedom getting richer and richer. Even where material circumstances offered zero concrete reason to believe that prosperity was close at hand, few parents questioned the assumption that their children would grow up to lead lives of greater wealth and comfort than they had, which in turn had been much greater than what their parents knew during the Great Depression. A trajectory of progress trending ever upward.

When I was an adolescent, between the fall of the Berlin Wall in 1989 and the terrorist attacks of September 11, 2001, the general mood I felt in the adults around me—energetic optimism with respect to national progress—always felt wrong. It felt like living in a house that I could see was built on a decaying foundation while everyone around me hummed a happy tune. This produced a crawling sense of unreality shared by many in my generation, which birthed grunge music and, slower and later, the literary Gothics that would flower in the 2010s and 2020s, as it became less and less possible to ignore the noises of termites gnawing.

When it became clear that many young people looked forward to a lower standard of living than their parents had known, with no likelihood of improvement—something I remember feeling personally from 2008 onward—suddenly it was perceived as less odd (and less indulgent) to write Gothics. The old evils—disease, racism, xenophobia, misogyny, resource hoarding, environmental destruction, child abuse—are still with us, and there no longer seems to be much of a survival advantage in denying it as we once did, lest we should discourage burgeoning progress. Now that the plagues have returned and life expectancies are creeping downward instead of upward in many developed countries, perhaps this trend will accelerate.

Anyway, this is a big part of why Poe's literary inheritance retains its fascination for me as a writer, for my peers in the writing world, and for the authors I edit and the readers who receive their work. Because this is our milieu. Because our situation involves more-than-occasional horror and absurdity. But even in an age of a relatively sunny outlook like the 1890s or the 1990s, we would still have been mortal; none of us has much more than a century to walk this earth. So the Gothic has a perennial quality, recycled and reinvented in age after age, and the stories of Poe retain cultural relevance, along with their sprawling lineage of descendants. The societies we construct will always remain vulnerable to shocks and instability—and even when that is not as apparent on the surface of things as it is right now, so will these meatsacks we carry around on our skeletons.

Poe's Neighbors

I am the editorial director of Lanternfish Press, which was founded in 2014 to publish literature of "the rare and strange": literary fiction, but with a Gothic or speculative twist. We also publish Clockwork Editions, reprints of mostly Victorian-era novels and stories. Over my last ten years working as an editor, I have watched various types of Gothic become more common and pervasive in the contemporary literary scene. It seemed to take over YA first, with the acceleration of dystopian nightmare narratives: a prevalence of dark futures. I do not know if this is because young people have a quicker radar for where the zeitgeist is headed or because, while fiction overall started trending in the same direction at once, YA books can be slightly quicker to produce. Anyway, as soon as it became part of my job to call for submissions of literary fiction infused by the Gothic, I started receiving an avalanche of words from Poe's descendants. Many of them do not look or sound much like him. I see brilliant interpretations of the Southern Gothic by young Black authors (read Kayla Chenault, for example); I see revivals of the postcolonial tropical Gothics that flourished in the middle to latter part of the twentieth century and influenced the generation of young writers in the United States who came of age with me. I see space Gothics and urban Gothics; Mexican Gothics like those of Silvia Moreno-Garcia and Isabel Cañas; suburban Gothics; midwestern Gothics; Gothics of everyplace imaginable.

In addition to the subjectively felt sense of economic and existential precariousness that I discussed in the previous section, another thing these proliferating new Gothics seem to have in common is that, although they range across a huge variety of settings, they are all rooted in a deep sense of place. Whatever their setting is, it is important. You can't have Gothics without atmosphere—literally; you can't have them without weather of some kind, without a climate, without rampant nature or a tumbledown house. The Gothic is an embodied form of horror, horror soaked into the physical bones of things. One trend I have seen and look forward to seeing more of is climate-change Gothic. An era of apocalyptic climate change is as natural a habitat for the Gothic as a region of suffocating heat so old it seems eternal. I would love to know how Poe would have written climate-change horror. And I love seeing how young Gothic writers are embracing this topic today, with equal parts poignancy and gallows humor.

Lanternfish Press makes its home in the city of Philadelphia.

We are, in a sense, Poe's neighbors. Our offices are a twenty-minute walk away from the house on Spring Garden Street where Poe once lived. We are separated from him by a mile of distance and 180 years of time. But that's hardly anything; the past does not die in Philadelphia. It lives right alongside the present. If there were ever a city ideally suited to the contemporary development of the Gothic, it's this one. Nostalgia is so heavy here it can be paralyzing. It lays thick on the dusty wares in dim storefronts that have been untouched for decades, with fading signs in 1970s fonts. It sparkles in the chrome of mid-twentieth-century diners that are still packed with patrons on Sunday mornings whether the food is good or not. It spooks you in the silhouette of the broken tailor's dummy that leans askew in a narrow attic window. Here, when a raven flies up and perches on your windowsill and quoths "Nevermore," it's hardly even surprising.

Philadelphia was home to Edgar Allan Poe from 1838 to 1844, during which he worked as an editor as well as a writer. Stories of this time include some of his most memorable, including "The Fall of the House of Usher," "The Pit and the Pendulum," and "The Masque of the Red Death." Literary culture still flourishes in Philadelphia, and anyone who works in the realm of Gothic fiction here cannot help but feel his influence emanating from the house at 7th St and Spring Garden that still stands today as the Edgar Allan Poe National Historic Site. You can visit and tour that house where he used to live and write and where his cousin-wife Virginia, whom he married when she was thirteen years old, fell sick with the dreaded scourge of nineteenth-century urban bohemians, tuberculosis.[4]

I will pass over how creepy it is that he entered into a moderately incestuous marriage with a girl who was only thirteen at the time; you can find plenty of discussions of this topic showing appropriate levels of outrage and disapproval as well as suggestions that their marriage may never have been consummated or not until years after it took place. By the time the couple lived in Philadelphia,

---

[4] Silverman recounts that Poe had witnessed the first sign of this affliction: "Virginia while singing began to bleed from her mouth" (179).

Virginia was in her late teens and early twenties: finally a young woman. It was just then, in the full flower of youth, that she began to rot before Poe's eyes. She took a room of her own in the house on Spring Garden; the couple slept separately, whether to allow her more rest or to avoid contagion or because sexuality had never been a primary focus of their relationship in the first place, I have no idea.

There were so many visitations of epidemic in early Philadelphia, as there were in many crowded places before the advent of antibiotics and as there will be again after antibiotic-resistant strains of disease reach their peak.[5] The difference in Philadelphia is that, for some reason, we held onto the box of Victorian medical instruments we used to use back then and the tissue samples we took. They live at the Mütter Museum, a shrine to morbid oddities that tourists are seldom surprised to discover. Pennsylvania Hospital, founded in 1751, still stands, and we still use it as a hospital. Maybe that is part of why Philadelphia is a city particularly inclined to the morbid and nostalgic. It is older than most cities in the United States, and the Gothic thrives on visible, tangible echoes of the past. Philadelphia had lived experience of a mercantile economy before capitalism supplanted that. It also experienced being the cultural and political capital of a fledgling nation for a hot minute before losing those titles to New York and Washington, DC. Now we are left with only the memories of greatness hanging over us in the form of sycamore trees and monuments.

---

[5] Gothic precursor to Poe and Philadelphia native Charles Brockden Brown penned *Arthur Mervyn; or, Memoirs of the Year 1793*, a novel that featured a particularly infamous yellow fever epidemic. Poe's "The Masque of the Red Death," published in 1842 while Poe resided in Philadelphia, is thought by some to have been inspired by this same epidemic. See these examples of publications that liken the Red Death to yellow fever: SK Vora and SV Ramanan, "Ebola-Poe: A Modern-Day Parallel of the Red Death?," *Emerging Infectious Diseases*, 8, no. 12 (2002): 1521–1523, doi: 10.3201/eid0812.020176 and Molly Caldwell Crosby, *The American Plague: The Untold Story of Yellow Fever* (New York: Berkley Books, 2007).

This city cannot escape its past. I am not sure it would ever want to.

I moved to Philadelphia when I was twenty-seven years old and broke, and my head was a demon-haunted attic. I moved away and back several more times, always returning to this famously gritty and chaotic city. From the start, it struck me as having its own unique Gothic aesthetic, brewed at the intersection of subtropical humidity and the rust belt's air of abandonment amid post-industrial decay. Whole neighborhoods of abandoned buildings with "bleak walls" and "vacant eye-like" windows. The lush overgrowth of vegetation that happens in August—plants that are not lovely so much as rank, suppurating, distorted, filling the air with an odor of green ripeness and rot, tangling over derelict railroad tracks and the desolate waste-lands of former manufacturing districts.

I say none of this in order to criticize my beloved city. As I recently saw a meme put it, I can only wish you the joy of loving something in life as much as people from Philadelphia love being from Philadelphia. There is something blithely honest about how Philadelphia does its growth, its death, its rotting, and its rebirth out in the open. It does not pretend, like most of the United States, to have no ghosts. It is clearly haunted, and the people who live here are clearly okay with that.

And so the Gothic flourishes here. For a recent example that illustrates both (a) how the Gothic grows wild in haunted places and (b) how it reflects or thrives on economic desperation, take Philadelphian Stephanie Feldman's 2022 novel *Saturnalia*.[6] A near-future tale of an impoverished young fortune-teller fleeing alchemical monsters brewed in the halls of old boys' clubs, with climate change, flooding, and the return of plagues as a backdrop, it is rich with the Gothic ingredients that are ever-present on the streets of Philadelphia and in the wider news trends of our contemporary world.

I feel lucky to live in a place where these ingredients come together, ferment, and bloom into gorgeous corpse flowers of Gothic

---

[6] Stephanie Feldman, *Saturnalia* (Los Angeles: The Unnamed Press, 2022).

fiction. The Gothic is alive and well in Philadelphia and not just at Lanternfish. Though we do cherish it particularly. We are getting ready to move to a new office at the moment, and we are felting garlands of ravens to decorate the ceiling. We will have a skull on a shelf, of course, and at least one image of opulent Victorian decay hung on the wall. This morbidity is, for us, not a serious thing at all. Not one of us walks around luxuriating in melancholy or imagining horrors all the time; I am the only one on staff who even wears black clothing frequently. Yet simultaneously, it reflects flashes of a mood as serious as mortality itself—just like the works of Poe.

9

A MURDER OF RAVENS

Thomas Devaney

I have spent a decade away from actively reading Edgar Allan Poe. I am not a Poe scholar, but at one point, I simply immersed myself in Poe, and then I believed I had shut the book—I had moved on. And, to some extent, I have. Yet, recently, I realize that Poe has moved on with me, the enduring specter of an enterprising soul.

Some of my Poe connections include teaching his work in a course that explored the vernacular-based music of American poetry at Haverford College, co-curating an exhibit of artifacts and archival manuscripts for his bicentennial celebration at the Rare Books Collection at the Free Library of Philadelphia in 2009, and conducting an experiential based tour of the Edgar Allan Poe National Historic Site in Philadelphia focused on the empty rooms of the house in 2004.[1]

My approach has always been to take Poe seriously. He was a wildly ambitious writer and editor: remarkably industrious, a masterful craftsperson, an alchemist of musical and suggestive effects— employing a deft use of *orality* and *variation in repetition* among

---

[1] For more information on the "Quote the Raven" exhibit at the Free Library of Philadelphia, see my pamphlet "Edgar Allan Poe at 200: The Absolute Literary Case," Yumpu, 2009, https://www.yumpu.com/en/document/read/3791975/edgar-allan-poe-at-200-aeuroethe-absolute-literary-caseaeur.

them. He read everything and scrutinized it all.

As Poe puts it, the essential poetic principle is "the rhythmical creation of beauty."[2] To this, I would add that what activates this effect is a deep feeling for a piece's *totality*. This is especially true in Poe where the force and "imaginative unity" of the whole is constantly in play.[3] It is one reason why quoting select Poe passages can lose some of their luster. Of course, this is true of many engaging poems and stories, but tradeoffs must be made so we can talk about them. By its very nature, the poetic principle traffics more in *being* than in *knowing*, yet it is in this immersion in *being* that furnishes us with a broader sense of these astonishing interior worlds.

Throughout my journey with Poe, I've discovered two undeniable things. First, I've learned that I can't consume large volumes of his work in one sitting, akin to my experiences with H. L. Mencken and Ambrose Bierce. Second, I am now aware how my experience of reading Poe has consistently surpassed my initial perceptions. Still, it should surprise no one that when one plays along the margins of *the known* and *the unknown* as Poe fearlessly did numerous possibilities remain in play.

Poe is a corkscrew into our cultural psyche, and I do not say that lightly. I am terribly aware that his engagement with psychic poison is a tremendous force, both his own and that of the culture. In the realm of Poe, we are compelled to confront our personal psychological voids; no one can claim neutrality. Poe endures as a perennial observer of our shadow selves.

The core store of Poe's work remains adroit and agitating. It still cuts to the core, evoking both alertness and disquiet. But it's fair to ask why the persistent perversity of his strangeness hasn't just fizzled out over time. How does this curious collection of work manage to

---

[2] Edgar Allan Poe, "The Poetic Principle," in *The Complete Works of Edgar Allan Poe, Vol. XIV: Essays and Miscellanies*, ed. James A. Harrison (New York: T. Y. Crowell, 1902), 275.

[3] Gaston Bachelard, *Water and Dreams: An Essay on the Imagination of Matter*, trans. Edith R. Farrell (Dallas: Pegasus Foundation, 1983), 45.

maintain its potency and peculiarity?

One theory is that it is simply found in ourselves. Another possibility is offered by William Carlos Williams who writes that "It is a *beginning* Poe has in mind, a juvenescent local literal."[4] *Juvenescent* being a renewing element, of which much more can be said. A localized disturbance consuming itself and an animating force materializing out of the chaos again and again. The overall purpose here, Williams believed, was that Poe was seeking a way to "find a way to tell his soul."[5]

My life has taken another direction, so I cannot write a book on Poe. But I would love to write a speculative essay on Poe and Pessoa, my starting point being that Poe the poet, Poe the editor, Poe the critic, and Poe the writer are all different characters in the manner of Fernando Pessoa's heteronyms: Alberto Caeiro, Ricardo Reis, Álvaro de Campo, and so-called Pessoa himself, Bernardo Soares. Also, how could I write about Poe and not write about my own whiteness vis à vis Toni Morrison's *Playing in the Dark*? Here I might also circle back to untapped layers in John T. Irwin's chapter "The White Shadow" and push further into Jung's shadow shelf, which would lead me to Charles Brocken Brown—to the headlands of the Gothic in north America. He may have done it better, but Poe did not do it first.[6]

I recently delved into Peter Kafer's compelling book *Charles Brockden Brown's Revolution and the Birth of American Gothic*. One of many questions Kafer poses is this: "How could such a place—the home of William Penn and Benjamin Franklin—give birth and

---

[4] William Carlos Williams, *In the American Grain* (New York: New Directions, 1956), 217.

[5] Ibid., 221.

[6] John T. Irwin, *American Hieroglyphics: The Symbol of the Egyptian Hieroglyphics in the American Renaissance* (Baltimore: Johns Hopkins University Press, 2016), 205–222.

nurture the Gothic imagination?"[7] Though Poe is hardly addressed in the book, I walked away from Kafer's study seeing so many shades of Brown in Poe. Kafer even suggests that Poe paid Brown "the highest Poeian compliment of plagiarizing from him, directly in 'A Tale of the Ragged Mountains,' and indirectly in numerous wilderness scenes and perhaps in selective renditions of the insane imagination."[8] Alas, what I find most significant is the underlying narrative of successive historical horrors, what Kafer aptly describes as "the requisite Gothic imagination to sense the dark histories already weighing down on the American republic."[9]

Poe's Tales from the 215

Poe's fingertip feeling for the phantasmagoria is exquisite. His stories and poems are infused with its enigmatic nature. There is an active strand in Poe, which lies in that steely moment when the troubled person, yes, it is usually a man, (and yes, he is usually an unusually white man) discovers that the enigma he has sought to unravel has instead grown more perplexing. Despite this, being of sound mind and body, he persists in his singular pursuit. The imp of the perverse is real; our dreams don't lie. But let me backtrack for a moment, about a decade or so.

In the mostly cloudy winter of 2004, my mild curiosity in Poe shifted into a thoroughgoing immersion. Collaborating with curators at the Institute of Contemporary Art in Philadelphia, I was invited by Ingrid Schaffner to submit a proposal for a project for their exhibition called *The Big Nothing*.

The show was "a major group exhibition exploring themes of nothing and nothingness in contemporary art."[10] Here is my project

---

[7] Peter Kafer, *Charles Brockden Brown's Revolution and the Birth of American Gothic* (Philadelphia: University of Pennsylvania Press, 2004), xvi.

[8] Ibid., 198.

[9] Ibid., xxi.

[10] "The Big Nothing, May 1–August 1, 2004," Institute of Contemporary Art, University of Pennsylvania, https://icaphila.org/exhibitions/the-big-

description for what became "The Empty House Tour" at the Edgar Allan Poe National Historic Site in the summer of 2004: "The Poe House tour explores the empty space of the house as well as phantom black cats, the walled-in window, and surprise-whispers revealing Poe's continuing presence."[11]

During my tour of the Poe House, in Poe's empty room on the second floor, I invited everyone to take a seat on the floor facing the east wall. From my first encounter, I was struck by a 4 x 8 foot plastered-over section of the wall. I learned that there had once been a window there until an addition was built onto the house. Across its surface, the matte plaster area was translucent.

I was enticed by what I would come to call the "walled-in window." After several months of ruminating on the wall, I made plans to use the space to project an imaginary slide show presentation.

While introducing the slide show, I noticed people start to turn around to look for a projector. There was none: only the Park Ranger (who happened to be an estranged childhood friend) standing in the doorway and, when they turned back around, me standing on the opposite side of the room in front of the mysterious blank wall.

Two of my four slides included 1.) A flow-chart of stories written in Philadelphia and 2.) A photograph of Colonel Richard Gimbel.

SLIDE ONE: An elaborate flow chart depicting the staggering all 380 items—over half of Poe's literary output—he wrote while living in Philadelphia. Not explicitly or broadly acknowledged, his six-year sojourn in Philadelphia represents the most productive output of Poe's brief career.

Here the much anthologized "Ligeia" is pointed out. At mid-screen "The Fall of the House of Usher"; at the lower right "William Wilson." Again, in the lower right section, "The Island of

nothing/#:~:text=The%20Big%20Nothing%20is%20a,and%20nothing-ness%20in%20contemporary%20art.

[11] Thomas Devaney, "The Empty House," *The Sienese Shredder* 2 (2008), http://www.sienese-shredder.com/2/devaney.html.

the Fay." At the bottom of the screen below "A Descent into the Maelstrom" is "The Pit and the Pendulum." "The Black Cat" is in the left-hand corner near "Israfel." And in the upper center is a constellation of Poe's detective stories, including "The Murders in the Rue Morgue," "The Mystery of Marie Rogêt," and "The Gold-Bug."

SLIDE TWO: A photograph portrait of Colonel Richard Gimbel, one of the heirs to the Gimbel Department Store family, foremost collector of Poe manuscripts and artifacts (real and forged alike) and the person who did even more than Poe himself to make the Poe House *the Poe House* in Philadelphia. While Poe only lived in the house for a single year (1843), Gimble owned it for several decades and used it as a repository for his voluminous archives.

Gimbel is slightly jowly. His eyes are warm and sleepy. He is wearing a black bow tie and a white dinner jacket. His unrealized ambition was to "Make this city more Poe-Conscious." Gimbel was clear on this: "Before I die I hope to make Poe and Philadelphia synonymous." [12]

Whenever I mentioned Gimbel's idea, many people in the room literally laughed out loud. Despite his exceptionally prolific time here, in the public imagination Poe is most immediately identified with Baltimore, not Philadelphia.

From Gimbel's Poe collection emerged a spirited speech. A toast-master's speech he delivered at the Yale Library in 1959. The toast begins:

To the inventor of a device more important to our whizbang age than the electric light—the detective story, that greatest palliative for the tired businessman, in the field of which more books

---

[12] Gimbel, Richard A., unpublished note, undated, Folder Gimbel on Poe, Colonel Richard A. Gimbel collection of Edgar Allan Poe materials, 1809–1995, Free Library of Philadelphia, Rare Book Department, Philadelphia, Pennsylvania.

have been published & sold than in all other literary categories combined.[13]

And it closes:

> To Edgar Allan Poe we raise our glasses, [and here I prompted all gathered in Poe's empty house to raise their imaginary glasses] filled with Amontillado from his cask of genius, and wish him well, whose heartstrings are a lute. Not "nevermore" but "evermore." We salute you![14]

I wished to recognize Gimbel's efforts to commemorate the extensive collection of Poe's Philadelphia writings, which consists of 380 pieces, his tales from the 215 (the area code for Philadelphia), composed between 1838 and 1844. Gimbel was also a Poe completist. It was no small thing unto itself and especially so considering the hairy and sizable nature of the unsigned work. Gimbel was also a collector of Thomas Paine and an ardent collector, in true connoisseur fashion, on the history of aviation, collecting everything *up to*— or all before—the Wright Bros.

Jumping ahead, in the winter of 2009, I organized a one-day program at the Kelly Writers House at the University of Pennsylvania called "A Murder of Ravens."[15] The program featured multiple readings and discussions focused on "The Raven" to mark Poe's 200th birthday. I especially appreciated Daniel Hoffman's marvelous reading of the poem that evening.

In Hoffman's *Poe Poe Poe Poe Poe Poe Poe*, a single phrase stands out to me: Poe's "special light, which is lurid and rippling with energy."[16] It is a vivid encapsulation of Poe. And upon reflection, I've come to realize that Hoffman's book title is also a concrete poem,

---

[13] Richard Gimbel, "Edgar Allan Poe: A Toast," *The Yale University Library Gazette* 33, no. 4 (1959), 138.

[14] Ibid.

[15] For program details, visit The Kelly Writers House Calendar at https://writing.upenn.edu/wh/calendar/0109.php#15.

[16] Daniel Hoffman, *Poe Poe Poe Poe Poe Poe Poe* (New York: Avon Books, 1978), 64.

with Poe appearing seven times in succession. Yes, there are the seven wonders of the world and seven days in the week (both quotidian and so structured by a divine force), but the number also represents fullness in life and *a cyclical continuation*, which is echoed in the repetition of the name. Poe himself would undoubtedly swell into a recital on such numeracy.[17]

Before writing my reflection here, I decided to reread "The Raven." And I was struck by three things: one is how much it reads like a stripped-down tale. The compression is exquisite—a middle weight boxer or prima ballerina assoluta in finest form. As such, the poem's armature has been reduced to its essence—so our experience is hotly felt in the moment.

The second thing that caught my attention is the landing lines of each main stanza, starting at "Once this and nothing more" and culminating in a series of "Quoth the Raven 'Nevermore.'" What strikes me is a steady crescendo followed by a sharp decrescendo effect related to silence created at the end of those refrains. As we read "Only this and nothing more," followed by "Nameless here for evermore," and then "Merely this and nothing more," I noticed how the silence increased each time, creating a space between the stanzas for us to dwell before moving on. The silence of each of those refrains has its own emotional effect. Perhaps the most meaningful pause occurs mid-poem after "Merely this and nothing more." But after that, the opportunities for pauses and silence drop quickly off. Finally, in my most recent reading of the poem, I notice how it keeps us firmly in its lyric grip, making it a living presence in the here and now. The absence of resolution only adds to this effect. It's like the sonnet form, which has been aptly described as a "moment's monument."[18] It allows the speaker and reader to remain locked in a never-

---

[17] To listen to Hoffman's Poe recitation as well as the remainder of the program, visit Penn Sound at https://media.sas.upenn.edu/writershouse/A-Murder-of-Ravens_Reading_KWH-UPenn_1-15-2008.mp3.

[18] Dante Gabriel Rossetti, "Introductory Sonnet," in *Ballads and Sonnets* (London: F.S. Ellis, 1881), 161.

ending battle, which feels like an eternal, damning hell. Find us here:

> And the Raven, never flitting, still is sitting, *still* is sitting
> On the pallid bust of Pallas just above my chamber door;
> And his eyes have all the seeming of a demon's that is dreaming,
> And the lamp-light o'er him streaming throws his shadow on
> the floor;
> And my soul from out that shadow that lies floating on the floor
> Shall be lifted—nevermore![19]

Randall Jarrell once wrote "any poet has written enough bad poetry to scare away anybody."[20] In the case of Edgar Allan Poe, that is true. Yet the spell-casting pleasures of Poe's greatest poems are immense. Unlike many writers, Poe's best-known poems also happen to be his best. His most exquisite poem of all is "The Raven."

Poe's work is notable for its implausibility. This is both a criticism and a major factor in his enduring popularity. The stories are not just tall tales of dangerous happenings and improbable yarns of parlous events; rather, their disquieting power of his writing, with their extensive dream-works and exploration of the workings of the human psyche, lies in how Poe skillfully builds ladder after ladder of tenable inferences to meticulously depict what might otherwise be considered, beyond belief.

Plausibly, yes, late on a terribly dreary night you, or any of us, might be reading about the death of a person, say, the death of a woman. And the melancholy tale might provoke your own tangled-up grief (lament within a lament) about someone you once loved, and actually still love, but who is now gone; and yes, plausibly, a raven

---

[19] Edgar Allan Poe, "The Raven," in *The Collected Works of Edgar Allan Poe*, ed. T. O. Mabbott, vol. 1 (Cambridge: Belknap Press of Harvard University Press, 1969), 369.

[20] Randall Jarrell, "Some Lines from Whitman," in *Poetry and the Age* (New York: Alfred A. Knopf, 1953), 101. The remainder of this chapter is from my unpublished talk, "A Murder of Ravens," which I gave in 2009 for the Kelly Writers House event.

might by chance fly into your living room on such a night (because you let it in) and because the creature is there for a highly particular, though ultimately undisclosed, design.

So on such a god-awful night, with such heat in your heart, you heard this disturbance, and though mildly sleepy, you go to check it out anyway. Here is the classic horror movie set-up: You are walking right into it. Perversely, everyone else seems to know what is going on except *you*. Every bleeding danger flag is flying in the midnight air, but the alarms are signaling in vain. Ever cool-headed in these moments, Poe has his bereaved lover soldier on:

> Back into the chamber turning, all my soul within me burning,
> Soon again I heard a tapping somewhat louder than before.
> "Surely," said I, "surely that is something at my window lattice;
> Let me see, then, what thereat is, and this mystery explore—
> Let my heart be still a moment and this mystery explore; —
> 'Tis the wind and nothing more!"[21]

Yes, it is windy brother, but no, that is not the wind. Everyone knows what happens next: the raven's arrival has become one of the most memorable animal visitations ever published. There are eternally different meanings to any such visit, yet all agree upon one point: such visitations are beyond the sphere of our normal linguistic articulation. It's a psychic passion play.

So when a wild animal comes a-knocking—in this case The Bird of Ill Omen—you know something is up. *Someone* is trying to tell you *something*. You probably already know it, but you need to hear it a few more times; yes, a few more times. It is preposterous that the raven's harsh three-syllable refrain "Nevermore" should also imperfectly approximate Lenore's two-syllable name, but it does. As it happens, the duration of each word is the exact same length. But this is not a social visit. The fowl is not here to chat. It is here to seal the deal: Lenore is gone. For your own part—not only do you not flee—but, in fact, you escalate the situation.

---

[21] Poe, "The Raven," 366.

The narrative is tight and well-crafted. Still, it does not fully or nearly account for the poem's extraordinary powers. Perhaps the liveliest aspect of "The Raven" is that its lines continually swell. It is a pushy poem. It is a relentless poem. It is one that Allen Ginsberg once remarked upon in a grad class I had with him at Brooklyn College (brightening behind his big glasses) that has "Rhythm out the ass." On the poem's unforgettable refrain "Nevermore," Poe himself commented that "the pleasure is deduced solely from the sense of identity—of repetition."[22] Elsewhere, in a much-quoted passage from "The Poetic Principle," Poe is exacting as a razor-edged pendulum: "I would define, in brief, the Poetry of words as *The Rhythmical Creation of Beauty*. Its sole arbiter is Taste. With the Intellect or with the Conscience, it has only collateral relations. Unless incidentally, it has no concern whatever with Duty or with Truth."[23]

To feed a desire for a behind-the-scenes look of his increasingly famous piece, Poe penned "The Philosophy of Composition." Among other things, the essay stands as a bold statement on aesthetic thinking. But it is here also that Poe purports to precisely describe the rational procedures he used to "design" his thrilling poem. Sections of the text are as madcap as some of Poe's characters: "the work proceeded, step by step, to its completion with the precision and rigid consequence of a mathematical problem."[24]

This is brilliant stuff and certainly a plausible vision that one writer may entertain, after the fact, about his compositional methods. Still, in his meticulous quest to demystify "The Raven," Poe actually deepens the lore and the mystifying air surrounding his poem. It is another dazzling performance.

It was also a savvy bit of self-publicity. In part, the essay has helped assure the longevity of Poe's signature poem. But with Poe,

[22] Edgar Allan Poe, "The Philosophy of Composition," in *The Complete Works of Edgar Allan Poe, Vol. XIV: Essays and Miscellanies*, ed. James A. Harrison (New York: T. Y. Crowell, 1902), 199.

[23] Poe, "The Poetic Principle," 275.

[24] Poe, "The Philosophy," 195.

all of his wayward and intentional forces converge in "The Raven." Literary reputations are notoriously fickle, and for Poe, this has been painfully true. To say that he has not always been embraced by the higher-ups, the mandarins of English literature, is an understatement. The list is impressive; Henry James and T. S. Eliot, at times, have bluntly dismissed him. In recent memory, Harold Bloom discounted Poe to the end. He writes:

> Poe's survival raises perpetually the issue as to whether literary merit and canonical status necessarily go together. I can think of no other American writer, down to this moment, at once so inevitable and so dubious.[25]

Of course I won't argue with Professor Bloom on Poe. It is but grist for the mill. Poe, being among the most self-seriously superior of critics (not unlike Bloom and James), anticipated such critiques. Poe is easy to belittle but hard to resist, if not dismiss. But I will concede to Bloom, Eliot, and James that I too occasionally have my doubts. Case in point: in moments I have had a sinking feeling that "The Raven" itself is not even a poem at all. It is rather a kind of aberration: a collective Jungian dream we have all had. Even people who know nothing of Poe know the poem. It is the rarest of birds: the poem you do not even have to read to know. It spans the generations.

My favorite contemporary version of this is Tim Burton's arresting short "Vincent."[26] The highly stylized black-and-white animation is an artistic conversation: from Poe to Vincent Price's Poe to Burton's own Poe, which involves all the above Poes and more (a living intertext via the seven arts). Burton points the way again to how Poe continues to speak to new audiences. In the film's last frame, we find the young Vincent lying dead in the spotlight. This is right after his no-nonsense mother enters stage right to mess up

[25] Harold Bloom, "Inescapable Poe," *The New York Review*, October 11, 1984, https://www.nybooks.com/articles/1984/10/11/inescapable-poe/.

[26] "Vincent," directed by Tim Burton (1982; Burbank, California; Walt Disney Productions), Film.

the fun. In perfect form, Vincent Price narrates the movie, which closes on these lines: "And my soul from out that shadow that lies floating on the floor / Shall be lifted—nevermore!"

Regardless of its canonical status, "The Raven" is deeply embedded into our cultural DNA. While truth may still be stranger than fiction, it pales in comparison to the outlandish operatic rendition of "The Raven" in *The Simpsons*. The show taps into our peculiar and menacingly weird zeitgeist, and the Treehouse of Horror episode, narrated by James Earl Jones, stands out as one of the most successful Poe adaptations for television. [27]

In the delightful realm where Edgar Poe's masterpiece intersects with the unique strengths of *The Simpsons*, an unexpected harmony arises. Despite its peculiar nature, Poe's work manages to captivate our senses by coaxing us into temporarily forsaking our skepticism.

The genius of Poe, and Matt Groening's team, lies in their ability to make the seemingly improbable not only possible but also necessary and entertaining.

Now, let me leave you with a closing thought: a disconcerting notion that arises from delving deep into the works of Edgar Allan Poe. It is difficult to name this eerie occurrence, which might be identified as the co-walker experience. There's much more to say, but this phenomenon, as depicted in stories like "William Wilson," involves the emergence and regularity of unsettling coincidences. It is as if the most implausible scenarios gradually transform into probable realities as each moment passes by. Immersed in the enigmatic worlds crafted by Edgar Poe, there are rare but real moments where one cannot help but encounter a creeping sensation that mirrors the experience of reading a captivating tale, only to find oneself ensnared within its very narrative. It is an eerie phenomenon that seems to transcends space and time, one that Jorge Luis Borges, a masterful

---

[27] *The Simpsons*, season 2, episode 3, "The Raven" in "Treehouse of Horror," directed by David Silverman, written by Edgar Allan Poe and Sam Simon, featuring James Earl Jones, Nancy Cartwright, Yeardley Smith, and Dan Castellanetta, aired October 25, 1990, in broadcast syndications.

storyteller influenced by Poe's legacy, skillfully amplified in his own literary creations. In works such as "Tlön, Uqbar, Orbis Tertius" and "Pierre Menard, Author of the Quixote," Borges delves into the realms of intricate narrative constructions, forging a potent alliance between his unique voice and Poe's disquieting spirit. However, it's in the mesmerizing tale of "The Circular Ruins" that Borges weaves a tapestry that is equal parts his own brilliance and Poe's enduring influence. This uncanny fusion serves as an exploration that leaves us breathless, as both "William Wilson" and "The Circular Ruins" investigate the depths of identity and reality, inviting us to question the very fabric of our existence.

No, I do not mean you identify with a character, I mean *you are* the character. It is your 200th birthday and you have been dead for 160 years, but now a band of your followers are clamoring over your bones. Some want to dig up your grave and move your remains from one east coast city to another.[28] Why does not this lunacy seem stranger than it is?

And even now (and I am not making this up), someone or something is digging on the other side of the brick wall in front of the table where I am writing, where I was writing this. It is weird. It is very weird. With Poe, coincidences only take you so far: you are either all the way in or you are not—there is no middle ground.

Another revealing Poe coincidence happened on New Year's Day 2005. I was about to take my seat for supper with a few friends. One of the hosts Conny Purtill, a graphic designer, casually asked what I was working on. I mentioned something on Poe but did so reluctantly as I do not like to talk about what I am writing before it is finished. But Conny was genuinely curious. So I politely added that it was on "The Raven" and wished to leave it at that.

Conny disappeared. Dinner was almost ready and smelled like heaven. It included a gorgeous macaroni pie, a shiny ham, collard greens, cheddar and scallion biscuits, buttery corn bread, and a brownie recipe courtesy of *The Alice B. Toklas Cookbook*. But then in a moment, Conny was back standing in front of me. He had a book. "Here it is,"

---

[28] See Ian Urbina, "Baltimore Has Poe; Philadelphia Wants Him," *The New York Times*, Sept. 5, 2008, https://www.nytimes.com/2008/09/06/us/06poe.html.

he said in an oddly serious tone. He was holding the shiny, shoebox-like book out towards me. Pointing to a page, he said, "I love this poem. That's why we put it here." I recognized the volume, it was the 2006 catalogue for the Whitney Biennial, which I did not realize Conny had designed.[29] I was slightly light-headed from the aroma in the house, but there it was again: "The Raven." Conny related that in an early meeting with the curators about the book the conversation turned to the idea of "the contemporary." One curator thought we had passed it; another said it had yet to start. At that point (Conny did not elaborate) he simply said they all started talking about Edgar Allan Poe. Somehow after that, they all agreed to put "The Raven" in the book without explanation. Before Conny told me this story, I did not want to speak, but after, I simply could not.

Poe's writing is a masterclass in close-up character storytelling. Each element serves to enrich the tale. It is not just that Poe's plots take unexpected turns, but it is more that they never turn back around. Yet this isn't a flaw; it's by design. As Poe once said, "Every plot, worth the name, must be elaborated to its denouement before anything be attempted with the pen."[30] It is astonishing to contemplate how Edgar Poe's stories, despite their lack of neatly resolved conclusions, possess such captivating allures. One might easily assume that the only loose ends being tied up in these stories are those ill-fated characters who find themselves physically bound. And let's face it, kids and the kids inside us love a good scary story. However, within the tremendously strange realm of Poe's reach, we are not mere spectators but active participants, entangled in his intricate webs. Poe skillfully orchestrates these predicaments, anticipating our decision to close the book or courageously delve deeper into the cold and clear depths of his tales. The moral is this: Keep the book open, refuse death. Hear the echoes of your own troubled heart.

---

[29] *Whitney Biennial 2006: Day for Night* (New York: The Whitney Museum of American Art, 2006), 56–59.
[30] Poe, "The Philosophy," 193.

10

EDGAR ALLAN POE IN THE SECONDARY CLASSROOM: LITERARY IMPOSTER TURNED ENGLISH TEACHER

Emily Michael

Classic literature has never been, and might never be, my forte, despite being an English Language Arts (ELA) teacher. At the start of my teaching career, I was nervous about not being a literary genius and felt overwhelmed by some of the curricula in front of me. With a background in professional writing and journalism, I knew that I had the skills necessary to help students become better writers, but I never had a deep connection to literature. While I have always enjoyed reading, I preferred to do so on my own terms and had a limited palate: romance and historical fiction.

I spent my last two undergraduate years focused on the small university newspaper and writing press releases for my public relations internships. I coasted through my required 300-level literature courses with the help of a few good friends and professors who tolerated my overall disinterest in classic novels and poetry. I faked my way through *Crime and Punishment*, skipped many Friday morning literature classes, and depended on my stronger writing skills to maintain a solid GPA that led to my Bachelor of Science degree in

English with a concentration in professional writing.

On one snowy January Saturday night, I bumped into a former vice principal of mine who said she needed a long-term substitute to teach a life skills course to at-risk high school students. I told her I had been reconsidering the education field, and she said she would pull some strings if I would be willing to try it. I immediately said "yes" and jumped headfirst into "teaching" the following week. It did not take long for me to realize that secondary education was where I belonged. By February, I started looking into a Master of Arts in Teaching (MAT) program and signed up to take the one test I needed to prove that I had the background knowledge to become a secondary English teacher. The test, scheduled for March, was loaded with literary questions, referring to authors, time periods, and genres that I definitely heard about in my previous courses but never paid much attention to. Luckily, I passed the test by one point and proved that I was a qualified English teacher candidate. I spent the rest of the school year helping ninth through twelfth grade students with diverse needs pass their classes, my specialty and personal favorite course to assist with being English. This opportunity also allowed me to re-cross paths with my former high school English teachers, who once again made me feel welcomed and supported, although this time as a colleague rather than a student. Later that year, I received my acceptance into the teaching program and started graduate level courses the week after Memorial Day.

Throughout my entire teacher preparation program, the biggest obstacle for me was not classroom management, lesson planning, formal observations, or building strong relationships. The biggest obstacle for me was connecting with literature on a deep enough level that my students would trust me to be the one teaching it. At this point in my journey, I was really kicking myself for not paying better attention or participating more in my American and British literature undergraduate courses. Now, I was on my own to analyze and pick apart the classics.

I relied heavily upon the support of my mentor teachers who had been teaching the same short stories and novels for years. I figured out enough to teach units on *Flowers for Algernon*, *To Kill a Mockingbird*, and *1984*, and I breathed a sigh of relief when my mentors did not make me teach the intense stuff like Shakespeare or Poe. However, my lessons, with complex and sensitive topics, reinforced my understanding that I had no choice but to become a literary aficionado. Teenage students can see right through an adult who does not know what they are talking about. And who wants to learn from a grown-up like that? I never wanted to fake my understanding of a text like I had as a student. I did not want to be a literary imposter.

After graduating, I accepted a job offer to teach ninth and tenth grade Merit and General English in one of Maryland's westernmost high schools located in the Allegheny Mountains. I met with other ELA teachers in July of that year, working on a new curriculum with a new-to-the-county textbook. In hindsight, this experience provided me with great insight. I was collaborating with teachers who had taught English at many different grade levels in Maryland, Florida, and even Germany. We were making decisions together about what our students would benefit from reading. Naturally, those intimidating classic authors such as William Shakespeare and Edgar Allan Poe were at the forefront of the conversation.

English teachers are interesting, territorial, opinionated creatures of habit, I have learned. Sit in on a curriculum meeting and hear classroom teachers declare, "*Gatsby* is for eleventh grade or higher. *Night* is for tenth graders. I already have the books on my shelf." Even four years into my career and working in a middle school, I was told what texts were "allowed" to be read in my classroom. Educators choose from required, suggested, and supplemental text lists. In Western Maryland schools, most of these texts are the same: a Shakespearean play each year of high school, Poe's short stories in middle school, and excerpts from Abolitionist, Holocaust, and Civil Rights literature every year.

The curriculum of my first year included a long list of literary works I had never heard of; plus, I had to start off with none other than "The Fall of the House of Usher." To be quite honest, I dreaded the labor I knew I would have to put in to not only read this "short" story myself but also to dive in deep enough that I would be able to teach it with passion. In order to prepare myself, I watched a few random YouTube videos and read tidbits from biography.com to brush up on the life of Poe. My first lessons were surface level and bland, and by paragraph fourteen, many of my students had dozed off, drooling on the pages of their Pearson textbook to the sound of an audio clip. Looking back on that particular morning, it is a true shame that the narrator's premonition that "the lady, at least while living, would be seen by me no more" did not grab anyone's attention, including my own.[1]

It took years and countless first-year teacher after-contract hours for me to finally appreciate the works of Poe, but I view my situation as something I have in common with my students who are "reluctant" readers. What held me back from loving Poe sooner was the intimidation of reading something outside of my comfort zone, and I can guarantee that that same intimidation of something new and strange is exactly what holds back young readers. Poe's unique language and writing style can be difficult to approach, even dreadful for some, but like most things, with time and practice, the unexpected can happen. Understanding this intimidation is what helps me to hook my students and receive buy-in from them. The outcome is exciting: a classroom full of Poe lovers, year after year.

Back to the drooling tenth graders. I wrapped up class the second morning of "Usher" and knew I needed to switch gears. I desperately searched teacherspayteachers.com to find something engaging that I could purchase from a more knowledgeable and experienced educator. I found an extremely modified, abridged version of the story that cut out hundreds of Poe's original lines. While I was worried that I was taking the easy way out, I justified my decision to move forward with the shortened version for a variety of reasons. First, it used Poe's original language, just fewer lines, so

---

[1] Edgar Allan Poe, "The Fall of the House of Usher," in *The Collected Works of Edgar Allan Poe*, ed. T. O. Mabbott, vol. 2 (Cambridge: Belknap Press of Harvard University Press, 1978), 404.

students would still be able to identify his unique style. Second, I had a large population of special education students and students reading below grade level. Considering I only taught general and merit classes rather than honors-level students, almost all of the teenagers who walked through my doorway were reluctant readers. This abridged text would be more appropriate and accessible for their skill sets. My final reason is probably most important: I could better understand the story *myself.*

For this particular part of the curriculum, my role was to help students identify and analyze elements of Gothic literature. We looked closely at bleak settings, tortured characters, strange or violent plots, dramatic descriptions, gloomy moods, and recurring symbolism.

My students immediately perked up when I said I was giving them an abridged version of this daunting story and that we would be out of the textbook for a few days. I printed off 100 copies of the ten-page packet, which took away some of the intimidation factor. We re-started the story by popcorn reading, which is when students take turns reciting paragraphs, and quickly identified the setting, characters, and mood. Students were assigned a writing task in which they developed a short essay by picking the three most prominent elements of Gothic literature in the abridged version of "The Fall of the House of Usher." They provided relevant textual evidence to support their analysis. Students focused heavily on the creepy-mansion-in-the-countryside setting, Lady Madeline's tortured character (who buries their sister and potential lover before ensuring she is dead?), and dramatic descriptions of the Usher characters' bizarre appearances and strange behaviors. While most students do not catch on to Roderick and Madeline's likely incestuous relationship, it usually only takes a moment or two after I re-read the lines describing "a tenderly beloved sister—his sole companion for long years—his last and only relative on earth" for students to realize that they might be something more than siblings.[2] Each time I teach this

---

[2] Poe, "The Fall of the House of Usher," 404.

version, I make sure to ask students what Roderick and Lady Madeline would have to do if they wanted the Usher name to live on. The innuendo is almost always enough to make them raise an eyebrow or throw out the term "inbreds!"

Fortunately, I had an opportunity to redeem myself shortly after my first attempt at teaching Poe. This particular school worked on a semester schedule, and I repeated the same curriculum in the spring. I remained in this position the following year, teaching the same texts and skills for another two semesters. Three of these semesters overlapped with the peak of the COVID-19 pandemic when I experienced teaching in-person, virtually, and hybrid. Each time I taught "Usher," I was able to add more despite the obstacles of teaching during the most trying of times. I started the unit by reading a short biography that highlighted Poe's human side before we looked at him as a writer. The idea of a drunk, poor, lost soul wandering the streets of Baltimore—a mere three hours from where we reside—captivates students. With mental health becoming such a crucial and overwhelming subject for modern teenagers, many students can make connections between their own struggles or the struggles of their loved ones to the struggles of Edgar Poe. When teenagers realize that Poe was not a fancy, popular, wealthy man but a human who had suffered great loss, pain, and rejection his entire life, they open their hearts a little more.

Each year that I teach Poe, and even each individual class period, I change things up based on my clientele. I go into the unit knowing that I am going to have to sell it because the majority of teenagers take one look at "old English" and decide that it is naptime. Luckily, the genre sells itself. Students are ready, or so they think, for more mature subject matter, and I pace my lessons to focus on the horror genre right around Halloween. I prioritize dedicating at least one class period to talking about Poe's life. YouTube, biography.com, poets.org, and other platforms help students independently research different aspects of Poe's life after I lecture about the basics. Some groups of students could research for hours, driven by their own personal interest in the subject matter, but others still need pushed further to connect. The PBS documentary *Edgar Allan Poe: Buried Alive* is another resource that helps visual learners understand not only Poe's life but also the time in history during which he was writing.[3] By this point, I also mention Poe's connection to the Baltimore Ravens and gain the attention of a few student athletes.[4] After a day of lecture, video clips, and independent research, I introduce the literary elements that are the focal point of the unit. My curriculum has changed recently because I have moved to the eighth grade, and my students are required to read "The Tell-Tale Heart." Like "The Fall of the House of Usher," the students identify and analyze many major elements: plot, characterization, unreliable narrator, imagery, suspense, and theme. Now I have become so familiar with the psychological tale that I could spend weeks working through it in my classes, and I feel more comfortable every time I teach it. I often joke that my first period class gets the worst version of my teaching and my last period class gets the best. However, each time I read and teach a work of Poe's, I notice something different and exciting.

My personal goal is to find ways for my students to enjoy and appreciate my content area and subject matter, but it is also crucial that I appropriately fill the role of classroom educator and teach to a set of standards. One of my top priorities as an English Language Arts teacher is making sure students can use their reading skills for comprehension. Required secondary courses in Maryland public schools follow standards that guide educators in lesson planning and identifying focus skills. For my current content and curriculum, I follow the eighth grade Maryland College and Career Readiness Standards, which cover reading literature, reading informational texts, and skills specific to writing, language, speaking, and listening. In ELA, it is expected that students build upon these skills year after year. The ELA standards become a little more complex as the student

---

[3] *Edgar Allan Poe: Buried Alive*, directed by Eric Stange (PBS, American Masters, 2016).

[4] "Naming the Team," Baltimore Ravens, accessed February 2, 2023, https://www.baltimoreravens.com/team/history/naming-the-team.

ages through grade levels. Within school systems, specialists and supervisors use the state standards to create specific curriculum requirements and a grade-specific scope and sequence document that classroom educators in every county are expected to follow. In many districts, based on my own experience, teachers are often included in the conversations about these documents, but ultimately, teachers must follow what is given to them. This helps to hold teachers accountable for addressing standards, exposing students to appropriate readings and activities, and ensuring the same novels, short stories, and topics are not repeated in different grade levels.

In order to assess standards-based skills within my own classroom, I created note-taking sheets that have a combination of comprehension, vocabulary, re-call, and personal connection questions to guide students in their learning process. I can quickly check these records at the end of each class and reinforce the concepts until the skills are mastered and the topic is understood. For example, when I introduce Poe for the first time to a class, I use the 3-2-1 questioning strategy but backwards. During that class period, students identify one thing they already know about Edgar Allan Poe and two things they want to know about him. Most know nothing at all, so they will simply acknowledge that his name is in the textbook. Some remember "The Raven," which is typically covered in seventh grade classes, usually only for a day or two. At the end of class, they must list three things they learned about Poe that day. Most students mention their new knowledge of his substance abuse, his mysterious death, and his shocking marriage to his thirteen-year-old cousin, Virginia Clemm.

Unveiling just the basic yet unique details of Poe's life truly opens the floodgates to energetic class interactions. Most students do not have the background knowledge to understand that it was more common and accepted for individuals to marry within their family during the 1800s, but they are well-aware of the consequences of alcohol dependence and drug use, the sadness that stems from familial alienation, and the hardships associated with poverty. Once they comprehend the complex situation that includes his mother-in-law/aunt Maria Poe Clemm, they are able to resonate more with

Edgar's background, like an old friend.

Occasionally, teachers are gifted a group of students who love to read aloud. They are eager, outgoing, confident, and ready to roll. However, more often than not, teachers must manage complex groups of students who do not wish to read in front of their peers. Each group must be handled differently depending upon the classroom rapport and types of learners. Therefore, I implement whole-group reading differently with each class. Sometimes we Round-Robin read, sometimes students pick the paragraph they want to read prior to reading aloud, and other times I read to them. The goal is that, by the end of the year, students will be able to read a grade-level text independently or with a partner and implement the strategies we used together. "The Tell-Tale Heart" is the only exception I make to reading aloud. We *always* listen to the audio on the first read. The audio version provided by our Houghton Mifflin Harcourt (HMH) textbook is about twenty minutes long, and the narrator's voice adds to the suspense and tone of the story. I usually let it play straight through, as long as students are awake and following along. Then, we pick the story apart, paragraph-by-paragraph, and watch the plot unfold.

The HMH textbooks we use are "consumables," and students have their own copies. Therefore, they are able and encouraged to take notes in the margins and highlight powerful lines in a text. Most of the time, I guide students in their annotation process by pausing after a paragraph and asking questions that will lead them to what Poe would want them to find. For example, paragraph one of "The Tell-Tale Heart" introduces readers to the first-person narrator who insists he is not crazy. I re-read the opening paragraphs and direct students to highlight first-person pronouns and descriptions that reveal the narrator's insanity. Most students are intrigued by this concept since our brains are wired to trust characters, especially narrators, until they do or say something questionable. The students are slightly confused yet appreciative that the narrator reveals his flaw instantly, and they want to know the alleged great reason he had for committing murder.

I continue my own dramatic re-reading of the entire story, pausing to shine a spotlight on the narrator's repetitive behaviors, the description of the old man's eye, the dismemberment of the corpse, the narrator's confident yet erratic behavior when the cops arrive, and the eventual guilt that takes over. My favorite informal check for understanding is when I ask my students to summarize the entire tale in one sentence and re-tell it to the science teacher next door. The added twist this school year is that we were deep into Poe literature when Netflix released the docuseries on Jeffrey Dahmer.[5] Between serial killer TV shows at home and the horror genre at school, students have plenty to comment on the subject matter.

My students' workload really increases once I am positive that they have an understanding of the story. We open class each day with basic recall questions about characters' actions, words, and behaviors, and then they prove what they know. I create additional note-taking sheets on which I ask students to provide textual evidence relating to key elements such as the unreliable narrator, imagery of the eye or the heartbeat, and the theme of how guilt can drive someone to both insanity and confession. Students are required, per the curriculum, to complete a selection test with a multiple-choice format, Part A and Part B comprehension and vocabulary questions. Most of these questions require students to look closely at Poe's language choices and grammatical style. The main grammar focus is his use of dashes, which represent interruptions or pauses, reflective of not only the narrator's mental state but, perhaps, Poe's mentality as well.

For upper-level eighth grade students with higher Lexile reading levels, I revisit the abridged version of "The Fall of the House of Usher" that I taught long, long ago. By this point, students are excited about Poe's writing, his unexpected plot twists and bizarre characters. I use it as a supplemental text to reinforce the same literary elements and provide additional exposure to Poe as most upper-

---

[5] *DAHMER: Monster: The Jeffrey Dahmer Story*, directed by Jennifer Lynch, Paris Barclay, Clement Virgo, Gregg Araki, and Carl Franklin, featuring Evan Peters, aired 2022, Netflix.

level students will continue to take more challenging English courses in high school and beyond. In my current district, "The Fall of the House of Usher" is reserved for general eleventh grade English, so many of my high-flying readers will not typically come across the title if they plan to take Advanced Placement courses their junior year.

My favorite project at the end of our Poe readings is a choice board on which students are able to display their knowledge of the subject matter in a way that best suits their style of learning. The choices include a traditional essay, a slideshow presentation, a speech, a piece of artwork, a comic strip, or a creative writing piece. Each option connects to the reading literature standards for grade 8, with students making connections between their own project and the themes, symbols, dialogue, characters, plot, or other literary devices found within one of Poe's works that we discussed in class. Students also have the choice of which text they analyze—"The Tell-Tale Heart," "The Fall of the House of Usher," or "The Haunted Palace," the poem inset found in "Usher." The majority of students feel passionately about one piece or another, which provides entry points and makes this project engaging for all students.

Another strategy I use in the classroom is gathering student feedback on almost every topic we cover such as the use of a unit reflection. At the end of each unit or before we move on to new subject matter, I create a Google form to obtain important feedback directly from the students on my lessons, the texts we read, our activities, and their overall understanding. I ask students to be considerate yet honest because I value their feedback.

This year, I was able to gather data from students in two of my eighth grade English Language Arts classes. This population includes students from diverse socioeconomic backgrounds with reading levels ranging from second to twelfth grade. These students do not receive reading intervention instruction and, therefore, were exposed to "Usher" as a supplemental text. Some of them read "The Raven" as seventh graders, but none of these students has experienced a "normal" year of middle school instruction or curricula due to the COVID-19 pandemic, which closed schools during March of their fifth-grade year. Their state standardized test results show that, as a group, they have weaknesses in reading comprehension and vocabulary skills. Our school has identified extensive reading comprehension and vocabulary gaps as focus areas and has implemented data-driven reading lab courses that are designed to meet each student's individual needs.

The informal survey I created and assigned to these students revealed interesting insights. I maintained conversational language for my questioning with hopes that students would feel more comfortable responding honestly. Most questions were written as multiple choice or on a scale. Thirty-three students recorded responses. When asked how much they knew about Poe at the start of my class, only one student answered that they "knew a lot about him." Twenty students claimed to "know a little about him," and twelve students said they knew nothing about him. Before we started the horror unit, 45% of students answered that they were "really excited and looking forward to" reading stories by Poe, and 55% of students said that they "didn't really care." I was very impressed that zero students selected the response of "I was dreading it." Student data revealed that "The Tell-Tale Heart" was the crowd favorite, with a whopping 82% of students picking that title opposed to the 18% who said "The Fall of the House of Usher" was their preferred Poe text. 45% of students indicated that, after participating in my class, they felt that they "knew a lot about Poe and like his stories" while 48% of students "know a little about [him], but like his stories." This data makes sense to me as a teacher because my curriculum requires that I teach more about the readings than the author. When asked whether they feel more open to reading additional Poe works in future classes or on their own time after participating in my class, 79% of students answered "yes" and 21% of students answered "no." There are those reluctant readers!

Surprising to me, only ten students indicated that they spoke about our Poe readings and lessons to a grown up at home. Maybe that is a teenager thing, but I also believe it has something to do with students' family dynamics. The one student who previously answered that he "knew a lot about Poe" prior to my teachings comes from a home with members who have solid educational backgrounds. His two parents and two older brothers are college-educated. Neither of his parents is from Western Maryland, and they earned university degrees out of state. One of his responses explains that he was excited to read part of "The Fall of the House of Usher" because of its advanced level. He was also eager to read "The Tell-Tale Heart" because his mom talked to him about it before and knew it would be coming up in his middle school classes. To me, this interaction between mother and son further proves that teenage students with support at home often experience great success in the classroom. A few other students mentioned that their parents knew some of Poe's poetry but did not say much else about it. A female student whose parents are extremely involved in her academic and extra-curricular life recorded another intriguing response. She indicated that when she told her parents at dinner one night what we were reading in ELA, they were slightly concerned. She further explained that she only told them a summary of the story, and when she disclosed the title and who wrote it, they understood the connection between the disturbing content and the notorious author.

Other students who did not communicate with their parents or guardians about Poe described how their reading experience made them reflect upon themselves. One student wrote that Poe's stories made her think about her own dark life experiences. She questioned whether his stories had a deeper meaning behind them or not. Another student explained that Poe's stories made her feel like there was more behind his words relating to mental health than some readers may be able to tell. Other students explained that knowing a little bit about Poe's childhood and young adult life helped them understand why he wrote "messed up stuff." All English teachers know that some topics and writers can trigger a trauma reaction from readers, and I do my best to handle any concerns accordingly for individual students. I am sure to involve my guidance counselors, special educators, and administrators if I notice a student needing emotional support because of any sensitive subject matter. When students with mental health concerns display generally undesirable or office-managed behaviors in the midst of a Poe unit, I inform administrators that topics discussed in my class may play a role in those behaviors, but students always decline that correlation themselves. While I have never had a student directly connect a mental health crisis to having read a Poe story, I make it a habit to give trigger warnings prior to topics such as murder, incest, and cannibalism prior to any readings or discussions. I believe this practice is a proactive way to protect my students' mental health, so they are aware of what topics lie ahead.

The most common theme and feedback I receive from students, whether immediately following the unit's closure or years later, is that Poe is memorable. Over half of my students from the 2021–2022 school year answered that their favorite story from the entire eighth grade curriculum is "The Tell-Tale Heart," which is impressive considering it is followed by more relatable social topics and high-interest subjects like Anne Frank's experiences.

My most recent data showed that approximately half of my students believed that teaching the life and works of Edgar Allan Poe is an effective topic to help students become more engaged readers. While their buy-in and appreciation of specific literature makes the teaching process much more enjoyable for everyone involved, eighth grade students are not professional educators who understand effective teaching materials. In my personal opinion, watching a group of reluctant thirteen-year-olds get positively rowdy about a story with unusual and challenging language is proof enough that involving the works of Edgar Allan Poe is a crucial step in a child's literacy journey. Although my role in my students' literacy journeys feels small, I try to encourage all readers in my classes to recognize the power of language. The language of Edgar Allan Poe is proof that words are powerful. He is a household name because of this. Whether they learn it from me or another teacher or Poe himself, I want students to recognize the power that their own language can have, no matter life's circumstances.

My personal experiences with Poe have come full circle. Reading is not for everyone. School is not for everyone. Classic literature is not for everyone. Poe is not for everyone. But he can be! If they have a reason. My reason for Poe is my students, and I am gratified that many students in my classes found their own reasons, too.

11

HOW THE WOMEN WHO LOVED EDGAR HELPED ME TO LOVE HIM TOO

Deborah T. Phillips

"I couldn't stand Edgar Allan Poe in school."

I started several hundred tours with that statement when I worked at the Poe Museum in Richmond, Virginia. The looks on my listeners' faces varied, most being mildly amused and intrigued while others were befuddled or even outright O F F E N D E D. My point in making this confession was not to lose my audience but to attempt a connection with the surly and bored-looking teenager on the group's fringe or the disinterested spouse dragged in by an overenthusiastic partner. This hook usually worked in a small way; I would detect a mild look of surprise, and they would become increasingly engaged over the next hour. It was clear from my body language and enthusiasm from the beginning that I was passionate about this guy, his work, and his life.

What had changed my mind? Through my work in public history, it was actually Edgar's mother Eliza, that "brilliant gem in the theatric crown," who guided me back to her son and helped me to appreciate his genius.[1]

I specialize in living history interpretation, and my repertoire includes three very special women who loved Edgar: his mother Eliza, his fiancée Elmira, and his wife Virginia. These women have served as my muses, igniting my curiosity and inspiring my passion for Edgar's work by allowing me to perceive and interpret him from multiple perspectives. I have had the opportunity to view him through the lens of a mother, who loved her little boy unconditionally; a lover and fiancée, who loved with a broken heart the man her family and fate denied her; and a wife, a veritable child, who grew up with his torments and genius and loved him to her last breath. These insights have informed my approach when interpreting him to the public, and I have enjoyed guiding thousands of people toward a greater understanding and appreciation of his genius through empathy rather than the shock value of his most horrific tales.

The first—and only—time I read Poe in school was in seventh grade, and I was not a fan. I decided early in the school year that I did not like my teacher, Mrs. Jones. I cannot remember anything in particular she did to earn my dislike, and she is probably a very effective and kind teacher. For my part, I had always loved school and learning; my mom worked in the library at my elementary school, and I spent a tremendous amount of time looking at encyclopedias, reference books, and anything else that caught my attention. I was what teachers called "bright." By middle school, I was turning into a bit of a know-it-all brat. I maintained excellent grades and a good rapport with all of my other teachers, but something about Mrs. Jones rubbed me the wrong way. The only lesson in class I remember enjoying was about haiku. I liked playing with the form and wrote one about Kurt Cobain; she critiqued it, and I dimly recall that she critiqued him. That may have been the problem, actually.

I remember Mrs. Jones really liked Edgar, but I do not

---

[1] From a letter printed in *The Richmond Enquirer* quoted in Geddeth Smith, *The Brief Career of Eliza Poe* (Rutherford: Fairleigh Dickinson University Press, 1988), 122.

remember her teaching much about his life. I grew up just south of Richmond, his hometown and home of the Poe Museum. A field trip there may have helped put the experiences that shaped and informed his writing in perspective for a bunch of twelve-year-olds, but that was an opportunity missed. We read many of his works in that seventh-grade class—at least two poems and four stories. I thought "Annabel Lee" was beautiful but sad. The only tale I appreciated was "The Pit and the Pendulum"—spoiler alert: the protagonist escapes at the end. What really, truly turned me off of Edgar was the treatment of the cat in "The Black Cat." I had a cat at the time, one who survived my sister's ex-boyfriend's sick prank of putting her in the freezer, and I remember being furious and shocked by Poe's tale. I went home and snuggled Stormy, who likely struggled, and assured her that I would never let anyone ever hurt her again. I denounced Edgar Allan Poe and swore never to have anything to do with him again, irrevocably and forever.

Despite this response to Poe's story, I had no real aversion to horror or the weird when it came to entertainment. I was six when I first read L. Frank Baum's *The Wonderful Wizard of Oz*, and some of the bizarre scenes not included in the 1939 film weirded me out—in a good way. For example, there's a scene where Dorothy and her companions are trying to climb a hill but are foiled by "Hammer Heads," little flat-headed armless people that seem benign at first but have the ability to extend their necks extremely rapidly and far in order to attack with their heads, which they do to the Scarecrow and Lion. I found this mildly horrifying; they were one of several strange creatures encountered only in the book. I enjoyed detective stories featuring the Hardy Boys and Nancy Drew and couldn't read enough books by Mary Downing Hahn, Christopher Pike, and of course, R. L. Stine. Between the ages of eight and eleven, each month brought a trip to K-Mart and a promise from my mom that I could buy the new *Goosebumps* book if I behaved. She drew the line at *Fear Street*, absolutely forbidding me from reading them, so of course, I borrowed them from friends and the library, hid them, and read as many as I could. Every Saturday night I eagerly waited for the spine-chilling introduction to *Are you Afraid of the Dark?*, and I watched numerous detective shows with Mom, including PBS' Masterpiece Mystery! (featuring a creepy intro with artwork by Edward Gorey), Jeremy Brett's various Sherlock Holmes manifestations, *Cadfael, Columbo, Poirot*, and more. I loved *Alfred Hitchcock Presents, Night Gallery*, and *The Twilight Zone*. By middle school, I had developed the relatively unhealthy habit of staying up extremely late on summer nights to watch horror movies on classic movie stations. This is how I discovered such movies as *The Exorcist* (1973), the original *Poltergeist* movies (1982, 1986, 1988), *The Shining* (1980), *Psycho* (1960), *The Haunting* (1963), and Vincent Price classics like *The House of Wax* (1953). The foundation definitely existed for me to at least appreciate Edgar Allan Poe, but my own prejudice hindered me from seeing his genius at that time of my life.

I have often reflected that I may have appreciated Edgar more if I had revisited him in high school, when I was more mature, but he was not even mentioned as far as I can recall. I vividly recall reading Hawthorne, Fitzgerald, Hurston, Wright, Thoreau, and Salinger, but absolutely no Poe and, again, no field trip to the Poe Museum located just a couple of miles away.

Although a history major and English minor in college, I had not reencountered Edgar in any meaningful way. In 2007, my husband and I were planning our honeymoon to Charleston, South Carolina, and I was eager for new reading material. I had thoroughly enjoyed Matthew Pearl's novel *The Dante Club*, a mystery which features gruesome murders based on the circles of Dante's *Inferno*, so I bought a copy of his newest novel, *The Poe Shadow*.[2] I devoured it on our honeymoon because I found the mystery surrounding Poe's death interesting. I was convinced for years of the cooping theory as a result of that book, and in hindsight, I consider this moment a gentle reintroduction to Edgar.

In mid-2008, I became the education manager for the St. John's

---

[2] See Matthew Pearl, *The Dante Club* (New York: Random House, 2003) and *The Poe Shadow* (New York: Random House, 2006).

Church Foundation and was learning all things Patrick Henry, my favorite "Founding Father." The oldest church and cemetery in Richmond, St. John's Church is the site of Henry's famous "Liberty or Death" speech given in March 1775, and the Foundation offers both public and private reenactments of that event with ten actors portraying well-known figures who were in attendance, including Henry, Thomas Jefferson, and George Washington. While talking to the actors, I discovered that several of them portrayed their characters elsewhere, using scripts they had composed through careful research. They even made a little bit of money doing so.

That fall, my director approached me and asked if I would be willing to portray Eliza Poe, Edgar Allan Poe's mother, who is buried in the cemetery of St. John's Church. Each October, the St. John's Church Foundation offers a cemetery program featuring several "spirits" who talk to guests about their lives and deaths before ushering them into the church for additional programming.[3] Based on my resume, my director knew that I sang, but she did not know how much I loved performing; I had acted in church and school plays for most of my life. I agreed to play the role, only a little discomfited that I was to portray the mother of *that* guy who wrote such awful things. I was excited to perform and to blend two of my greatest loves: performance and history.

The Foundation's dress fit with some alterations. I researched Eliza online, devised my five-minute spiel, and with some red food coloring applied to a handkerchief, my first kitschy performance of Eliza Poe was ready to go. From what I gathered, Eliza was a "triple threat": a talented actress who could also sing and dance. Her story was both inspirational and tragic: she was an actress from at least the age of nine, an orphan at eleven, a wife at fifteen, a widow at

---

[3] St. John's Church in Richmond, Virginia, still offers a cemetery program each October, more extensive than in 2008 and now titled "Fancy Me Mad." The current program features approximately ten spirits, including a special presentation by an actor depicting Edgar Allan Poe. For more information, visit the church's website at https://www.historicstjohnschurch.org/.

eighteen, and a spouse again at nineteen when she wed David Poe, Jr. She gave birth to three children, but her husband abandoned the family in New York City, and she died tragically soon after at age twenty-four in Richmond of consumption, what we now call tuberculosis. In hindsight, my first program was probably cringe-worthy, but it attracted some attention; a representative from the Poe Museum reached out to St. John's Church Foundation about a partnership for the bicentennial of Poe's birth. I portrayed Eliza, and two Poe Museum staff members, impersonating Edgar and his wife Virginia, served as guides for walking tour groups. Perhaps a bit to my surprise, I enjoyed myself immensely and felt a strong urge to continue to tell people about Eliza's story. I asked my director if, as part of St. John's Church Foundation's living history offerings, I could create a half-hour program as Eliza Poe to present graveside in the spring. She agreed, and I was excited to research and share Eliza's story, one which I personally found so inspiring.

Soon after, much to my surprise and delight, I located a biography of Eliza Poe: *The Brief Career of Eliza Poe* written by Geddeth Smith, a historian and actor. It was out of print, but my director found and ordered a copy for my research; I read it within a day. Well-written and thoroughly researched, Smith's book is a compassionate and meticulous evaluation of not only Eliza's life but also theater culture in the Federal era. Eliza's story was absorbing; I felt inspired by her determination against so many odds as well as her perseverance and dedication to her craft and children. Armed with Smith's book, my knowledge of the era's language due to my love of Jane Austen's novels, and the anthropological training I had received in undergraduate and graduate programs, I composed a script. Around this same time, I contracted a respiratory illness; I was twenty-four years old, the same age Eliza was when she died of consumption, and I could not stop coughing. My mother warned me that I was becoming too invested in my role.

St. John's Church Foundation debuted my Eliza Poe graveside program in the spring of 2009 to a small but enthusiastic audience. The script was pretty good; I incorporated a monologue from Eliza's repertoire which Smith had reproduced in his book as well as one of the songs, which I found digitized at a university. Each month my audience grew in number, and soon groups were inquiring about private performances. As part of their recognition of Poe's bicentennial, even *Jeopardy!* referenced my program: "Take a tour of St. John's Church Cemetery, where Eliza, this relative of Poe's, is buried, led by an actress portraying her."[4] To my chagrin, no one knew the question: "Who was his mother?"

I began to understand and empathize with Edgar more; according to many reports, Eliza kept him and his younger sister Rosalie near her in Richmond during her final illness, which meant they likely witnessed her bloody coughing bouts. Rosalie was less than a year old when her mother died, and little Edgar was almost three years old; by all accounts he was a bright little boy. My earliest memories were from around that age; thus, I reasoned that surely he was impacted by watching his beautiful mother waste away from tuberculosis and that this circumstance would have an impact on little Edgar.

I delved into researching the relationship between son and mother. As an adult, Edgar did not retain any vivid memories of her. In 1835, Edgar wrote a letter to Beverley Tucker and revealed, "In speaking of my mother you have touched a string to which my heart fully responds. To have known her is to be the object of great interest in my eyes. I myself never knew her..."[5] As these lines attest, we cannot discount the effect that emotional trauma can have on infants and toddlers in their later development; many studies show how very young children who have experienced loss or trauma later display signs of depression and/or addiction. When I realized the impact

---

[4] *Jeopardy!*, Episode 5718, aired June 17, 2009. It was the $1600 clue in the category titled "Celebrating Poe's Bicentennial"—the remaining Double Jeopardy! categories were inspired by Poe allusions: The Belles, The Raven, The Purloined Letter, The Premature Burial, and The "Gold" Bug.

[5] Edgar Allan Poe to Nathaniel Beverley Tucker, December 1, 1835, in *The Collected Letters of Edgar Allan Poe*, ed. J. W. Ostrom, B. R. Pollin, and J. A. Savoye (Cambridge: Harvard University Press, 2008), 78.

watching his mother die could have had on young Edgar, it felt like an epiphany. From great trauma can come great art. Through the lens of his mother, I felt true compassion and empathy for little Edgar. I returned to his writings and read both well-known and many lesser-known tales such as "Berenice" and "Morella." I enjoyed them immensely. Although it may be surprising after my initial encounter with a Poe tale, to this day, "Berenice" is my favorite horror story by him. I felt like I had a better understanding of why he featured beautiful women dying young.

My circumstances shifted somewhat when I left St. John's Church in 2010 to work for a local non-profit tour operator that specialized in step-on guide services as well as living history. Richmond Discoveries offered me an opportunity to expand my knowledge, explore the entire Richmond region, and create whichever living history characters I wanted.[6] My new boss loved my Eliza Poe program, but what I had created belonged to St. John's Church. I decided to dive back into the research and expand the script, so I purchased my own copy of Smith's book and spent several months on my own time re-researching and rewriting Eliza Poe; I learned that I needed to own the rights to my program and set a precedent I follow to this day. My wonderful mother-in-law sewed a gown for me based on the only known portrait of Eliza, and my new script featured six songs and two monologues from Eliza's repertoire.[7] She became a popular program within a short time for groups of all types.

When I perform Eliza, if there is time, I take questions in-character before breaking character to briefly discuss the impact her life and death had on Edgar. In the midst of reimagining the character,

---

[6] While employed at Richmond Discoveries, I was featured on a podcast in the role of Eliza Poe. See "Eliza Poe/Debbie Phillips," History Replays Today: The Richmond History Podcast, podcast audio, August 15, 2015, http://historyreplaystoday.org/49-eliza-poedebbie/.

[7] To view the portrait and those of the other women mentioned in this chapter, visit "The Women in Poe's Life," The Poe Museum, March 25, 2021, https://poemuseum.org/the-women-in-poes-life/.

I had my first son and found my empathy for poor Eddy deepen as I realized how perceptive infants and toddlers are. One of my primary goals in interpreting Eliza continues to be to help others understand some of the source of Edgar's deep pain and obsession with death. His mother, brother, wife, and foster mother all died of tuberculosis—the first three at the age of twenty-four with him reputedly by their sides. That kind of repeated trauma is sure to leave a mark. It is easy to feel sympathy for him when one realizes how constant the threat of death and separation from his few loved ones was for him.

I was just embarking on my rewrite of Eliza Poe when another Poe-connected living history opportunity arose; it seemed like the universe was pushing me toward him. In the summer of 2010, a local ghost tour operator called Haunts of Richmond asked me to portray Edgar's fiancée Elmira Royster Shelton in the "Haunted Homecoming," a new interactive walking tour in Shockoe Hill Cemetery, where about half a dozen people connected to Edgar are buried.[8] Elmira interested me; she and Edgar were engaged as teenagers and then again a few months before he died. Like her, I knew what it was like to experience a heart-rending breakup with a high school sweetheart who had a way with words. Also, our romance was instantly rekindled when we met again years later. I felt an affinity with her.

Haunts of Richmond had a great script, co-researched by the Poe Museum, and the program sounded fun, so of course, I said yes. This tour ran for several years and was very popular: actors portraying Edgar and his wife Virginia led guests from grave to grave, encountering the "spirits" of such people as his first crush Jane Stith Stanard, his foster parents the Allans, his old flame Eliza White, and Elmira as both a heartbroken teenager and a widowed matron. The tour followed the timeline of his life; even poor Virginia "died" and

---

[8] To see a short clip of me as Elmira Royster Shelton, visit "Debbie Tuttle Phillips on Virginia This Morning," YouTube video, 4:37, July 15, 2010, https://www.youtube.com/watch?v=Fr4ihLRIULQ.

was whisked away by a shrouded actor before Edgar and Elmira reunited prior to his "death." Much like with Eliza, I felt inspired by Elmira's story to research her further and create a new living history program for groups. I was curious to explore interpreting Poe through the lens of someone who loved him romantically as opposed to maternally.

I had a benefit with Elmira that I had not enjoyed with Eliza: she wrote letters and gave interviews over the years. She contradicted herself with regard to her relationship with Edgar, notably becoming more sentimental toward him as she aged. They were engaged to marry in early 1826 when he matriculated at the University of Virginia, but her father disapproved of the match and intercepted Edgar's letters to her, persuading her that she had been forgotten and convincing her to marry the wealthy Alexander Barrett Shelton. Edgar likely spent months at college wondering why he had not heard from his fiancée and returned home to find her engaged to Richmond's Most Eligible Bachelor. Once wed, Elmira learned that Edgar had not forgotten her and that her father had purloined Eddy's letters.

By 1849, nearly twenty-three years later, the widowed Elmira was living a quiet life in Richmond with an inherited fortune when Edgar appeared in her parlor one Sunday morning to renew his acquaintance. He shook up her world; Elmira had no intention of remarriage, but as many songs have expressed through the years, you never forget your first love. Her father was deceased; however, her brothers were not. They, along with her daughter, loathed the idea of her resuming a romantic relationship with Edgar. To be fair, he did not have the best reputation as a result of his struggles with alcohol dependence and pecuniary distress. Much to her family's chagrin, she agreed to marry him, and he bought her a thin gold wedding band engraved with his name, now in the Poe Museum's collection. Mysteriously, whilst en route to Philadelphia for a lucrative editing job and then New York to retrieve his mother-in-law/aunt Maria Clemm for the wedding, Edgar died in Baltimore. Elmira read about his death in the newspaper only days before their wedding was to take place. On my tours at the Poe Museum, many people look at the daguerreotype of her from around the time of Edgar's death and remark on how unattractive she is; to the contrary, I see a quiet beauty riven and shook by a life of heartbreak. Maybe I am biased. "Poor Elmira," I find myself saying frequently when I talk about her.

She was certainly a source of inspiration to Edgar. While they never married, many scholars (including myself) argue that Elmira was the source of several of his most beautiful love poems. She herself denied this, yet these stanzas from Edgar's 1827 poem "Tamerlane," his first published work, seem evidence to the contrary:

Yes! she [was] worthy of all love!
Such as in infancy was mine
Tho' then its *passion* could not be:
'Twas such as angel minds above
Might envy—her young heart the shrine
On which my ev'ry hope and thought
Were incense—then a goodly gift—
For they were childish, without sin,
Pure as her young examples taught;
Why did I leave it and adrift,
Trust to the fickle star within?

We grew in age, and love together,
Roaming the forest and the wild;
My breast her shield in wintry weather,
And when the friendly sunshine smil'd
And she would mark the op'ning skies,
I saw no Heav'n, but in her eyes—[9]

Beautiful lines made more meaningful when one realizes that teenaged Edgar frequented the woods of Richmond as well as the

---

[9] Edgar Allan Poe, "Tamerlane," in *The Collected Works of Edgar Allan Poe,* ed. T. O. Mabbott, vol. 1 (Cambridge: Belknap Press of Harvard University Press, 1969), 30.

famous garden of Mr. Ellis, his foster father's business partner, when he was courting young Elmira. Ignorant of her father's interception of his letters, Edgar must have considered Elmira "fickle" when he returned from University to find her engaged to another. In my script for Elmira, I utilize much of Edgar's poetry to make connections between their mutual heartbreak and its impact on some of his most stirring verses.

Performing as Elmira allows me to speak about Edgar's life much more than I can as his mother, and her perspective allows me to see him better as a man rather than a wounded adolescent. Elmira's interest in Edgar is romantic. While I would not necessarily say I have a crush on a dead guy, I can definitely see why Elmira fell in love and was willing to incur her family's wrath for him later in life. By channeling my own feelings through somewhat similar circumstances with my husband, I feel I am able to express the loss of that love to audiences while conveying Edgar's genius.

In early 2022, Poe Baltimore approached me to create a program as Virginia Clemm Poe, Edgar's cousin and child bride, for the bicentennial celebration of her birth that summer. I had not considered creating her as a program before, primarily because I had outlived her by several years, but I agreed because I could see how her life—and death—affected Edgar. Virginia was certainly one of his most important muses, and it was her five-year-long struggle with tuberculosis and what Edgar called "the horrible never-ending oscillation between hope & despair" that drove him to drink.[10] Excessive drink contributed to behaviors that won him little sympathy from his detractors. Frequently I have heard people cavalierly describe him as "an alcoholic madman," and I have developed the habit of leaping to his defense by describing what his wife's illness did to him and how he developed unhealthy methods of enduring, or coping with, what was a prolonged, tragic situation. Looking at Edgar through

---

[10] Edgar Allan Poe to George W. Eveleth, January 4, 1848, in *The Collected Letters of Edgar Allan Poe*, ed. J. W. Ostrom, B. R. Pollin, and J. A. Savoye (Cambridge: Harvard University Press, 2008), 641.

the lens of his cousin and wife gave me an opportunity to tackle some of the more unsavory aspects of his life: the accusations of pedophilia, alcoholism, and infidelity.

When I compose a living history script, I strive to see the world from my subject's position as much as possible to create the most convincing portrayal I can. This is not an easy task; it requires extensive research into the subject through her own and others' words as well as a thorough understanding of the mores and history of the time. As a researcher living in the twenty-first century, I am sometimes required to perform mental acrobatics to fathom the belief systems of individuals from earlier centuries. I found this to be the case when writing my script for Virginia; by all accounts, she devotedly loved her husband, despite behaviors that were troublesome, to say the least. We have few letters from her and no journals or diaries. How would I talk about Edgar's sins and vices as his young childish bride? The answer seemed natural to me: with candor and empathy.

Virginia was about eight years old when Edgar moved in with her family in Baltimore, and they married five years later in 1836 in Richmond; she was thirteen, and he was twenty-seven. The sexual nature of their relationship is unknown; he lived with her as a big brother for several years before their marriage, referring to her as "Sissy." Her mother lived with them throughout their married lives, and they did not have children. As I have pointed out countless times, their relationship *should* make us uncomfortable in this day and age. Yet it is important to remember how little agency women had in the early nineteenth century and that Virginia's mother, Maria Clemm, advocated for the wedding. A woman in that time with no male relative to support her was as good as dead unless she were independently wealthy, and Maria was far from that. A child of thirteen, Virginia did not have the legal or social ability in that time to decline the marriage if she had wished, and she does not appear to have done so. According to their friends, the couple were perfectly matched and very happy for nearly five and a half years until the ravages of disease descended on their lives.

Deborah T. Phillips as Virginia Clemm Poe
for Poe Baltimore's Virginia Poe Bicentennial Gothic
Tea Party and Reception, August 13, 2022.

Courtesy KalinThomas.com

The last five years of Virginia's life were particularly difficult for her and Edgar as he struggled to cope with her lingering consumption. Edgar could not help his wife; it is like seeing light bulbs turn on above people's heads when I remind them that there were no antibiotics in the 1840s. He could do nothing for her but hold her hand and pray that her bloody coughing fits end soon. He drank, knowing he could not handle alcohol, because at least that afforded him a brief respite from the pain that was his life. After the publication of "The Raven" in 1845 launched him to (impoverished) fame, Edgar became a favorite at the literary salons of Anne Charlotte Lynch; he began a warm friendship with Frances Sargent Osgood, a talented poet. Though married to other people, Edgar and Frances began a literary courtship, printing compliments and poems to one another in *The Broadway Journal*; Virginia encouraged their friendship. Edgar was not drinking anymore because of Frances's friendship, and Virginia believed her to be a steadying influence despite whatever feelings of jealousy she may have felt. I struggled with the mentality behind Virginia's actions at first; I think Virginia knew her death was imminent, and she loved Edgar enough to want him to seek the company of those who made him happy. She recognized that being around her was torment for him, and with the unconditional love of a devoted spouse, Virginia sacrificed her feelings to help her husband endure and, hopefully, thrive.

It is fair to say that I have become quite a fan of Edgar thanks to the women who loved him. I have gained a better understanding of how his separation from each of them informed his writing. In my years as a tour guide around Richmond and at the Poe Museum, I have given tours to thousands of guests from around the world. I always incorporate some recitation and performance into my tours to engage my listeners with Edgar's work because I truly believe art is an effective means of teaching. More people than I can count have told me that my genuine enthusiasm and compassion for Edgar is contagious, and they will read him with a fresh understanding of the man behind the macabre. While I am thankful to Elmira and Virginia for the opportunity to tell their stories, I owe a special debt of gratitude to Eliza, for in addition to being the mother of a genius, she is also my premier living history character of nearly a dozen. I am hardly finished; I continue to research these women, tweaking scripts as appropriate, and have plans for at least two other Poe-related characters. If someone had told me twenty-five years ago that I would be on a first-name basis with Edgar and have a deep appreciation for the genius of his tales and poems, I would have laughed, yet here I am.

I still cannot read "The Black Cat."

12

PUTTING POE'S PROVIDENCE ON THE MAP

Levi Leland

The breath of autumn blew through my hometown of Coventry, Rhode Island. I was a seventh grader headed to my last class of the day. While science was not my favorite subject, it was Friday, and the thoughts of how I would occupy my weekend overwhelmed my eager brain. My peers and I were overjoyed to discover a substitute at our teacher's desk as we entered the classroom and found our seats. We all took a minute to settle down as chatter rang through the room.

Nothing could have prepared me for the flame that was about to ignite within my impressionable young soul when the substitute quieted us down to tell us her plans for the class.

I cannot recall the name of this teacher, but if I saw her face, I would know her instantly. She pulled out a hardcover picture book, and the class speculated as she introduced us to the author and illustrator. Confusion and more chatter spread through the room since we were middle schoolers—obviously too cool for kid's books. Besides, this was science class, not English. If we only waited to make our judgments until after she read the opening paragraph, we would have quickly realized that this was no children's tale. She read "The Black Cat" by Edgar Allan Poe, accompanied by the dark and imaginative illustrations by the artist Gris Grimly.[1]

I was entranced by this macabre story of a tormented man haunted by the demon of his murdered cat. The pictures were as captivating as the story, and I could not take my eyes off the book. There were four stories in total within the edition, but the teacher only read us that one, leaving me with a burning desire to know the other tales. I remember pulling out a piece of paper and jotting down "Edgar Allan Poe, Gris Grimly, The Black Cat" before altering all the plans I had made in my head for that weekend. I was set on finding a copy of this book for myself.

That illustrated edition was my first book of Poe's stories. I remember reading it over and over again while needing to know more about this Edgar Allan Poe guy behind the words. Growing up in the twenty-first century allowed me the convenience of a home computer, and I spent countless hours utilizing mine to research Poe. I was enthralled, absorbing everything I could about this bizarre figure from the nineteenth century. I recall seeing images of him and thinking that he looked like a character from one of his own stories. His image fit the aesthetic of a man capable of writing such horrific fiction. Everything about Poe mesmerized me. Adolescence is tough, and navigating your way through middle school is even tougher. There is this struggle to find your place among your peers and this longing to have something to relate to. Poe gave me a course. There was a familiarity about Poe that engrossed me, and even to this day, I still cannot put those feelings into proper words. Poe was a distraction from the anxieties in my life. Poe wrote, "words have no power to impress the mind without the exquisite horror of their reality."[2] In a perverse way, Poe's words allowed me the comfort of a better reality. His works made any horror faced in my life a little less severe by comparison. For these reasons, I was drawn to Poe.

---

[1] See *Edgar Allan Poe's Tales of Mystery and Madness*, illus. Gris Grimly (New York: Atheneum Books for Young Readers, 2004).

[2] Edgar Allan Poe, *The Narrative of Arthur Gordon Pym* (New York: Harper & Brothers, 1838), 109, https://www.eapoe.org/Works/editions/pymbc.htm.

The next book I acquired was a complete edition of Poe's works. It was a hefty hardback edition with a blue and gray jacket.[3] A red-eyed raven adorned the front cover. This book became my companion for the remainder of my middle school and high school career. That very edition sits proudly tattered on my bookshelf along with the vast collection of Poe books and materials I have come to acquire since. Every once in a while, I will read a tale or poem from that edition, conjuring up that nostalgia from my childhood.

Two years after learning Edgar Allan Poe's name, my mom took me to visit his grave in Baltimore, Maryland, at the age of fourteen. During that trip, the Poe House and Museum was a must on the itinerary. After our tour through the tiny home once occupied by Poe and his family, we met the curator, Jeff Jerome. As we conversed, I remember thinking how fortunate I was that an authority on Poe was giving *me* the time of day. Before leaving the Poe House, Jeff removed a sign from an old chair that read "Do not sit." He then prompted me to have a seat while telling me that the very chair was once owned by Poe himself. I reluctantly placed myself in the rickety old chair as my mom excitedly snapped a number of photos. I was euphoric over the whole experience, and to this day, it is still one of my greatest memories. As I reflect on those times, I can say with certainty that had it not been for those moments in my teenage years I may not have been so encouraged to remain devoted to Poe. My mom was always incredibly supportive of this new passion of mine and took me to Baltimore again the following year. During that visit, Jeff gave me an actual piece of the house that was salvaged from a restoration done years prior. I treasure that piece of crumbling plaster filled with horsehair from 1830. I never thought that I would one day own a Poe artifact so unique. Gestures like these kept my passion thriving.

In 2011, I had a second encounter with plaster and a Poe house. The Poe Cottage in the Bronx held an art contest while undergoing

---

[3] Poe, *Complete Stories and Poems of Edgar Allan Poe* (New York: Doubleday & Co., 1966).

restoration. The winners would get to go to the cottage, place their art in a time capsule, and plaster it in the walls of this historic home that served as Poe's final residence. With more than five hundred entries and only a handful of winners picked, I was the youngest, placing second with a pen and ink illustration of Poe surrounded by images inspired by his works. The visual arts were always a hobby of mine since I exhibited skill in drawing from a very young age. This contest not only reassured me of my talent but also made me realize how inspiring Poe really was to me. My first visit to the Poe Cottage was for this event. A crowd gathered outside to watch me and the other winners present their art while the media took pictures and videos. I will never forget plastering the walls of this sacred place. This moment affirmed that I was truly a part of something—that I fit in. There was this sense of community that I was elated to be a part of.

Subsequent trips with my mom over the next few years led us to the Poe Museum in Richmond, Virginia, and back to the Poe Cottage after the renovations were completed. As I crossed more Poe sites off the list, I realized how monumental it was for me to visit these places during the beginning stages of my Poe studies. I was gaining reliable information at an early age that allowed me a more serious perspective on Poe. Examining artifacts up close and in the flesh only fueled my passion and propelled me forward in the most productive of ways. The last standing Poe house/museum that I had yet to visit was the Edgar Allan Poe National Historic Site in Philadelphia, Pennsylvania, which I finally traveled to in 2017. It was after this visit that I could say officially that I had been to every Edgar Allan Poe museum in the country.

By the time I reached my early twenties, my tenacity and experiences acquainted me with many prominent names in the Poe community. While I was quite established in this world of Poe, I lacked a niche that set me apart from the rest. I knew I needed to find an outlet that could classify me as a legitimate authority on Poe. It was at this point when I started to focus on Poe's connection to Providence, Rhode Island, since I had so many tangible resources close to me that I was able to visit and appreciate in person. Poe's relationship with our city's celebrated poetess, Sarah Helen Whitman, was the reason for his extended time here in 1848. I had read about her in biographies of Poe, but they were always such brief passages that I assumed there was not much to elaborate on. After further investigation, I realized how wrong I was. It was at this moment I had what many would call an epiphany: Boston, Richmond, Baltimore, Philadelphia, the Bronx—each city I had visited that was associated with Edgar Allan Poe held its own significant claim to the great American writer while my own capital city was relatively quiet about its connection to Poe.

That needed to change.

Providence contains a wealth of history. Oral lore often mentions Poe's time in the city but is always saturated with fabricated facts and misinformation. Many who study Poe on a more serious level know that two versions of him exist. First, the alcoholic, drug-addled, death-obsessed madman that the general public is familiar with. This is the mythical version, the one that Poe's literary rival, Rufus Griswold, wrote about in his slanderous "biography" published after Poe was already dead and unable to defend himself.[4] Then there is the other version, the one that truer fans and scholars know: the genius writer who not only pioneered genres of fiction but also invented them, giving the reading public the type of storytelling that it never knew it needed. Poe was a hard-working husband who cared deeply for his family and strived for nothing but the ability to support them through his writing. This is the real Poe, the one I came to know over the years.

Many authorities on Poe make it their primary mission to set the record straight and separate these two versions. When I had that eureka moment, I realized that this was the foundation I needed to make a unique mark of my own in the Poe community. I realized

---

[4] Ludwig (Rufus W. Griswold), "The Death of Edgar Allan Poe," *New-York Daily Tribune*, Oct. 9, 1849: 2, https://www.eapoe.org/papers/misc1827/nyt 49100.htm.

that there was an opportunity right under my nose that nobody had yet seized. Providence needed a spokesman for Poe. Someone to help celebrate his ties to the city in a thorough and accurate way.

There was another layer to this endeavor, a figure who was just as worthy as Poe and in need of some serious recognition.

Sarah Helen Power Whitman was born in Providence on January 19, 1803. Her ancestors were among the first settlers led by Roger Williams in the early seventeenth century. Whitman's family name would grant her respect in the city, but she quickly proved that she deserved admiration on her own merit. Having married a law student from Brown University named John Winslow Whitman in 1828, Whitman moved with her new husband to Boston where she was introduced to some of the most profound ideas of her day. Her husband's affiliation with two different publications allowed Whitman to begin a career in writing, but by 1833, she returned to Providence a widow, where she would continue her pursuits within the restrictive presence of her mother and mentally ill younger sister.

Sarah Helen Whitman was a proponent for women's suffrage, a force in favor of abolition, a spiritualist, and a practicing medium who attended and hosted séances in Providence. She was a gifted woman of great intellect. She influenced and even mentored many prominent people who made it into the history books while she did not. Whitman was a progressive activist at the forefront of major movements happening in America and a beloved poetess in her day. She was well known before Edgar Allan Poe's attempt to sweep her off her feet, but today, she is generally known exclusively for her relationship with him. Another mission I set forth was to highlight Whitman's legacy inside and outside of her association with Poe.

There was no doubt that I had the experience, information, and passion as I occupied this small geographic slice of Poe history. I just needed an idea to spread the information I had acquired in an interesting way. That prompted me to create a website, edgarallanpoeri.com, as a dumping ground for all things Poe and Whitman in Rhode Island. I tracked down graves of people connected to both figures in cemeteries throughout the state. I traced significant sites and locations that had any relevance, photographed them, and added them to my website with a brief history to accompany them.

As the website began to grow, another idea struck me. What if I was able to tell this history in person? What if there was a way to bring people to these landmarks and talk about them right there in the footprints of Poe and Whitman themselves? As I traced the key locations in Poe and Whitman's romance, I found that there was this perfect one-mile loop. There was no doubt in my mind that my next venture would be "A Walking Tour of Poe's Providence." Now all I had to do was recite the history in a form of storytelling as gripping as a tale penned by Poe himself.

Having access to Brown University's special collection of Whitman's personal documents, journals, and letters was one of the greatest resources in my research.[5] As I scoured numerous boxes of folders, reading manuscript after manuscript, I was completely captivated. Reading about Poe's first sighting of Whitman as she recounts it in her own hand was something otherworldly. It brought the history to life like never before. I spent countless hours at Brown's John Hay Library, transcribing scribbles that would be essential in helping me create the script for what would become my walking tour. This experience in itself was quite surreal, as I was compiling a history right from the hand of someone who lived it.

The easiest part of writing anything about Poe is that the truth is stranger than any fiction one can imagine. Poe's biography tells a climactic story of a man struggling through life with just enough triumphs to make observers still root for his success. From September to December 1848, Poe's story in Providence creates a perfect arc. He came to Providence fully optimistic about making Whitman his bride. She rejected his proposals, but he persisted. Finally, she agreed to marry him on the conditions that she get her mother to consent to the union and that Poe abstain from alcohol. Both of

---

[5] For more information on these materials, see "Guide to the Sarah Helen Whitman Papers, 1816–1878," John Hay Library, Brown University Library. 2008, https://www.riamco.org/render?eadid=US-RPB-ms79.11&view=title.

these conditions were met, and the couple were set to marry on Christmas day. This love story was about to have its happy ending until two days before the wedding when Whitman received a note informing her that Poe had a glass of wine at his hotel and was seen intoxicated. Whitman confronted Poe, and he made his final plea to her as she fainted on the sofa. She was able to utter one final "I love you" to him before he was kicked out of the house by her mother. The couple never saw or spoke to each other again, and Poe died less than a year later. While this arc does not exactly have a happy ending, it is as if Poe inadvertently created the perfect template for a tragic short story in his own life. For someone creating a walking tour of this subject, I could not have had an easier job. I feel quite fortunate to live in a space with this connection to Poe and to be able to share this incredible story of this chapter in his life.

I remember scheduling my first tour in September 2021 after refining my script over and over again. I knew that I had created a tour worthy of my *own* interest, but my audience would be the true judge of how effectively I translated this history to the general public. The weather was near perfect. Summer was beginning to transition into autumn, and the crisp air had brought me back to my younger days where it all began with Poe. October always draws people to their darker curiosities—Halloween, of course, being the biggest influence on that tendency. As I was creating this tour, I thought about the appropriate time of year to guide it. In my mind, late September through mid-November was ideal. Not only is the weather impeccable for an outdoor walking tour, but the season attracts people to Poe more than any other time of the year. Another perk to the season is that Poe and Whitman's romance in Providence occurred at this very same time of year nearly two centuries ago. This allows my audience to connect to the history on a deeper level as they can envision this iconic romance under an accurate setting.

I had a very modest turnout of eighteen people for this first tour. We started at Whitman's residence on Benefit Street where the introduction between her and Poe began. I relayed how Whitman and Poe met and their subsequent romance. When "The Raven" was published in New York's *Evening Mirror* in 1845, Poe became a household name. His fame allowed him to begin a lecture tour as interest in the master of horror became nationwide. Providence's Franklin Lyceum hosted Poe for a lecture in December 1848, but it was the lecture of a popular poetess and mutual friend of Poe and Whitman, Frances Osgood, that first brought him to Providence in July 1845. During that very brief visit, Poe laid his eyes on the ethereal Sarah Helen Whitman while she tended her rose garden in the backyard of her home on Benefit Street. She had no idea that Poe caught this glimpse of her that evening, but this would be the precursor to a significant relationship between the two in the years to come. When Poe returned to Providence in September 1848, he officially began courting Whitman. That courtship rapidly progressed into an engagement, which initiated a wild and distracted story.

After my spiel, we made our way down to the rose garden behind the home where the ancestral roses that Whitman gardened herself are still in full bloom. While Poe never lived in Providence and never published any works here, his time here did result in at least one poem, his second titled "To Helen." This poem recounts his first look at Whitman in her rose garden under the midnight moon of that sultry summer evening. As I recited the first stanza from that poem which this very rose garden inspired, I could see the awe in my patrons' eyes. In that moment, they realized they were standing at the very spot where Edgar Allan Poe once stood, looking before a bed of roses that was memorialized in a piece by one of the world's greatest poets. At that moment, the audience felt a closeness to Poe that I am sure they did not expect.

During this romance with Whitman in the bustling city of Providence, Poe acquired two ounces of laudanum for an attempted suicide en route to Boston. Whitman's rejections of Poe's marriage proposals sent him spiraling into a hopeless fit of despair. At this point in his life, he tragically thought his best option would be the grave. Laudanum was a tincture of opium and alcohol used as a painkiller in the nineteenth century. Today, it can be equated to morphine. He swallowed one of the two ounces, intending to take the other and finish the job once he mailed a letter to Annie Richmond of Lowell, Massachusetts. Annie was another woman Poe was smitten with at the time. He thought that she was the one who could save him from all his woes.

That first dose rendered Poe too ill to even function, and he ended up sleeping off the effects, never able to take that second dose. His life was spared, and four days later, he sat for a daguerreotype photo right here in Providence. Sarah Helen Whitman later dubbed this photo "Ultima Thule," and it remains Poe's most iconic photograph today. This image was one of two that Providence had the great fortune of capturing of Poe during his time in the city. The other, known as the "Whitman" daguerreotype, was taken four days after the Ultima Thule, when Whitman finally agreed to marry him. This photo shows a much calmer, healthier-looking Poe in better spirits. We only know of six separate occasions when Poe sat for a daguerreotype in his life, so the fact that Providence served for two of those sittings is quite substantial.

A subsequent stop on the tour brings us to The Providence Athenaeum, a member-funded library opened to the public in 1836. The library operates under the same model today. In 1848, it served as a safehouse for Poe and Whitman to have their privacy from Whitman's scrutinizing friends and family. Around this time, Whitman had read "Ulalume," an unsigned poem in *The American Review*. Whitman fell in love with the beauty and sentiment of the poem, asking everyone she knew if they had read it, and she vainly questioned who the author was. One morning, while Poe and Whitman were in the Athenaeum, she asked him if *he* had read it. Without saying a word, Poe grabbed a bound volume off of the shelf in the alcove where they were sitting and opened up to the poem. He then took a pencil and signed his name at the bottom of the page. That volume remained on the shelf for over twenty years until Whitman went back to secure it into good hands within the library. The Providence Athenaeum has preserved it in its special collections since that day. One can still view it in person and examine the lightly penciled-in name of Edgar Allan Poe written in his own hand on the very bottom of that page.

Among The Providence Athenaeum's pantheon of life-sized busts, Edgar Allan Poe's sculpted likeness is perched right above the door as you enter and exit the library. This bust of Poe is copied from Edmond Quinn's bronze bust sculpted for the Bronx Society of Arts and Sciences for Poe's centennial in 1909. The Athenaeum's copy was duplicated from one in my personal collection, which I obtained from the Poe Museum in Richmond, Virginia, in 2012. It is only appropriate that Poe's likeness watch over the stunning library where he once walked with his Providence sweetheart while sharing poetry and literary ideas.

One of the final stops on the tour is the home of the Dailey family on Brown Street, which served as the final stop for Sarah Helen Whitman. At the age of seventy-five, Whitman was alone, and her health was declining. Her friends offered to take her into their home and care for her. Whitman graciously accepted this offer. She spent the remaining five months of her life under the tender care of Charlotte Dailey and her two daughters, Lottie and Maude. On her deathbed, Whitman continued to correspond with John Henry Ingram, a biographer set on writing the first definitive biography of Edgar Allan Poe. Before Whitman passed away on June 27, 1878, she requested that a formal announcement of her death be sent to the papers after she had already been buried. She also requested that no invitations to her funeral be sent out. These requests did not impede a large gathering of people at the Dailey home on the day of Whitman's wake and funeral. This is a prime example of the profound effect Whitman had on the city and the number of genuine friends she had by her side. I like to take this opportunity on the tour to emphasize Whitman's legacy *outside* of her connection to Poe, as this brief anecdote so perfectly exemplifies that point.

A question I like to ask my group before I begin a tour is "How many of you knew that Poe had ties to Providence?" Some people have no idea he was ever in Providence while others only know a brief, choppy account of his time here. However, after the tour is over, I am certain they walk away enlightened to the point of pure surprise. Something I am always excited about after conducting a tour is the feedback afterwards. One patron equated each stop on the tour to an episode of a Netflix show that they want to binge-watch, eagerly awaiting to find out what happens next.

I think Poe appeals to people in varying ways, but the core is always the same. Edgar Allan Poe is a figure we remember being shocked by. His life was surrounded by controversy and the bizarre while his writing remains unmatched. He is one of those writers in English class one remembers not being so bored by. One of my greatest advantages of creating a local tour about Poe's history in Providence is that, before now, Rhode Islanders thought they had to travel a substantial distance to be close to Poe history. I think this is the hook that pulls people to my tour.

His relationship with Sarah Helen Whitman proved to be one of the most important events in his life even though it was quite a tumultuous time for him. When Poe died less than a year after he parted ways with Whitman, she became one of his most staunch defenders until her own death. She not only corresponded with early Poe biographers to ensure an accurate portrayal of him but also published her own biography in 1860 titled *Edgar Poe and His Critics* as a direct response to the slanders and misinformation being spread about him after his death. Whitman set forth the mission that people are still following today, the one that I continue to achieve through my tour: separating fact from fiction, Poe the man and Poe the myth. If I can be a force in gaining the public's interest in Poe while relaying an accurate account of his life, I can say with conviction that I have done my part. At the same time, I am able to represent a profound figure with even more claim to Providence's history, Sarah Helen Whitman, bringing some well-deserved recognition to her, too. Aiding Providence in celebrating its rightful claim to Edgar Allan Poe has been one of my greatest accomplishments.

I think there will be a perpetual appeal to Poe. His name conjures up primal feelings of fear and mystery. When Poe captivated his audience through his writing, he affirmed a trait that is still so relevant today: people want to be scared. They want horror. They want to be transfixed so that they cannot help but to look, read, or listen. For this reason, Poe will always attract the public's attention. I have discovered that this is even truer when one can pinpoint a section of Poe's life to a location that is accessible to the audience. This allows a type of storytelling that touches more of the senses.

A Walking Tour of Poe's Providence has realized two successful seasons now.[6] I have guided over thirty tours for over one hundred patrons. In April 2022, I even guided the Poe Studies Association on a brief tour when they came to Providence as part of their conference in Boston. The Providence Athenaeum served as host, and it was my distinct pleasure to fulfill the Athenaeum's request to co-host this wonderful group of Poe enthusiasts. I walked them down Benefit Street from the Athenaeum heading north, the same route Poe took with Osgood during his first visit to the city. As we approached Sarah Helen Whitman's historic residence, I prompted the group to glance down Church Street, looking in the backyard. It was on that same walking route and in that same direction that Poe glanced, catching his first glimpse of Whitman. This experience reiterates my passion for not only telling the history of Poe in Providence but also allowing listeners to experience it. As long as I can continue to tread Poe's path in Providence, guiding people along the way, I am confident that I will walk until my legs give out.

In June 2022, I had the honor of guiding Jeff Jerome, now curator emeritus of the Poe House and Museum in Baltimore, on my walking tour. That experience evoked so many emotions for me, as did my first meeting with Jeff over a decade prior. For a moment, I paused in disbelief that I was now commanding Jeff's attention as he did mine when I was the young fan at the Poe House. When reality set in, I was still that young, ambitious Poe fan stumbling over my words in awe of the moment. It was a humbling experience for me as this relationship came full circle. I do not think there is a way for me to thank Jeff properly for his kindness and support. Part of

---

[6] To book a tour, visit Edgar Allan Poe: Rhode Island, https://edgarallanpoeri.com/contact/.

me hopes that my successes through my walking tour and other en-
deavors are confirmation that he has done a great justice to Poe in
ushering in the next generation of fans.

13

KEEPING POE'S MACABRE SPIRIT ALIVE IN THE BRONX: WORKING AT THE EDGAR ALLAN POE COTTAGE

Roger McCormack

In 1846, a small, white, Dutch clapboard cottage was situated thirteen miles north of Manhattan in the village of Fordham, then part of Westchester County, New York, and today part of the Bronx. Located in rural New York, the cottage looked out on an apple orchard and the rolling hills of Long Island in the distance. Built for farm laborers in 1812, it remained a modest, working-class home. In the mid-1840s, a few homes, a hotel, two taverns, a blacksmith shop, a railroad, and a college made up the village of Fordham. This was all.

From the porch, the residents would have heard the sounds of birds chirping, the New York and Harlem Railroad rumbling, and the bell tower at St. John's College tolling. Visitors who walked through the front door might have had to duck to enter the small room that served as both kitchen and parlor. They would have seen a rocking chair, a hanging bookshelf, a writing desk, Dutch silverware on the kitchen wall, and a cast-iron stove. They would have encountered the cottage's residents: Maria Clemm, her daughter

Virginia Poe, and Virginia's husband Edgar Allan Poe. Rather worse for wear, often sick and fretting about Virginia's health, Poe was going to the city less and less but still writing—always writing.

Today, the clean country air of Fordham that attracted Poe is no more. His former home sits a few hundred yards to the north, but it is no longer in the country. The views of the hills of Long Island and the sounds of the cadences of rural life have been replaced by stately Art Deco prewar apartment buildings, bodegas, honking cars, and the endless pell-mell of traffic on Fordham Road. The neighborhood is bustling, and the intense pace of the Bronx's development has made the Poe Cottage an incongruous site. In fact, the relentlessness of New York City's development almost doomed the cottage to destruction at the turn of the twentieth century. A far cry from the dusty country roads of Poe's day, it is located along one of the busiest roads in the Bronx, the Grand Concourse. Founded in 1909, the Concourse was modeled after the Champs-Élysées in Paris, intending to echo European grandeur with a New York twist. The road was designed by the French engineer Louis Risse, who, while hunting in the then mostly rural Bronx, noted a series of ridges headed South into Manhattan. He knew at once that this was the place to construct the monumental concourse of his imagination. Occupying the corner of Kingsbridge Avenue and the Grand Concourse, the cottage is adjacent to two subway lines: the Jerome Avenue line (Number 4 Train) and the Concourse line (D Train). To say that Poe would not have recognized Fordham even just fifty years after he lived there is an understatement. Similarly, today's visitors get the sense that they are literally being transported back in time—to a time when Fordham was a rural village and the small, Dutch farmhouse cottages were common sights. If the visitors walked into the cottage, they would still have to stoop to walk into the small kitchen and parlor, just as it was. The same Dutch silverware hangs on the kitchen wall.

You would still see St. John's College, of course, which had opened in 1841. However, it has expanded and is now known as Fordham University. Poe famously liked to hang out with the all-

Jesuit faculty and paid them the dubious compliment of describing them as "highly cultivated gentlemen and scholars" who "smoked, drank, and played cards like gentlemen, and never said a word about religion."[1] If Poe and the Jesuit priests of St. John's could know the cost of Fordham University's tuition today, they would roll over in their graves!

Everything has changed around it, but that little cottage remains frozen in time because the man who lived there over one hundred years ago—regarded as an idiosyncratic yet immensely talented writer during his lifetime—is today considered one of the most influential writers in the American canon. The cottage has remained because Poe has remained—in our collective imagination and in the Bronx.

Old ghosts haunt the Edgar Allan Poe Cottage of Fordham, Bronx, New York. Edgar Allan Poe famously lived in the cottage from 1846–1849 until the time of his mysterious death in Baltimore. It was his last home and later became the earliest Poe Museum in the United States. First opened in 1917, it is older than our friendly rival museums in Baltimore, Philadelphia, and Richmond and is one of only three existing Poe homes preserved to this day. It has been administered by the Bronx County Historical Society since 1975 when the Society took over stewardship from the Bronx Society of the Arts and Sciences, the organization (along with the New York Shakespeare Society) responsible for saving the cottage from destruction when the Bronx was being extensively developed at the turn of the twentieth century.

I have been the Director of Education at the Bronx County Historical Society since 2020, hired at a time when the entire world, not just the cottage, seemed to have stopped moving. Like Poe, I

---

[1] Marie Louise Shew Houghton reports that the Reverend John Henry Hopkins, an Episcopal priest, heard Poe make this comment in her letter to James H. Ingram dated February 9, 1875. See John Carl Miller, *Building Poe Biography* (Baton Rouge: Louisiana State University Press, 1977), 101.

was an exile and misfit of sorts: a recent master's degree program graduate who had been working on my family's vegetable farm in New Jersey while searching for a way to use my passion for literature and history meaningfully. Like Poe, I was also desperate for money, and thankfully, the Bronx County Historical Society, and with it, Poe Cottage, came along. In my role as Director of Education, I interpret the site and ensure the historical and literary significance of Poe and of the cottage is kept alive through special events, academic literature, and tours.

I give tours of the cottage to hundreds of people a year. Europeans come to explore the master of the short story and better understand his relationship to the Decadent movement of literature in France. A filmmaker came to the cottage a few years back to film it as part of a work on René Magritte, the famed Belgian surrealist, as Magritte *himself* visited in the 1960s and drew inspiration from the Gothic ambiance for his pioneering art. Poets of local and international renown come to glean inspiration by walking through Poe's writing room and often to read their own poetry—tangibly hoping to ensure that Poe's poetic spirit is kept alive.

Local school groups are drawn by the frightening tales they are reading in school, and old-timers from the Bronx like to come and reminisce about the seemingly widespread belief that the cottage is haunted. Poe's wife did die there after all and in a terrible way! The spooky Gothic aura is noted by visitors, who are both fascinated and appalled by reminders of Poe's emotional trauma and loss.

What all these people have in common, though, is Poe, and the impact his work has had on their lives. People feel a dark fascination with Poe's work, the tragic circumstances of Poe's life at the cottage, and the incredible grit he exhibited in producing classic works as he faced the ravages of his wife's death and his own alcohol dependence. Today we would say he was New York Tough.

Poe was a New Yorker long before the stereotype gained currency—combative, volatile, of questionable sanity. He was a kind of big city columnist, writing a column called "Doings of Gotham" for *The Columbia Spy*, a Pennsylvania newspaper. In these columns, Poe captured the essence of modern New York: "The streets are thronged with strangers, and everything wears an aspect of intense life."[2] It is a definition of city life that has not changed much since his time in New York: the Bronx today is a place of immigrants and strivers. It is rare to hear English spoken on the street and even rarer to encounter a quiet street.

The commercial and literary pressures of nineteenth-century New York, the foremost publishing center of the United States, were substantial. As they are today, readers were impressed by lewd gossip, miraculous events, and sordid tales of urban life. Poe had to produce for this audience in a cutthroat literary marketplace—something any writer in today's New York would understand—but was cunning enough to capitalize on a public eager for outrageous tales. Notably, Poe contributed to an early Orson Welles-like Martian invasion hoax trend, proclaiming a fictitious transatlantic balloon voyage in the pages of *The Sun* based in New York.[3] Though it was not until the twentieth century that such a voyage was undertaken with success, the hoax was believed by many as Poe's instinct for the fantastic and the unnerving was as keen in his work as a columnist as in any of his other writings.

Only a place as culturally effervescent as New York could provide a home for the vagabond that was Poe. Yet there is a dark side of Poe's New York life, aspects of which would be instantly recognizable to modern New Yorkers. He had come to Manhattan in 1844, a move forced by straitened circumstances in Philadelphia: as

---

[2] Edgar Allan Poe, "Doings of Gotham," *The Columbia Spy*, May 25, 1844, 3, The Edgar Allan Poe Society of Baltimore, https://www.eapoe.org/works/misc/gothamb2.htm.

[3] Edgar Allan Poe, "The Balloon Hoax," *New York Sun*, Express, April 13, 1844, 1, The Edgar Allan Poe Society of Baltimore, https://www.eapoe.org/works/tales/ballhxa.htm.

Poe scholar Scott Peeples notes, Poe might have been worried about starving to death.[4] New York was already the commercial and cultural heart of America in the mid-nineteenth century, displacing Boston and Philadelphia as the preeminent American city, and so it made sense for Poe to try to make a go of it there.

The city's inhabitants lived transiently, moving frequently from one apartment to another, as they do today. Poe was no different: he lived in five different residences before his move to the cottage in Fordham. The fears and hopes of contemporary Bronxites would have resonated with him. For one, Poe was a renter his entire life, like the vast majority of modern Fordham residents. Poe often had difficulty scrounging together the $10 monthly rent he paid for the cottage.

Many of the Bronx students I give tours to will open up about similarly traumatic housing situations. The Bronx today is also the poorest county in New York State—its residents are rent-burdened, fear eviction, and eke out difficult lives in a city known for inexorable change and ruthlessness. Students tell of being forced out by a greedy landlord, moving and losing friends, having difficulty adjusting to a new school—all in a city of supposed abundance and plenty. Like Poe, the New York and Bronx my students inhabit is a place of sanguine hopes and squalid reality. The mythic fears depicted in Poe's stories—premature burial, sentient houses, the loss of teeth, torture—paralleled the real fears—starvation, economic ruin, professional self-destruction—he knew all too much about.

Poe's dreams of commercial success were repeatedly dashed, and despite gaining fame and critical plaudits, he never was able to achieve the financial competency that had eluded him his whole life. The merciless quality of American capitalism reached its acme in nineteenth century New York where wealthy merchants lived cheek-by-jowl with impoverished Irish and immigrant laborers, all drawn to New York for the same reason Poe had come and the same reason

---

[4] Scott Peeples, *The Man of the Crowd: Edgar Allan Poe and the City* (Princeton: Princeton University Press, 2020), 119.

why millions of people come to New York today—in the hope of bettering one's life.

Like the schoolchildren to whom I give tours, I first became aware of Poe when I was young, and also like these students, I was similarly gripped by the claustrophobic horror, psychotic protagonists, and the Gothic bloody-mindedness of his tales, particularly "The Cask of Amontillado" and "The Tell-Tale Heart." As I got older, though, I began to appreciate the layers of Poe's stories, many of which explore urban and political themes. Poe of course is hard to pin down politically: he was a Southerner and a defender of slavery who loathed abolitionists and associated Boston and New England with literary snobbery and bad didactic literature. But probably because of his hardscrabble life, Poe saw through the illusion of an idea in vogue in the 1800s—American exceptionalism—and realized something elemental about the harshness of American life.

"The Man of the Crowd," for instance, in which the protagonist, a flaneur, follows a man through the streets of London, evokes modern ennui and urban alienation. The dystopian satire "Mellonta Tauta," written in the cottage and in which a woman from 2848 travels back to the nineteenth century, explores the themes common in Poe's oeuvre: that democracy is a race to the bottom (Poe often referred to it as "mobocracy"), that capitalism and progress are false gods, and that history itself is as much gossip as fact.

Poe's New York phase was a period of triumph and disaster. He wrote "The Raven" at the Brennan farm in what is today the Upper West side in 1845. The poem was the equivalent of a new Cardi B or Taylor Swift song today and allowed Poe to take the rarefied world of the New York literary salons by storm. He cut a Romantic figure, dashing in his elegant Richmond clothes, and carried out a number of flirtations (yes, while his wife was still alive). But—alas—like many writers, he found this rarefied world easier to enter than to stay put.

185

Poe was also particularly concerned with a savagery unique to adult life: that of professional rivalries and warfare. In the great tale of vengeance and revenge written at the cottage—"The Cask of Amontillado"—Montresor lures Fortunato into the wine cellar under the drunken pretext of finding another bottle of wine, mirroring Poe's virulent attacks on the "New York Literati" for mediocrity and the prostitution of talent to the demands of the market. Poe also had a thin skin and did not care to be insulted with impunity. Historian John Tresch writes that he "praised his friends" but "ravaged his foes," "torching his former partner Charles Briggs as derivative, vain, and 'grossly uneducated,' describing Hiram Fuller's *Mirror* as a 'desert of stupidity,' rapping Lewis Gaylord Clark as pointless and indistinct: 'he is as smooth as oil,' and his 'forehead is phrenologically, bad—round and what is termed bullety.'"[5]

All of this literary sniping, of course, was and is a hallowed New York tradition. Poe was as bitchy as Truman Capote and as scurrilous as Norman Mailer. Resentment at being kept out of the upper echelon of the New York literary world is a common enough complaint. Yet for all this coarse and characteristically nineteenth-century invective, Poe did write a tale for the ages with "The Cask of Amontillado"—only a writer of Poe's caliber could turn a jilted ego into a work that transcends the combative setting in which it was written to create a universally classic story of vengeance.

I stress to visitors that Poe would be at home in the modern world with its profusion of shoddy writing and mediocre phrasemaking—this affinity explains in part his continued fascination for a wide variety of audiences and signals that he was also a paragon of artistic and intellectual integrity. And as Truman Capote had his Gore Vidal—who famously remarked on hearing of Capote's death "It was a good career move," Poe had a number of nemeses, many

---

[5] John Tresch, *The Reason for the Darkness of the Night: Edgar Allan Poe and the Forging of American Science* (New York: Farrar, Strauss and Giroux, 2021), 278.

drawn from his New York milieu.[6] The most damaging association was with Rufus Griswold, poet and critic, who today we would say was a frenemy of Poe. Griswold smeared Poe in a libelous obituary that marred Poe's reputation, reversing the usual formula of artistic obscurity in life: posthumous fame.[7] Poe, like the Bronx, was resilient. His reputation has survived the vituperations of mediocrities, and his place in the American canon is secure.

Probably overwhelmed at the pace of life in nineteenth-century Gotham, Poe swiftly moved to the outskirts of the empire city. His child bride and first cousin Virginia had contracted tuberculosis while they were living in Philadelphia, and Poe, Virginia, and his Aunt Maria relocated north. After renting a few homes nearer to the city center, the family thought that the clean country air of Fordham would help Virginia recover. Alas it did not, and she perished in the cottage on January 30, 1847.

Virginia's young age and the fact that she was her husband's cousin never fails to elicit a collective "Ewwwww!" from my students when they tour the cottage. They love to see the bed she died in, though, preserved in the small downstairs bedroom where Virginia succumbed to her illness. But there is a sweet and tender side to this politically incorrect marriage. Poe cherished his time with Virginia and "Muddy," as he endearingly called his Aunt Maria Clemm, whom he viewed as a mother. Poe reveled in their tortoiseshell cat, Catterina, and enjoyed tending to the cherry trees and dahlias on the broad lawn of the cottage. (I, too, take great pleasure in the companionship of my own black cat, named Poe. But rest assured, he has both his eyes.) Many visitors are moved by the depths of Poe's devotion to Virginia and his toil to provide for her comfort in the

---

[6] Gore Vidal qtd. in Richard Bradford, *Literary Rivals: Feuds and Antagonisms in the World of Books* (London: The Robson Press, 2014), np.

[7] See Ludwig (Rufus W. Griswold), "The Death of Edgar Allan Poe," *New-York Daily Tribune*, Oct. 9, 1849: 2, https://www.eapoe.org/papers/misc1827/nyt49100.htm.

last days of her life, striving to keep her warm with only his cloak from West Point and Catterina. Poe wrote despondently after her funeral in his poem "Deep in Earth": "Deep in earth my love is lying / And I must weep alone."[8] And in a letter after Virginia's death, Poe wrote:

> I became insane, with long intervals of horrible sanity. During these fits of absolute unconsciousness I drank, God only knows how often or how much. As a matter of course, my enemies referred the insanity to the drink rather than the drink to the insanity. I had indeed, nearly abandoned all hope of a permanent cure when I found one in the *death* of my wife. This I can & do endure as becomes a man—it was the horrible never-ending oscillation between hope & despair which I could *not* longer have endured without the total loss of reason.[9]

The poems and tales of loss Poe wrote at the cottage resonate in particular with many who visit, particularly the elegiac "Annabel Lee." In the poem, inspired by the decline and demise of Virginia, Poe writes:

> A wind blew out of a cloud, chilling
> My beautiful Annabel Lee;
> So that her high-born kinsmen came
> And bore her away from me,
> To shut her up in a sepulchre
> In this kingdom by the sea.[10]

And Poe goes on, in a beautiful passage conveying the depths

---

[8] Edgar Allan Poe, "Deep in Earth," in *The Collected Works of Edgar Allan Poe*, ed. T. O. Mabbott, vol. 1 (Cambridge: Belknap Press of Harvard University Press, 1969), 396.

[9] Edgar Allan Poe to George W. Eveleth, January 4, 1848, in *The Collected Letters of Edgar Allan Poe*, vol. 2, ed. J. W. Ostrom, B. R. Pollin, and J. A. Savoye (New York: The Gordian Press, 2008), 641.

[10] Edgar Allan Poe, "Annabel Lee," in *The Collected Works of Edgar Allan Poe*, ed. T. O. Mabbott, vol. 1 (Cambridge: Belknap Press of Harvard University Press, 1969), 477.

of his devotion for Virginia:

> But our love it was far stronger by far than the love
> Of those who were older than we—
> Of many far wiser than we—
> And neither the angels in Heaven above,
> Nor the demons down under the sea,
> Can ever dissever my soul from the soul
> Of the beautiful Annabel Lee:—[11]

Poe had come to cherish his domestic life and was assailed by dread at the sure knowledge that it would end with the death of Virginia.

Maria Clemm mattered to him as well. Widely acknowledged as keeping Poe on the straight and narrow, Maria ensured the cottage was kept "so purely clean," as described by one visitor as "so neat, so poor, so unfurnished, and yet so charming a dwelling I never saw."[12] Poe paid tribute to Maria in "To My Mother" in a characteristically emotional way:

> My mother—my own mother, who died early,
> Was but the mother of myself; but you
> Are mother to the one I loved so dearly,
> And thus are dearer than the mother I knew
> By that infinity with which my wife
> Was dearer to my soul than its soul-life.[13]

The countless struggles of Bronxites inspire me to preserve the

---

[11] Poe, "Annabel Lee," 478.

[12] Mary Gove Nichols, qtd. in George E. Woodberry, *The Life of Edgar Allan Poe: Personal and Literary*, vol. 2 (Boston: Houghton Mifflin Company, 1909), 218, 214.

[13] Edgar Allan Poe, "To My Mother," in *The Collected Works of Edgar Allan Poe*, ed. T. O. Mabbott, vol. 1 (Cambridge: Belknap Press of Harvard University Press, 1969), 467.

many legacies of Poe and to ensure that his struggles and literature do not pass from the collective understanding of Fordham and the Bronx. For instance, at a recent event at the cottage celebrating Poe's birth, the Queens Poet Laureate Maria Lisella gave a reading reflecting on her late husband, the Bronx poet and activist Gil Fagiani. Gil lived on Fordham's Creston Avenue, a block from the steps of the cottage, and bore witness to the darkest days of the Bronx, when arson and housing abandonment were abetted by greedy landlords seeking insurance payouts. Gil conquered heroin addiction and was active in the earliest community efforts to combat the blight of opioid addiction. The similarities between Poe's own struggles—personal and professional—and those living in the Bronx today reinforce their resiliency as they strive to attain that elusive American dream dangled in front of those who want to believe in American exceptionalism.

And of course there are the many Poe relationships that have flowered since I started at the historical society. We maintain genial relationships with our Poe partners in Philadelphia, Richmond, and Baltimore. All of the Poe museums frequently travel to one another's sites to lecture, tour, and learn from the specialized knowledge and individual lens on Poe's life each museum provides. In particular, my partnership with Enrica Jang, the incomparable executive director of the Edgar Allan Poe House and Museum in Baltimore, has taught me an invaluable amount about Poe in a brief time.

In 2022, Poe Baltimore loaned an exhibit on the deaths of Edgar and Virginia Poe. The exhibit explores the mysterious death of Poe in Baltimore, of which no convincing cause of death has been adequately proved. The most common cause attributed to his death is alcohol dependence, but the exhibit explores the various theories and the reasons for the bevy of sensational tales of Poe's demise. In addition, the display reminds visitors of Virginia's indispensable role in his life, providing him with much-needed emotional support and, at times, serving as his muse. These deep and fruitful professional relationships enhance a knowledge and appreciation of Poe's work and contribute to the enduring fascination with Poe's life, literature, and times.

During my tours, I emphasize that Poe was the original archetype of what became associated with the Hemingway figure in American literature: hard-drinking, self-destructive, and creatively brilliant. But he was a fighter. At the time of his death he had departed Fordham for a tour of the South to pursue a long-deferred dream—making his own magazine, which he titled *The Stylus,* a reality. Poe intended the magazine to be a serious literary endeavor. It would publish only the best of American literature and criticism. Poe had made raising the standards of American literature a life's work, including battling for higher pay for writers who often faced deplorable financial straits if they wanted to live off their writing alone. He was also known as the "tomahawk man" for his polemical criticism of work he considered mediocre or work that was praised because it was written by the rich, the well-born, or the well-connected. His magazine would never stoop to such puffery.

Lamentably, this magazine never came to pass. As part of this tour, Poe stopped in his former hometown of Richmond, rekindling a childhood romance with Elmira Royster. She agreed to marry him, and Poe headed back to the small cottage in Fordham to settle his affairs before returning to Richmond to start a new life with Elmira. His route took him through Baltimore where he disembarked from the train for unknown reasons. He was found a week later, delirious and raving. In a few days, he was dead.

But great writers are immortal.

Those of us at the Poe Cottage have done our part to keep Poe alive. We have petitioned the city for funds to ensure the cottage is preserved, written grants to ensure reserves to fund emergency repairs and maintenance, and striven to provide a robust series of educational programming. In the end, we can only hope to be good stewards of Poe—his literary significance and his life in the Bronx—and ensure the Poe Cottage remains a source of community pride and a tale of successful historic preservation.

14

A PUBLISHING HOUSE THAT POE BUILT: RED STYLO MEDIA

A Conversation with Enrica Jang and Jason Strutz

Enrica Jang: I am the writer of graphic novels and comics series. I own a small independent publishing company, Red Stylo Media, and for the last thirteen years, we have published comic anthologies, independent comics series, and operated as a packaging service for other independent comics creators. We are a small shop that does just about everything, even plush toys. I do lead a double life; I am a writer and a publisher at night and on weekends, but by day, I am the Executive Director of Poe Baltimore and the Edgar Allan Poe House & Museum in Baltimore, Maryland. My experience as a writer and editor led to my employment at Poe House in 2017.

Red Stylo has published a series of literary horror-inspired comic anthologies. Our first book, *The Poe Twisted Anthology* (2011), is a collection of original comic stories inspired by Edgar Allan Poe.[1] I had already been working on my own independent series, but *Poe Twisted* was the first book that I took on editing. I am a longtime lover of Poe's work. I went into the project already recognizing Poe's popularity. From a business standpoint, I was trying

---

[1] *The Poe Twisted Anthology*, ed. Enrica Jang (New York: Red Stylo Media, 2011).

to tap into an existing fandom while also bringing in original comics inspired by that literary love, always aware that there would be a built-in interest. That was very much intentional. What was accidental was seeing that model work so well with Poe; that was sort of a reason in itself to continue. Now we have books inspired by Shelley's *Frankenstein*, Shakespeare's plays, and Dante's *Inferno*. In addition, we have published several more literary anthologies. But all along ours is a publishing house that Poe built.[2]

Later I adapted Poe's "The Cask of Amontillado" for comics and wrote a graphic novel that is a sequel, *The House of Montresor* (2014).[3] I am very proud to point out that my books were sold in the Poe House gift shop before I was hired as director. My art partner on these projects, and now a featured artist for Poe Baltimore, is Jason Strutz.

Jason Strutz: I am a comics illustrator, writer, graphic designer, and creator of a variety of art-related and creative life projects. I have worked at sign shops and comic shops, making a living doing comics and art part-time, and once my partner and I had our daughter, she became my part-time job.

Enrica and I met at a comics convention. She invited me to do some small bits for *The Poe Twisted Anthology*, which kicked off the anthology series from Red Stylo, and continued to contribute to the anthologies with stories in *Shakespeare Shaken*, *Unfashioned Creatures*, and *A Soul Divided/Caged In Flesh*. I later illustrated our adaptation of *The Cask of Amontillado* as well as our sequel *The House of*

---

[2] See *Unfashioned Creatures: A Frankenstein Anthology*, ed. Enrica Jang (New York: Red Stylo Media, 2014); *Shakespeare Shaken*, ed. Enrica Jang (New York: Red Stylo Media, 2012); and *What Fresh Hell Is This?: Comics Inspired by Dante's Inferno*, ed. Genevieve Trainor (New York: Red Stylo Media, 2019). For more information on these works as well as additional titles, visit https://redstylo.com/project_category/literature-inspired-anthologies/.

[3] See Enrica Jang and Jason Strutz, *The Cask of Amontillado, #1* (Pittsburgh: Action Lab, 2016); Enrica Jang and Jason Strutz, *The House of Montresor* (Pittsburgh: Action Lab Entertainment, 2016).

Montresor. When Enrica joined Poe House, she approached me about doing illustration and design work for some fundraising events and publications. Later I worked on the art for The International Edgar Allan Poe Festival and the recent "Edgar and Virginia Poe Death Exhibits," a series of illustrated panels which tells the stories of the strange circumstances of Edgar's and Virginia's deaths and *many* burials. It's been nearly six years now working on Poe House projects and about thirteen years working with Enrica.

Enrica: My first experience with Poe was in either middle school or high school. I cannot say he was a deep dive for me, but I loved the stories and also heard all of my favorite modern horror writers talk about Poe as an inspiration for them. He was always in the background. As we moved into *The Cask of Amontillado* and *The House of Montresor,* I learned a lot more. Now, after my work for Poe House, I probably know too much about Poe!

The idea for *The House of Montresor* started with a graduate school assignment for a completely different kind of writing. I was pursuing a professional writing MFA and taking courses in different kinds of scripting: white papers, comics, multi-media. In one of these courses, I was assigned Poe's "The Cask of Amontillado" for an assignment to break down the narrative into a proposal for a computer game, which was awesome for me since I already loved Poe.

My approach initially was conceptualizing whether the object of the game was to rescue Fortunato or catch his killer. Then I had to imagine all the different puzzles that would be built into it and write a scene. At the time, I was already doing some comic script writing. My coursework in graduate school led to an eventual internship at Marvel Comics, which started me on the road to publishing.

Reflecting upon these circumstances, I think that story was in the works from the beginning: the scene I scripted for the game course ultimately became the first scene for *The House of Montresor.* In time, I figured out that my graphic novel was going to be a sequel: the narrator in Poe's story tells it in real time, eventually reaching the scene where he lures Fortunato into the catacombs. It is sinister, and the tension is building. The reader senses something is wrong. The reader's grasp of the situation is happening almost in real time with the victim. What does happen is horrible, but that is not the real twist: Poe's narrator tells us that all we've just "witnessed" happened fifty years ago! Montresor got away with murder. No one can rescue Fortunato before he suffocates behind the bricks; the deed is done. The reader feels this drop in the stomach. At the end, many questions arise: Why did he do it? Why is he telling? Who is he telling? Is it merely a confession, gloating, or is there more? I knew I could build a story in that space—what is going on five decades later?

Jason: Hopefully, people trust that we do not have zombies popping out of brick walls or that someone saves Fortunato.

Enrica: We stay true to Poe's original story while still taking the narrative to a new place. That was always the goal.

Jason: We were lucky we did not have to do a whole graphic novel to tell the Poe story. It was short enough to fit into a reasonably-sized comic issue and to either refresh people's memory of the Poe classic or introduce them to the original before continuing it. There was no way to know people's experience or familiarity with the story before moving on to the sequel. Maybe they had read this story in middle or high school and thought, "Oh yeah, the brick wall one."

Enrica: I think, from a narrative point of view, it is important to visualize what is happening. And it brings home the horror. Consider the force of will it takes to commit that kind of atrocity, to make someone suffer that way. The reader imagines Fortunato's initial panic and imagines how terrible it is to experience the relentless building of the wall in front of him, brick by brick. When the reader thinks about how awful that must be, Poe gets even darker.

195

Jason: Visually, when it came to that moment, I knew the last brick that goes in has to be at Fortunato's eye level so that he can look directly at it.

Enrica: The moment when the brick is going into the wall and the light is about to be lost is this great moment in the illustration: Fortunato meets his doom!

Jason: I remember our collaboration on both of these projects as being pretty smooth. I received the script for "The Cask of Amontillado" adaptation. When adapting existing content, the writer has to do the work of picking out characters, including character descriptions and costume descriptions. Then I, the artist, generate prospective sketches for what these people look like, how they are dressed, and what their environment looks like. Then we negotiate between our visions. Before I start laying out panels or trying to tell the story, I need to have a command of the writer's vision.

Enrica: For me, adapting Poe's story began with picking out the various scenes and beats that lend themselves visually to the progression of the story. Because motion cannot be conveyed in panels, we have to find a way to intimate the action. I remember one of the early challenges was how to emphasize visually the remoteness of where Fortunato and Montresor were going. We had to do some world-building and architecture of Montresor's house and how he descends with Fortunato away from the crowd and into the catacombs. In addition to visual appeal, the reader must understand what happens as the two descend, not just into scary darkness but farther and farther into a place where no one will hear them. Fortunato could scream all day long, for days, and no one would find him. To engineer how that should look in the panel takes ingenuity. We needed a couple of meetings to figure out the best way to indicate that distance, depth, and space. One of my favorite pages is the descent down the page as the two make their way into the catacombs.

Montresor and Fortunato descend into the catacombs.
The Cask of Amontillado, illustrated by Jason Strutz
(Red Stylo Media 2015).

Jason: It is a vertical panel that goes all the way down the page and shows how deep they are. It shows a couple of different views of a spiral staircase to indicate where they start and where they end. I received the instruction, "They spend three panels walking down a spiral staircase." For horror work, I am always trying to find the creepy angle on a scene, using framing, color, and viewpoint.

I think of comics as writing the book at least twice, if not three times. The writer writes the script, but it is not done yet. Once the writer receives the page sketches, they have to do the art direction job of reviewing the visual component and asking, "Is this the best way to do it?" It is another negotiation between our visions. I know that there were times when I did something with the art on the page and Enrica amended the script to fit and other times when I had to adjust my plan to her vision. The third time this book was "written" was when Enrica incorporated the final changes she desired, including editing when there were just too many words to fit in a panel.

Enrica: Jason could have done that more, I think! When I think about revising that work now, I would be more judicious about my edits and cutting some of the dialogue. But all writers want to do that.

What I like about Jason's work for the book is his choices. There was my art direction, but then there was Jason's art execution, which was multiform. It is one thing to illustrate and letter; it is another thing to do the color. A significant part of a dark book like this is the interplay of color and light. We had long talks about the firelight on the bricks and the moisture on the walls as well as the textures and the shadows. Jason made some really great decisions regarding how the light played or faded as Montresor and Fortunato walked down that staircase or down the tunnel.

Jason: Light was a major element in designing what these books would look like. Seventies Euro-horror movies such as *Blood and Black Lace* and *Black Sabbath* directed by Mario Bava as well as German expressionist films like *The Cabinet of Dr. Caligari* directed by

Robert Wiene inspired me. Those films feature crazy shadows and strange colored lights that do not really make sense within the world. I tried to add that kind of atmosphere, dynamism, and mood. I wanted to show how that would work in the various locations, especially because this story could be set roughly at the beginning of the use of electric light but there would be a variety of different light sources: the fire and lanterns in the beginning and then artificial sources of light when the story jumps forward in time.

This approach follows my type of style as well. I deliberately hid some details. Because I like to do the color on these books, I can plan out what is going to be shown and what is going to be concealed. I do not have to hope that somebody else perceives what I am trying to do as I would if I were to hand off the illustrations for color.

Enrica: Jason wears many hats. For any page of comics, the illustrator, inker, colorist, letterer, and perhaps a flatter could be several people. Jason was responsible for all of it.

Jason: I did the lettering on both *The Cask of Amontillado* and *The House of Montresor*. I admit that I have anxiety about handing my illustrations over to a letterer and that person saying to me, "You didn't leave enough room for the balloons!" The way I did this book and continue to do comics now is to sketch layouts of the story and insert the lettering at *that* stage. I save time because I can verify what fits before I spend the time attempting to finalize the art on anything. Frankly, part of me does not quite understand how to make comics and then give it to two or three other people. I am always worried that what I get back will not resemble anything that I thought it was going to look like. This perhaps results in me being what some may refer to as a "control freak" on the art side of the books in which I am involved.

Enrica: Welcome to the world of being a comics writer. Having to hand off what is in your brain to someone else to render it visually is a vulnerable place to be.

Jason: At this point, many of the comics I work on are written by myself as well. I can only curse myself now if I do not anticipate something that has to be changed. However, I can also forgive myself if I write too much. I have the luxury to go back and say, "All right, this works better another way."

Enrica: This collaboration resulted in a work that I know did not look how I'd originally imagined it, but now that it exists, I can't precisely recall how I used to see it anymore. Whatever nascent idea had existed was supplanted by what is on the page now. That is not always the case. If a writer can embrace the work of collaboration and it makes them forget their own preconceived notions, that is a success. This is a very long way to compliment Jason. I felt like what eventually made it to the page and how we finished it is how the book is in my head now. This is how it exists now.

We ask each other sometimes, after seeing where the work has led us and doing more creative projects inspired by Poe's biography rather than his writing, looking back more than a decade later, if we should have included more Easter eggs, or references to actual things that happened to Poe, in the previous work. But...I do not think it would have a big effect on the way we did the story.

What I understood about Poe before I learned specifics about his biography was that he was misunderstood. Whatever people thought they knew about Poe there were more layers and untruths and unknowns. I became aware of the conspiracy theories around Poe right about the time we were delving into our work: that he was misunderstood, even rejected at times, that he did likely struggle with depression or addiction, that kind of thing. Overall, his personal reputation was maligned. I did not know all the specifics, but I was aware of those layers. But while I agree we would likely capitalize on opportunities to put in more Easter eggs related to Poe's biography, mostly I think my appreciation of his work has deepened. I feel that as much as there are layers to his biography the layers to his work are more apparent to me now. As a kid reading him in school, I appreciated the theatricality of Poe, the horror and the fun, gleeful, gallows humor of the work. When I grew up, I detected more of the sadness and grief, the layers of loss.

We think about going back to the project at different times and continuing to build it. I have a whole Montresor comics series on the backburner. Of course, working at Poe House, there are any number of inspirations and ideas. Also, my position there provides a vantage point for how competitive the market is. Poe is and has always been a very potent force in comics.

Jason: There was a great series of Poe adaptations by the late artist Richard Corben. He has adapted "Berenice," "The Conqueror Worm," and even "The Cask of Amontillado." His adaptations inspired me; they are grotesque. They are more cartoony than mine, but I like the direction he took the stories.[4] The comics medium really lends itself to Poe-style work. The type of creeping horror conveyed through his language works well in comics. Anybody doing a horror comic has some level of debt to what I call "cerebral horror." The comics medium lacks much pacing control, meaning the creators do not control how fast the pages get read and flipped. This eliminates many "jump scare" opportunities, which means the content must provide the horror in a more cerebral way.

Enrica: I am noticing more instances of Poe as a character. Poe himself becomes a character in his own adventures and not necessarily the biographical, or real, Poe. I try to make a point to read these comics to get the full breadth of what is out there.

Jason: Poe is a good blank slate for alternative history or an

---

[4] For examples, see Richard Corben, *Edgar Allan Poe's Spirits of the Dead* (Milwaukie, OR: Dark Horse Comics, 2014) and Richard Corben and Rich Margopoulos, *Haunt of Horror: Edgar Allan Poe* (Milwaukie, OR: Dark Horse Comics, 2006).

alternative take on characters because we know the milestones in Poe's life. Unfortunately, much of his personality and biography has been filtered through his literary enemies.[5] That is where we get the image of Poe as a degenerate. Falling down drunk all the time. This reputation does not seem to make sense considering the amount of work he accomplished.

Enrica: I think Poe would have been furious at the notion that he has been characterized as disheveled. There were such episodes, but they were noted because they were so out of character for him. He wanted to be seen as a gentleman. He was careful to try to curate that image, and he would have been mortified by the stories that he was discovered in the gutter.

Jason: I have been on a few of the tours through Poe House. A giggle goes through the room when the docent reminds people that Poe was an attractive guy at the time. He was young and not some crazy monster. On those tours, visitors seem to react to this assessment of his appearance as "hahaha, that can't be true." They have preconceived ideas of what Poe is. That makes him a good character to use in a variety of adaptations. The name is known, but the real history is mostly unknown.

Two of the projects I've worked on for Poe House incorporate comics. Most recently, Enrica and I created five-panel exhibits about the actual lives of Poe and his wife Virginia for the International Edgar Allan Poe Festival in 2021–22.

Enrica: It was a fun opportunity to return to the comic scripting process in order to identify the highlights so that Jason could illustrate the panels. Initially, I had imagined that Jason would do more

---

[5] The most infamous instance was perpetrated by Rufus W. Griswold when he published an obituary under a pseudonym. See Ludwig (Rufus W. Griswold), "The Death of Edgar Allan Poe," *New-York Daily Tribune*, Oct. 9, 1849: 2, https://www.eapoe.org/papers/misc1827/nyt49100.htm.

of a series of spot illustrations or vignettes, but the panels are sequential like comics.

Jason: Enrica handed me the timeline of events and some key images of the deaths of Poe and Virginia. I wanted the panels to flow from panel-to-panel, telling more of the story within each piece. It was a return to a kind of a very short form comics for the exhibit.

Enrica: Sequential art is a great medium to try to tell strange, complicated histories. Whereas biographers take several inches of text on the page to explain movements and contrasting ideas, sequential art can do the same in a single, compelling page. In the interest of getting as much information as possible to someone visiting a museum or to someone learning these stories for the first time, comics are well suited to sharing that information and getting the maximum amount of information to different people, even disparate generations, at the same time.

Jason: It is a very pure form of storytelling. Humanity-wise, we basically started by making comics on cave walls. It is an immediate way for people to digest storytelling. People who may not be able to read a certain language can look at a sequential piece of art and know what is going on for the most part, making it accessible to almost anyone. Poe's fictional works really lend themselves to sequential art in that they are based on the characters and on the emotion. I'm proud of both series we completed and look forward to more.

Enrica: The exhibits are beautiful, and they are traveling. First in Baltimore, then they went on to the Poe Cottage at Fordham in New York followed by Richmond, Virginia, for the Poe Museum's 100th anniversary capstone event.

Jason: I like the world of Poe. He has a compelling history, but he has a lot of mystery in his private life as well. Because of the time that he lived and the type of life that he led, there is a lot of room for interpretation, especially stylistic interpretation of illustrations of his life history. Revisiting these mysteries is endlessly compelling; we are always finding new angles to look at his life. To do art around that—the unknown—is always an intriguing thing to do, for me at least.

Enrica: I like the phrase "to do art around that" because there are several stylistic choices that can be made based on these elements of his biography that are subject to interpretation. Is there anything about Poe's writing that creates this aesthetic for you as well? Or do you find yourself pulling on threads already present?

Jason: His writing has some detail, but it is not exhaustively detailed. Therefore, the work is open to so many different ways of interpretation, and that, again, mirrors his life: we have some details, but we do not have a full picture. Horror and unknown type things are interesting to me. Being able to work in those spaces around the facts that we know is compelling. We can always come up with a new angle, which could be humorous, creepy, or ominous. Visually, even Poe himself is a distinctive looking guy, depending on the image or the illustration of him and at what time of life. An artist can do a lot with that sort of iconography. I have drawn a lot of wildly different sketches for Poe projects.

Enrica: It also makes it daunting. Reading Poe is such a personal experience, and there is not a lot of direction from him. He is verbose and emotional and evocative but not a lot of description necessarily. So the reading of Poe is intensely personal. Therefore creating adaptations of Poe's work or providing a story placing a twist on one of his works is almost to invite comment immediately. The reader renders a verdict: they accept it if it fits their conception. I suppose it is that typical "The book was better" reaction from readers. Once one reads something and imagines it, that person is committed to that vision. If there is dissonance, good luck in the comment section.

Jason: A good challenge. And has been so for thirteen years, a very lucky number. I enjoy working with you and Poe. You always come up with interesting projects to do and give me some good challenges.

Enrica: Well, thank you. I feel lucky to do this work and continue to enjoy working with you, too. From our Poe books and now museum exhibits and events. It's a pretty great gig.

Jason: It is an ongoing conversation that has not exhausted itself yet. We will see what happens next!

15

SOMEONE'S RAPPING AT THE DOOR, SOMEONE'S RINGING THE BELLS...LET HIM IN: HOW I BECAME A POE BIOGRAPHER

Mark Dawidziak

I now realize that the ominous rapping and tapping sounds began when I was seven years old and had seen my first monster movie. That momentous occasion occurred almost sixty years ago, and, like a werewolf caught by a full moon, I found myself transformed. Yet it wasn't moonlight that did the trick. It was something more powerful, more magical. It was the cathode ray tube beaming mind-boggling black-and-white images into my second-grade consciousness, filling it and thrilling it with fantastic terrors never felt before. Up to that moment, comedy—specifically the delicious brand of lunacy featuring comedy teams—dominated my television viewing and occupied the top spot in a heart yet untouched by the tell-tale variety. Well, that's what passed for children's entertainment on the TV sets of the early 1960s. In a world that didn't know Nickelodeon, the Disney Channel, or even PBS, the New York stations gave us the comedy of our parents and, in some cases, our grandparents. By the age of seven, therefore, I had been in the near-constant company of Laurel & Hardy, Abbott & Costello, and the Three Stooges.

In fact, Bud Abbott and Lou Costello, best known for their "Who's On First?" baseball routine, were largely responsible for setting me on the path that would bring me face to face with Edgar Allan Poe. I eagerly anticipated a Saturday afternoon showing of a film I hadn't seen before, *Abbott & Costello Meet Frankenstein.* To be sure, I was there for the *Abbott & Costello* part of that title. I did not even know what a Frankenstein was, let alone why in the world anyone would want to meet him. When it was all over, comedy had gained a rival for my affections. Unlike most blends of horror and comedy, the horror in this 1948 film was played straight. The comedy was left to Bud and Lou, so the horror was every bit as effective as the humor. Staring at the television screen in the living room of that suburban Long Island home, I fell under the spell of not only Frankenstein but also the Wolf Man and, most seductively of all, Bela Lugosi's Count Dracula. From that childhood's hour, I was and always have been a horror fan. We didn't have the term "monster kid" back then. That's what the grown-up versions of those kids call themselves today. We just said we loved horror and demonstrated that love by collecting and building Aurora monster models, delighting in the weekly broadcasts of monster movies on such TV showcases as *Chiller* and *Creature Features,* and hunting the newsstands and drug stores for the latest issues of our beloved monster magazines. Notice a theme? Added to this macabre mix were regular visits to the creepy and kooky Gothic sitcom homes of *The Munsters* and *The Addams Family,* along with wonderfully eerie trips to *The Twilight Zone, The Outer Limits,* and Collinsport, the Maine town featured on the supernatural soap opera *Dark Shadows.*

What's all of this got to do with Poe? We're getting there. Or, more to the point, I was getting there. *Dark Shadows,* which became a full-blown pop-culture phenomenon in the late '60s, featured nods to, among other Poe stories, "The Cask of Amontillado," "The Pit and the Pendulum," "The Tell-Tale Heart," "Ligeia," and "The Premature Burial." All of those pop-culture delights recalled so fondly, whether frightfully funny or fabulously frightening, in some way were stamped by Poe's influence. All during this time, I was, of course, vaguely aware of Poe, even if I hadn't quite acknowledged the source of all that rapping and tapping I found so irresistible. At the age of sixty-six, having written the biography *A Mystery of Mysteries: The Death and Life of Edgar Allan Poe,* the monster kid now fully realizes the subject of that book always had been hanging around, lurking so very close by in those, yes, dark shadows, waiting for me to acknowledge his presence, recognize his influence, and summon him from the murky corners.[1] It was a gradual process but an inevitable one, thanks to that first encounter with the horror realm. Poe could not be denied.

With each step, the fascination deepened. There was the raven on *The Munsters,* inhabiting the living room clock and regularly finding a reason to croak "Nevermore!" There was Poe, strategically occupying the top-center position on the cover of the Beatles LP *Sgt. Pepper's Lonely Hearts Club Band.* And there were the Universal Poe movies of the 1930s with Lugosi and Boris Karloff as well as producer Roger Corman's 1960s films with Vincent Price. While hardly models of fidelity to the stories and poems, these cinematic treats did give Poe a pop-culture street cred that fueled the desire for better acquaintance.

That opportunity arrived in the form of the Scholastic Book catalogue distributed in a seventh-grade classroom at St. Anthony of Padua School in East Northport, New York. One of the featured books was *Ten Great Mysteries by Edgar Allan Poe,* and it included "The Murders in the Rue Morgue" and "The Purloined Letter." At about that time, I was discovering the Sherlock Holmes stories and adding mystery fan to my profile. So, this Poe not only was a master of the macabre; he was a pioneer in the field of detective fiction. The plot indeed was thickening. Scholastic also offered a volume titled *Eight Tales of Terror,* which included "The Fall of the House of Usher," "The Masque of the Red Death," and "William Wilson." Both those little well-worn paperbacks remain with me. They are the foundation on which a vast Poe library was built.

---

[1] Mark Dawidziak, *A Mystery of Mysteries: The Death and Life of Edgar Allan Poe* (New York: St. Martin's Press, 2023).

Scholastic book covers for the Poe anthologies titled *Ten Great Mysteries by Edgar Allan Poe* and *Eight Tales of Terror*.

Courtesy Mark Dawidziak

High school English classes added an appreciation of Poe's poetry. College literature classes cultivated an admiration for his criticism, essays, letters, and (didn't see this coming) many humorous pieces. And now was acknowledged the presence of Poe, the complete writer. Now I was haunting used bookstores, searching the crammed shelves for odd volumes from editions of his collected works—discarded treasures that contained writing not found in the standard "complete" collections of stories and poems. In my thirties, I set out to read everything Poe had written. In my forties, I consumed every biography and critical examination I could add to the ever-expanding library. In my fifties, my wife, Sara Showman, and I started offering a selection of Poe stories and poems through our Largely Literary Theater Company located in Cuyahoga Falls, Ohio. Sara magnificently interprets "The Masque of the Red Death," "Alone," and "The Bells." I do the best I can with "The Raven," "Annabel Lee," and "The Cask of Amontillado" (with Sara providing the voice of "the noble" Fortunato) in *The Tell-Tale Play*.[2]

My day job as film and television critic brought me into contact with writers, actors, and directors quick to acknowledge their great love of Poe: Ray Bradbury, Stephen King, Anne Rice, Robert Bloch, Wes Craven, and Vincent Price, to name a notable few. No opportunity was lost to discuss Poe's work and personality. That's something else I only fully realized after *A Mystery of Mysteries* was completed. I was working on this biography long before I knew I would be writing it. The keen observations from these horror specialists helped me interrogate the Poe stereotypes and better understand that complete writer I began to perceive in college. These insights can be found throughout the book.

Vincent Price was the earliest recorded interview taped for my Poe biography. I had interviewed him twice before, so there was no hesitation or apprehension about approaching him that January 1985 evening in the elegant ballroom of the Beverly Hills Hotel.

---

[2] For more information about the company and our productions, visit the Largely Literary Theater Company's website at http://www.largelyliterary.com/.

Impeccably dressed and looking as if he just had strolled off a movie set, the genial star of Corman's *House of Usher* and *The Masque of the Red Death*, quickly warmed to a favorite topic:

> Do you want to know what made Poe such a master of the horror story? In addition to being a great observer of human nature, he had great curiosity. He was intensely interested in everything, so everything informed his art: history, science, languages, criminology, flora, anything, everything, and, above all, the human psyche. It all informed his work, and that's what you need if you're going to write well in this deceptively complex area we call horror. You must have that driving curiosity and sense of wonder about the great things we're capable of . . . and the bad, as well. You can't just be interested in scaring people or sending chills down their spine. That's what separates the best horror stories and makes them literature. You have to know that about Poe the man in order to appreciate Poe the writer.[3]

That's the kind of perception that will give you more than a little appreciation for the Price of Poe.

Price once observed that people who limit their interests limit their lives. Poe clearly wasn't one of those people. A few years after this close encounter of the third kind with Price, a conversation with Bloch, the author of *Psycho*, forged a link with that earliest of pop-culture influences, comedy. We know Poe had a terrific sense of humor, Bloch pointed out, not because he wrote humor, but because he wrote horror. Humor and horror are flip sides of the same coin, and it's absolutely required that one has a sense of humor in order to achieve greatness in the horror field. "It's an essential part of the basic equipment that you need to do this," the fellow who created Norman Bates told me during that talk in the lobby of a Virginia hotel.

> So horror writers are almost always very funny people, and that always surprises people. A sense of humor is about the last thing

---

[3] In-person taped interview with the author, Beverly Hills Hotel, California, January 1985.

people attribute to Poe, but if you know anything about writing horror, it's the first thing you would attribute to him. He wasn't funny despite writing great horror. He wrote great horror because he was funny and because he was a lot of other things. You must look past the relentlessly marketed image.[4]

That grandfather of the Goth image is highly marketable, without doubt, but it also has reduced Poe to a caricature and a grotesque one at that. He's the sickly, melancholy, pasty-faced, hollow-eyed figure sitting forlornly among the cobwebs in a creaky attic, a raven perched on his shoulder and a bottle of cognac in reach. With a red-eyed black cat prowling nearby, this mistaken and misshapen version of Poe is hunched, stoop-shouldered, over manuscript pages as he spins fantastic tales in a fever-dream state. It's as if we're viewing Poe reflected in one of those fun-house mirrors that madly warps, distorts, and exaggerates the human form captured in its run-riot realm.

With each of these conversations, the shadows around Poe were further dispelled. The myth of the gloomy, depressed, possibly mad genius was replaced by a complex, dedicated, and incredibly prolific artist. Although the master-of-the-macabre stereotype definitely has its roots in some aspects of Poe's personality, he was far from friendless or perpetually morose. In addition to being witty and often playful, he could be charming, courtly, and captivating. He also could be petty, overly sensitive, and self-destructive. So the people who limit their interest in who Poe actually was limit their perception and understanding of him. All of the forms of writing he pursued so brilliantly were genuine reflections of his personality. Mystery? He possessed a logical and inquisitive mind that was challenged by puzzles and the search for answers. Horror? He was obsessed with the nature of death and haunted by his many losses. Poetry? He prized beauty in many forms and viewed himself, first and foremost, as a Romantic poet in the tradition of his hero, Lord

---

[4] In-person taped interview with the author, Hyatt Regency Hotel, Crystal City, Virginia, May 29, 1993.

Byron. Criticism? He had an exacting and analytical nature. Humor? You even can find evidence for this in the horror stories and criticism.

I, too, unquestionably (and unquestioningly) bought into the popular Poe image at first. Those misconceptions were helped along by high school English teachers erroneously encouraging me and my classmates to confuse Poe with his deeply troubled narrators. It was such an easy and alluring shorthand. Sure, that explains so much. Poe must have been drawing on his own personality when creating the obsessed narrators of "The Tell-Tale Heart," "The Raven," "The Cask of Amontillado," and "Annabel Lee." It's not only a wrong-headed assumption but also one that criminally short-changes the artist responsible for these short stories and poems. What I realized was that we do not lose Poe the frightmeister by discarding the myths and expanding our view of him.

Consider where Mark Twain and Poe stood in literary lore and legend at the beginning of the 1960s. Both were widely recognized American writers. Both had been assigned roles based on typecasting. Twain was the genial family author and folksy wit. Poe was that morose purveyor of nightmare tales. The decade that followed enlarged and expanded our view of Twain as long-suppressed writings revealed him to be an insightful, often dark, social critic. Poe emerged from the 1960s every bit as popular, but in the public consciousness, the same guy he'd always been or thought to have been.

We did not lose Twain the family author and folksy wit because we broadened our view of him and accepted there was so much more to him. That Twain remains with us. And we will not lose Poe the master of the macabre when we finally grant him his due as a versatile, scrupulous, and disciplined artist. We, in fact, will gain a more inspiring and realistic understanding of the writer who gave us the poems and stories. We will gain a more profound awareness of and admiration for the artistry. Seems we owe him that much.

Despite all of this, however, I never once thought about writing a biography on Poe.

When *Everything I Need to Know I Learned in The Twilight*

Zone, my lighthearted tribute to Rod Serling's classic anthology series, was published, it did well enough for St. Martin's Press to initiate a conversation about the next book.[5] I pitched the book idea I was sure would be a slam-dunk, can't-miss natural. Problem was the editor didn't like the can't-miss idea. He suggested a wildly different concept. I did not like his idea. I went to Plan B and tossed him my second-most effective pitch. He was too professional and erudite to say, "Meh!", but that's clearly what was behind the carefully and considerately phrased rejection. His counterproposal left me cold, so back and forth the volleying went, until it seemed obvious that we had reached an impasse and the discussion would need to be tabled for another day. That's when, just as we were about to say our good-byes, he said, "What about Edgar Allan Poe?" Poe?

Did he just say Poe? Hold the phone because I think I just about dropped the one in my hand. What made him say Poe?

For one thing, he said, it has been a while since the last popular biography of Poe was published. For another, interest in Poe remains constant. And, finally, "you have the ideal resume for this." I wasn't digging the proverbial toe in the dirt, but I didn't see it that way at all.

He explained: "You've written a horror novel and short stories. You've written non-fiction books about heavyweight horror topics, like *Dracula,* and mystery topics, like *Columbo.* You've written about a major nineteenth-century American writer, Mark Twain. You've written a literary biography. And, like Poe, you've been a critic for most of your professional life. You check almost all of the boxes."

Almost all. Not poetry, I humbly admit. I have a tin ear when it comes to writing poetry. Still, it took someone outside looking in to put all of this together. I didn't see this whole checking boxes thing. OK, he had my interest. Exactly what kind of biography was he suggesting? He was most interested in the enduring mystery of Poe's death. What happened to the writer during the missing days

---

[5] Mark Dawidziak, *Everything I Need to Know I Learned in* The Twilight Zone (New York: St. Martin's, 2017).

before he was discovered outside of an Election Day polling place in Baltimore on the damp, chilly afternoon of October 3, 1849? Which of the twenty-plus theories about his death actually caused him to stop breathing at the age of forty on October 7?

"Whoa!" I shouted into the phone. "Whoa! Whoa! Whoa! Back up the hearse. Are you suggesting I write a book that will definitively solve the mystery of Poe's death? Are you thinking the Poe equivalent of one those books that appears every couple of years claiming to have finally and conclusively solved the mystery of Jack the Ripper's identity? Are you thinking we can wrap up a cold case from 1849 with no surviving soft tissue, no autopsy, no death certificate, and almost no reliable witnesses? If that's what you're suggesting, you better find yourself another lunatic because this one is driving away." Subtle as I was, he sensed my reluctance. I was, after all, more interested in how Poe lived than how he died. I had become more and more fascinated with what must have been the real writer rather than that ludicrous fun-house-mirror image pop culture had made of him.

"Tell you what," I said after a little more discussion. "I won't make any promises that are impossible to deliver. But how about a biography that examines Poe's life through the prism of his death? I'll examine the various theories and see if modern forensics and scientific testing can eliminate any of them. And if I find compelling evidence for a leading suspect, I'll make that case even if it can't be conclusively proven. Along the way, we can knock down some of the myths, misconceptions, and mysteries that have attached themselves to Poe. How does that sound?"

That sounded good to St. Martin's, and a formal proposal was submitted and accepted. Right from the start, the stated goal was a popular biography. It was never my intention to write the standard academic work on Poe. There are better scholars for that undertaking. I wanted my book to be non-traditional in its approach. I had read and admired the traditional biographies. There is no shortage of them. The world didn't need another traditional study of Poe's life. I was going to take some chances with structure and techniques,

215

and I knew that wouldn't sit well with some expecting and preferring a conventional approach. You start this process fully aware of how conspicuous you are, leaping off the high diving board and hoping there is water in the pool.

Poe didn't seem to worry about such things, but then, Poe was a genius. I love the story of him meeting a young friend on the streets of New York right after completion of "The Raven." Encountering William Ross Wallace, Poe informed him that he had just written the greatest poem of all time. He then proceeded to read it to Wallace, who judged it uncommonly fine. Fine? Was that all he had to say? It wasn't merely fine, Poe insisted; it was nothing less than the greatest poem ever written. That's the great thing about greatness. He knew. He had composed a masterpiece, and he had full confidence in that accomplishment. We mere mortals are not possessed with that kind of ability or confidence. Let me put it this way, even if a small part of me dared to entertain such hopes, I wouldn't be stopping any friends in the street and proclaiming, "I've just completed the greatest biography ever written." I'd be worried about having done an adequate job, and I'd consider "uncommonly fine" a pretty nice compliment. But, again, Poe was a genius, and probing the creative process channeling that genius was a major goal for this biography. As a writer, how could you not be fascinated by Poe's creative processes?

One non-traditional aspect of *A Mystery of Mysteries* was the structure. I decided on a dual-timeline narrative with chapters alternating between Poe's increasingly desperate last months and various periods of his brief life. Following this design, the two timelines would meet in the final chapter when all of the evidence would be considered. From the start, it was not lost on me that one of America's most iconic writers died under eerie circumstances that reflected the two literary genres he took to new heights. The book takes pains to drive home that Poe died in a painful and bizarre manner that would not have been out of place in one of his own tales of terror. He also left us with a mystery...a double-barreled mystery to be precise. What was the cause of his untimely death and what happened to him during the three missing days before he was found, delirious and wearing ill-fitting clothes that were not his own? Yes, it's a moment steeped in mystery and horror.

Another departure for this biography was the use of interviews. This certainly is not customary in life studies of people whose lives ended so long ago that it's impossible to speak with anyone who knew them. Yet having been employed by newspapers for forty-three years, I was inclined to rely on the instincts and skills of a journalist. If anyone objects, well, I'll borrow what Stephen King said about not apologizing for his love of the horrific and the haunted: "It's what I have."[6] Therefore, my expert witnesses in this investigation included Poe scholars who were consulted as the leading authorities on aspects of his life, personality, and literary output. I asked each to speak as candidly as possible, hoping that the results would be as engaging as they were insightful. I was not disappointed. This approach might seem more suited to a newspaper story or a documentary film, but it allowed me to utilize their expertise in specific areas while also recognizing their immense contributions to Poe scholarship. My other interview choices, or witnesses, if you will, included forensic pathologists, museum curators, medical experts and historians, those horror specialists already named, best-selling true-crime authors, a specialist in forensic anthropology and archaeology, and a pioneering FBI agent. Each had something compelling to say about how Poe may have died, and each said it well, providing lively voices heard throughout the biography. Each, however, also had something illuminating to say about how he lived. Each had a piece of an ever-challenging puzzle. Each dispelled a few more shadows.

Did I settle on a favorite theory—one that, to me, makes a great deal of sense? Absolutely. Do I insist that this must be the real solution? Absolutely not. Indeed, I am not even sure I want it to be solved. The mystery of his death is an essential part of the Poe mystique, and it's entirely possible we'd lose more than we'd gain if the

---

[6] Stephen King, *On Writing* (NY: Scribner, 2000), 158.

cold case was put to rest. There's a maxim that assures us some mysteries aren't meant to be solved. And I'd like to think Poe wouldn't want us to solve it. I'm quite sure he would have thought that it would take nothing less than an Edgar Allan Poe to unravel it all.

My great hope for the biography has been that it will at least slightly dispel the false image even many ardent Poe fans still have of him: an enduring and persistent image that any biographer needs to explain and then try to explode. How did the caricature so pervasively overtake reality? It started with the infamous obituary penned by the very man Poe had expected to be his literary executor: poet, editor, and anthologist Rufus Griswold. Poe was unaware that Griswold had been nursing grudges against him for years. The day after Poe's funeral, on October 8, 1849, in Baltimore's small Westminster Presbyterian Cemetery, Griswold buried him again, under a mountain of grotesque lies, distortions, and fabrications. Writing an obituary that appeared in the evening edition of the *New-York Daily Tribune*, Griswold had no intention of honoring any prohibitions on speaking ill of the dead. "Edgar Allan Poe is dead," the blast at the recently departed began. "He died in Baltimore the day before yesterday. This announcement will startle many, but few will be grieved by it."[7] That was one of the kinder passages in Griswold's brutal attack. And it was just the first salvo. Griswold continued to flail obsessively at the corpse in future printed assaults, depicting Poe as, among other things, immoral, arrogant, unbalanced, dishonest, envious, conceited, and dishonorable. He created a wildly inaccurate image of Poe that hasn't been completely dispelled to this day. He was the first and greatest mangler-in-chief when it came to twisting our perception of the life and personality of Poe.

A pathetic irony emerges from examining everything Griswold wrote about Poe. All of the vicious volleys he aimed at Poe couldn't help rebounding and hitting an unintended target—Griswold

---

[7] See Ludwig (Rufus W. Griswold), "The Death of Edgar Allan Poe," *New-York Daily Tribune*, Oct. 9, 1849: 2, https://www.eapoe.org/papers/misc1827/nyt49100.htm.

himself. He did as much lasting harm to his own reputation as he did to Poe's, perhaps more. Griswold wanted to be remembered for his art as a poet and litterateur, having tried to establish himself as an arbiter of literary taste with the anthology *The Poets and Poetry of America*. Instead, if he's known for anything today, it's for the art of character assassination. He's remembered only because Poe is remembered. Griswold's name comes up again and again, but only in Poe scholarship, which, for the last eighty years, has been an ongoing effort to correct the record he muddled, muddied, and falsified. The first mighty effort to restore Poe's reputation appeared in 1941, and, in many ways, Arthur Hobson Quinn's *Edgar Allan Poe: A Critical Biography* remains the indispensable biography.

The backlash to Griswold's treatment of Poe began well before Quinn's book was published. Almost immediately, well-meaning friends and colleagues printed more flattering reminisces, but many of these accounts are often unreliable as well. On the literary front, the pro-Poe forces were led by his French champion, the poet and critic Charles Baudelaire, who labeled Griswold "a pedagogic vampire." He also denounced Griswold as a cur, famously asking, "Does there not exist in America an ordinance to keep dogs out of cemeteries?"[8] Despite their admiration of Poe, however, Baudelaire and other admirers contributed to what would become the stereotype. They did, after all, popularize the notion that Poe's characters were projections of his personality. Even as Quinn and later biographers strove to set the record straight, Hollywood and pop culture further entrenched the image of Poe as the melancholy, maybe mad, master of the macabre.

Fame, therefore, has been a decidedly double-edged sword for Poe. He continues to be known for just a handful of stories and poems, most falling on the spooky side of the street. We've reduced his identity to that small part of his literary output, letting it completely

---

[8] Charles Baudelaire, *Edgar Allan Poe: His Life and Works* (1856): English translation in *The Unknown Poe*, ed. Raymond Foye (San Francisco: City Lights, 1980), 81.

frame our perception of him. Yet, at the same time, that handful of stories and poems, many about the dead and dying, has kept him alive. It's this Poe that stares at us from T-shirts, coffee mugs, wall clocks, scented candles, and tea tins. It's this Poe we've turned into plush dolls, paper dolls, bobbleheads, and action figures. It's this Poe that appears on blankets, lapel pins, earrings, socks, and a staggering assortment of items available for purchase.

It's also this Poe that has developed into a renewable literary energy source, introduced and reintroduced to generation after generation as a standard curriculum favorite in junior high school, high school, and on to college. Few of us escape the summons of the rapping and tapping I first heard in childhood. One has to think that Poe would have mixed feelings about how he is remembered. On one level, he undoubtedly would be delighted to learn that he is remembered, his fame outlasting and outshining all of those contemporaries who were supposed to outlive him. But he also probably would be a little horrified to realize he was mostly and only known as a horror writer. Well, there it is: We've got good news and bad news for you, Eddy. Funny thing happened on the way to literary immortality. They forgot you could be funny. And a big reason they forgot is that marketing the Goth guy is so much darn fun. So, I don't expect one biography, or an army of them, to magically reverse the dark spell cast over Poe. No matter. Small victories are still victories, and there is the ongoing reassurance Poe offered in "The Pit and the Pendulum" that "even in the grave all *is not* lost."[9] That was true on the day they buried Poe in Baltimore. It was true when Griswold rendered him, to use a phrase from the poem "Lenore," "doubly dead."[10] It remains true today as Poe's works are widely read while Poe's shadowed identity is just as widely misread.

---

[9] Edgar Allan Poe, "The Pit and the Pendulum," in *The Collected Works of Edgar Allan Poe*, ed. T. O. Mabbott, vol. 2 (Cambridge: Belknap Press of Harvard University Press, 1978), 682.

[10] Edgar Allan Poe, "Lenore," in *The Collected Works of Edgar Allan Poe*, ed. T. O. Mabbott, vol. 1 (Cambridge: Belknap Press of Harvard University Press, 1969), 336.

16

ROLE-PLAYING AT POE

Andy Duncan

Ten years ago, I was assigned the role of Edgar Allan Poe. It was typecasting. Who better to play a Southern writer of Gothic horror, fantasy, and science fiction than a Southern writer of Gothic horror, fantasy, and science fiction?

Besides, I had my own raven.

The occasion was a weekend role-playing game. Two of my Frostburg State University colleagues wrote a grant to assemble a cast of students, faculty, and staff to inhabit a new educational game from the Reacting to the Past Consortium at Barnard College. Its title was *Frederick Douglass: Slavery, Abolitionism, and the Constitution, 1845*. A talented undergrad—now a professional actor and writer—named Brandon Chase was given the role of Douglass.

The action of the game swirled around Douglass's attempts to galvanize public opinion against slavery and the attempts of various factions to support him, thwart him, silence him, or ignore him. Every participant portrayed a real-life historical character or a fictional representative of some group: abolitionists, enslavers, politicians, influencers, crooks, walk-ons, hangers-on, random celebrities. I was in that last category.

My job as Poe was to ignore the politics while trying to talk every other character in the game into publishing and/or promoting my work and, ideally, slipping me some cash because, let's face it, that's the free-lancer's life, today as in 1845. I also had to write a poem based on the events of the weekend and declaim it at the formal lunch that concluded the event. Write it I did and declaim it I did but do not be disappointed, dear reader, that I long ago lost that manuscript. It was less Poe-ful than woeful.

What I chiefly brought to the game was my wife's life-sized plastic raven, a cheap Halloween decoration that might look convincing on a front porch, to passers-by on the sidewalk after sunset who wore eyesight-obscuring Jason masks. I toted that raven around all weekend, and it gained me more points than I deserved. The prop never made it back to Sydney's faculty office, somehow; I think she was glad to be rid of it. As I type this, I feel its presence behind me, perched atop a filing cabinet, watching.

The weekend was a great success, and our master of ceremonies—the game's co-author, Mark Higbee of Eastern Michigan University—pronounced himself delighted.

You may have heard of this game. It made headlines in 2022 when Reacting to the Past pulled it from circulation. "College students and professors complained that advocating for, or listening to, the views of white supremacists made them uncomfortable," reported *The Wall Street Journal*.[1] One problem, apparently, was that some students were *really getting into* the enslavers' position. The thought of that is so shuddery that my normal free-speech leanings are muted on this one; I grant the possible need for a cooling-off period in role-playing *that* issue as opposed to, say, *Acid Rain in Europe, 1979-1989.*

I recall no sympathy for the enslavers during our Douglass weekend, certainly not from me. No, what I *really got into* that weekend was the idea of Edgar Allan Poe—not *being* him, exactly, but for the first time in my life, feeling a strong kinship with him, as a direct descendant, a recipient of a legacy.

---

[1] Douglas Belkin, "Professors Drop Slavery Role-Playing Over Concerns It Upsets Students," *Wall Street Journal*, May 13, 2022.

I sort of feel I've been role-playing him ever since. And as my students today might say: That's a lot.

No wonder this essay was so hard to write.

I don't know why I denied Poe for so long. I am, after all, a professional writer of science fiction, fantasy, and horror, mostly at short lengths, and much of it dark, though my darkness tends toward the puckishly macabre—more Addams Family than Manson Family.

Still, it's Poe's field. In the 1988 essay anthology *Horror: The 100 Best Books,* World Fantasy Award-winning novelist John M. Ford contributed a piece that describes Poe's all-pervasive influence on Ford, on our colleagues, on me:

> There isn't anywhere you can go in this overcast, weedgrown, blood-fertilized field of ours that he hasn't been first...In the perfumed, moldy halls of horror, he is the doorkeeper, the cartographer, and the resident ghost.[2]

I've had a love-hate relationship with the Southern Gothic since I seriously started writing fiction in my mid-20s. I joke that my own upbringing was Southern Gothic enough. It wasn't, really, though I have written elsewhere about the more hair-raising aspects of my home state, my hometown, my home church, my home.

Suffice to say that when a historical marker was dedicated in 2019 in downtown Batesburg, South Carolina, commemorating the 1946 beating and blinding of Black war veteran Isaac Woodard by the town's police chief—an infamous racial atrocity that was pivotal in U.S. history—I was the only speaker that day who grew up in the town...and certainly the only one who could claim that police chief was a friend of the family.

Small wonder that so many of my published interviews show me playing pushmi-pullyu with the Southern Gothic and its founding avatar. Here, for example, is me in 2010, talking to Darrell Schweitzer in *InterGalactic Medicine Show:* "Initially, it seemed I was

---

[2] John M. Ford, "Tales of Mystery and Imagination (Review)," *Horror: 100 Best Books*, ed. Stephen Jones and Kim Newman (Toronto: Xanadu, 1988), 31.

always writing Southern stories and Southern folklore type stories...But I was also writing other stuff simultaneously—some of which ended up in *Weird Tales*—stories like 'From Alfano's Reliquary' and 'Grand Guignol,' what Mike Grimwood, who was on my thesis committee, referred to as my 'tales of the macabre,' the more Poe-like things, though Poe was a Southern writer too."[3]

Some of my fiction, yes, is overtly Poe-influenced, but when one has said that, one has perhaps not said much. Any story, if successful, has many influences. Allow me to belabor this point with a couple of examples.

For her 2008 project that became the Shirley Jackson Award-winning *Poe:19 New Tales Inspired by Edgar Allan Poe*, editor Ellen Datlow asked a clutch of potential contributors to pick a Poe story or poem and write a story inspired by it, while avoiding pastiche and Poe as a character. I looked at Ellen's list and realized that no one had claimed "The Gold-Bug," which interested me only because I remembered it was set in my native South Carolina. In fact, that's all I remembered about it.

So during lunch at the Subway in Frostburg, Maryland, I re-read "The Gold-Bug," in which the moody, brilliant Legrand and his two male sidekicks, including the unnamed narrator and a sadly stereotyped Black man, follow a series of clues through the Sullivan's Island wilderness and locate Captain Kidd's treasure. The second half of the story is nothing but Legrand windily telling the narrator how he solved the puzzle; this includes a detailed explanation of how a substitution cipher works and how the resulting gibberish can be translated back into English.

The story's long-term influence on everything from *Treasure Island* and Holmes and Watson to *The Da Vinci Code* is obvious, but as I re-read it for the first time since childhood, my abiding thought was "This is a geocaching story."

---

[3] Andy Duncan, interview by Darrell Schweitzer, *InterGalactic Medicine Show*, October 2010, http://www.intergalacticmedicineshow.com/cgi-bin/mag.cgi?do=issue&vol=i19&article=_interview.

In hindsight, this was a counterintuitive choice; I was, and am, the worst geocacher in North America, owing largely to my deep reluctance to stretch, kneel, crawl, get dirty, reach into holes in the ground, and, indeed, go outside.

But to a geocaching theme I now was committed and that meant my story had to be set in the present day, unusual for me. Because the twenty-first century widened my options, I decided to make overt the same-sex attraction that was only implied in Poe's original. So my Poe geocaching story became a Poe geocaching lesbian romance story. When I decided to set the story in Western Maryland, where I live, I knew it would have to end in the beguilingly creepy Cranesville Swamp, probably with my narrator taking a nocturnal walk—and that idea reminded me of the 1940s horror movies of the great *auteur* writer-producer Val Lewton, which are chockablock with lonely nocturnal journeys. So I decided my Poe geocaching lesbian romance story might as well be a Lewton tribute story as well.

Because of course I also wanted to include a substitution cipher, I kept at my elbow, as I wrote, Elonka Dunin's *Mammoth Book of Secret Codes and Cryptograms*.[4] I was trying to fake my way onto what my novelist friend Christopher Brown calls Team *Cryptonomicon*, but Dunin was, and is, the real deal.

The files I generated while working on this story are sort of ridiculous. For example, in the service of cipher construction, I made a list of lines of thirteen letters each:

- lookbehindyou
- gettwoobjects
- neverforgetme
- ididloveyouso
- turntopageten

---

[4] Elonka Dunin, *Mammoth Book of Secret Codes and Cryptograms* (Philadelphia: Running Press, 2006).

- itsatravelbug
- hifirstfinder
- pickupthebowl
- walkfivesteps
- fivestepsback
- therainisakey
- bringyourcoat
- whoiscrawling
- whoslistening
- heisbehindyou
- nightiscoming
- lookinlookout
- thirteentimes
- grindthebones

But the first one was, of course:

- edgarallanpoe

I also made a file, while re-reading "The Gold Bug," titled "Poe elements," which included another list:

- tarantula
- frenzied dancing/tarantella
- William Legrand
- Huguenots
- Charleston
- South Carolina
- Palmettos
- Fort Moultrie
- Jupiter
- Newfoundland (dog)
- death's-head

- secret writing/invisible ink
- beetle
- tulip tree
- skull
- skeletons
- Captain Kidd
- Bessop's Castle
- Sullivan's Island
- All in the Wrong by Arthur Murphy
- gold rush
- entomology
- seven metals of medieval alchemy and astrology: tin (Jupiter), lead (Saturn), mercury (Mercury), iron (Mars), copper (Venus), silver (moon), and gold (sun)
- philosopher's stone
- peacock's tail
- scarab
- antennae
- counter: a valuable token or coin of uncertain weight
- censer
- bacchanal

By the time I sorted all this out, of course, the *Poe* deadline was well past—Fwee! There it went!—so when "The Night Cache" finally was, if not finished, at least in a satisfying state of abandonment, I offered it to Nick Gevers of PS Publishing as a story original to my upcoming second collection. Instead, PS published it as a standalone novelette, which meant my collection now had a Table of Contents hole to fill with some *other* original story yet to be written.[5] Such is the life of the free-lancer, today as in 1845.

Suffice to say that my Poe-tribute Lewton-tribute geocaching cipher-cracking Western Maryland lesbian romance with (I forgot

---

[5] Andy Duncan, *The Night Cache* (United Kingdom: PS Publishing, 2009).

to mention) autobiographical elements and screwball comedy went on to be a World Fantasy Award and Shirley Jackson Award nominee, which, I'm ashamed to say, only encouraged me.

Another overt Poe tribute in my published corpus thus far is titled "The Premature Burials."[6] Three guesses which story inspired *that!*—in part, at least. It began as a rewrite of "The Three Snake-Leaves," one of the more obscure folktales collected by the Brothers Grimm, in which a beautiful and strange princess makes the outrageous demand of all her suitors that they be buried with her upon her death, whether they're dead or not. This demand turns all claimants away save one brave soul who gambles that the princess's imminent death is unlikely but who soon finds that he chose poorly.

This seemed a very nineteenth-century story to me, given the period fascination with premature burials and resurrection men. It also struck me (no judgments, please) as a pretty sexy story, overtly and covertly. For example, the prince is rescued by a talking snake that wriggles into his tomb and—well, never mind. I oomphed the sex in my story so I could submit it to an erotic-horror anthology Paula Guran was editing. Guran said it didn't fit her anthology, but she'd happily take it for the pioneering e-zine she was editing, *Gothic.Net*—if, that is, I'd cut some of the sex. Such is the life of the free-lancer, today as in 1845.

I also included shout-outs to James Thurber's "Mr. Preble Gets Rid of His Wife," another comedy of collaborative domestic grave-digging, and gave a cameo to the actual wrought-iron cemetery gate I walked through one afternoon in Wisconsin, on pilgrimage to August Derleth's grave. Arching across the top of the gate is this motto:

IT IS A HOLY AND WHOLESOME THOUGHT,
TO PRAY FOR THE DEAD

---

[6] Andy Duncan, "The Premature Burials," in *Beluthahatchie and Other Stories* (Urbana, Illinois: Golden Gryphon Press, 2000), 116–128.

I enjoyed telling friends that I was writing an Edgar Allan Poe-James Thurber-August Derleth-Brothers Grimm pastiche. None seemed surprised.

I also intended the story to be much longer because I was determined to give my main characters a posthumous third act via the Fox sisters, who (as you all know) launched modern spiritualism in 1848—but I gave up on that as I heard the eerie knocking of deadline.

The fact is, that as I flip through my three published collections and all the unfinished scraps and orts on my various writing desks, I see Poe's influence everywhere: obsessive, untrustworthy, logorrheic narrators; dead people who are more alive than the living; crumbling and labyrinthine settings inhabited by crumbling and labyrinthine characters.

Most of all, I see the endless chewing of gristly historical bits, all the stuff I did not make up—the traveling truck-bed electric chair of Depression-era Mississippi; the dime-museum Diorama of the Infernal Regions; the meeting, in a Haitian hospital yard, between Zora Neale Hurston and the patient presented to her as a capital-Z Zombie; the severed, pikestaffed head of the most venerated flagellant in the Tower of London, Thomas More. "You realize," murmured a Catholic friend, after I performed at the International Conference on the Fantastic in the Arts (ICFA) a grisly excerpt from my story "An Agent of Utopia," "that Catholics consider More a saint?" I smiled and replied, "Yes"; he smiled, nodded, backed away, and said no More.

Like Poe, too, I publish lots of things in lots of places: fiction, criticism, journalism, "casuals," humor, public speaking, public readings. For years, I've been immersed in the very Poe-like pursuit of documenting regional ghost stories, monster stories, unsolved murders, UFO sightings: all flavors of weird legend and lore to be found across Western Maryland and our borderlands.

I am, in short, a professional American writer like the one Poe modeled for us—though, like Poe, one with a rather macabre sensibility.

229

In my fiction, again like Poe, I favor atmosphere, mood, voice and language over, well, anything else. In a recent essay, I wrote:

> If I realize that I have hit on the right voice, then I know I'm onto something—even if I have to go back and rewrite the plot, rewrite the structure, rewrite the characters, just to fit the voice. If the voice is good, the story is good.[7]

Even Duncan scholars, should they exist, probably don't know it, but my overtly Poe-related writings include one theatrical effort that was performed exactly once. My ten-page sketch *The Tomb of Ligeia Mare*, written at speed for the 2016 One-Act Play Festival at the ICFA, has a science-fiction premise.

> Place: A wintry cliff overlooking a polar sea on Titan, Saturn's largest moon.

> Time: The 22nd century, give or take.

The loudest of the three characters is Verden Fell, a "tycoon of vast wealth, arrogance and bombast" meant to be a parody of Donald Trump, in those long-ago days when some of us could laugh at him. Fell is on Titan to bury his late wife, Ligeia, after "the most expensive funeral in the history of the solar system…at a cost that would have bankrupted most planets." Those are the words of Fell's long-suffering assistant, Rowena, whom I saddled with all the exposition, mostly delivered to the audience. She acidly continues:

> The tomb is an egotistical Gothic monstrosity, of course—we are talking about a FellCorp project, after all—but Ligeia was something of an egotistical Gothic monstrosity herself. A tall, raven-haired woman of fathomless dark eyes and icy beauty, Ligeia liked to recite Poe from memory. That was understandable,

---

[7] Andy Duncan, "Channeling Voices," in *Pocket Workshop: Essays on Living as a Writer,* eds. Tod McCoy and M. Huw Evans (Seattle: Hydra House/Clarion West Writers Workshop, 2021), 62.

I suppose, with a name like hers. But dying young, from consumption, struck many as overkill.

Fell's plans are quickly derailed by the discovery of an ancient, extraterrestrial burial site ("Bones have no place here! You're supposed to be building a crypt!") and by the return of Ligeia, who possesses first Rowena and then the project's chief scientist, Dr. Tremaine. The terrorized Fell dies in a fall (more overkill), and the two survivors, who are also lovers and plotters à la Clouzot's *Les Diaboliques,* gloat over their victory: "With luck, we'll be deep in the Danish rainforests before the lawyers even have their first conference call." Their exit lines are from Poe:

> …the play is the tragedy, "Man,"
> And its hero the Conqueror Worm![8]

This summary is as close to a revival as *The Tomb of Ligeia Mare* deserves—though it was fun while it lasted, about fifteen minutes. Not until I revised this essay did I realize the whole performance, filmed by Bill Clemente, haunts YouTube.[9] All credit goes to the director, Kelli Shermeyer, and the cast: Stephanie Neeley and Frances Auld as Rowena and Dr. Tremaine, respectively, and Nebula Award-winning science fiction writer James Patrick Kelly as Fell, whose squalling, spiraling exit from the stage was almost as prolonged and noisy as Trump's is proving to be.

The Tomb of Ligeia Mare is the sort of happy, giddy, almost-extemporaneous experience that traditionally happens to a fiction writer—especially a speculative-fiction writer—on the convention circuit. My great mentor, John Kessel, speculated once that my convention schedule was my chief writing muse; and my wife, Sydney, often says that if I had money enough and time, I'd spend every

---

[8] Edgar Allan Poe, "Ligeia," in *The Collected Works of Edgar Allan Poe,* ed. T. O. Mabbott, vol. 2 (Cambridge: Belknap Press of Harvard University Press, 1978), 319.

[9] *The Tomb of Ligeia Mare,* YouTube video, 16:05, March 27, 2016, https://www.youtube.com/watch?v=xsuu3CmPWDI.

weekend of my life at some con hotel, wearing a name tag. Neither of these remarks was meant as a compliment, but I'm proud of them anyway.

I returned to ICFA in March 2023 after a pandemic away, and my exhilaration hasn't ebbed yet—not just because no one brought up *The Tomb of Ligeia Mare*, though I was grateful for that certainly, but because I had the chance to see old friends, meet new ones, introduce the former to the latter, talk shop for days, and in general, feel like a needed member of a vibrant community rather than a muttering, scribbling hermit who spends way too much time inside his own head.

Have we left the topic of Poe behind? We have not. He died about a century too soon, but how Poe would have loved the convention circuit!—the myriad opportunities to read one's work aloud, to pontificate during panels (from the dais and, even more thrillingly, from the audience), to self-promote and/or self-destruct, to noisily join movements and even more noisily quit them, or just to plant oneself in the lobby or the bar or the green room or the hospitality suite and jack into the community vibrato, the fleeting thrill that the entire convention—nay, the industry—nay, the *cosmos*—Eureka!— revolves around *you!*

I never feel more kinship with Poe than when I'm in full-blown convention mode. You seldom catch me wearing a kilt or Spock ears or dressed as a pirate or Sailor Moon or a space cadet, but I'm still role-playing all the way.

In our living room hangs a souvenir from my earliest days on the capital-C Circuit. I brought it home from the 1995 ICFA—the first year of my long association with that aforementioned annual gathering in Florida. I mainly went because John Kessel told me I'd probably like it (an understatement) and because my favorite living cartoonist, Gahan Wilson, was Guest of Honor.

I was a clueless graduate student, wholly unpublished except for journalism—that is, for disreputable ephemera, today as in 1845— and so I arrived at the con hotel a day early, knowing no one, and mostly roamed the halls, hoping someone might talk to me.

Seeing a propped-open door, I walked through it and found myself in a big room set up for an art show, a maze of temporary walls. Hanging on them were dozens of original Gahan Wilson drawings. Several feet to a side, much larger than the published versions, these were framed, museum-quality works in pen and ink and pastel, their captions handwritten across the bottom.

I slowly roamed the exhibit, taking my sweet time in front of each piece. I examined them up close and from a distance. I savored every moment of that private viewing, that wholly unauthorized VIP preview experience.

And repeatedly, my path kept crossing that of the only other person in the room: a bald man in a safari jacket, holding a clipboard, who stopped in front of each piece and jotted a note. I assumed he was a conference official, some sort of curator, and I expected him to ask me, politely, to leave and to come back when the exhibit was open.

Instead he just smiled at me and nodded and stepped back to let me pass. I smiled and nodded in return. The next time we met, I made way for him, and we exchanged another smile and a nod. This happened several times. We moved about the room in an utterly companionable silence.

Finally, I found myself in front of a drawing of a funeral. Pallbearers and mourners were clustered around the casket, peering at the closed lid, expressions of dismay on their faces—and as these were lovingly detailed Gahan Wilson faces, they were very expressive indeed. The caption read: "I think it's his beeper."

I laughed out loud, whereupon my unseen, previously silent companion spoke up from the other side of the room. "Thank you!" he said. "I was hoping you would laugh at *something*. I'm glad I'm not a *complete* failure!"

It was, of course, the artist himself, who proceeded to give me a private, one-hour tour of the exhibit, stopping before each image to tell me where the idea came from and what headaches the art director had caused and to point out whatever part of the drawing had given him (he claimed) the most trouble. (I saw no signs of trouble.)

233

It was an extraordinarily generous investment of his time.

For his Guest of Honor talk later that weekend, Wilson stood beside an easel with a three-foot-tall sketch pad and told a standing-room-only audience the story of some of his favorite cartoons. As he talked, he sketched each with a Sharpie, then flipped back the page to make room for the next drawing. At the end of the talk, amid wild applause, he said, in an offhanded, almost inaudible way, "If anyone wants any of these drawings, you are welcome to them."

Fanboy me was sitting in the front row, of course, and as one of the first people at the easel, I claimed my favorite and asked Wilson to sign it for me.

And that is why our living room, today, is dominated by a Sharpie sketch of a hulking, scowling ape sporting a teacup-sized pillbox hat as its tiny mustached minder obliviously turns a crank. It's the Organ Grinder of the Rue Morgue.

I wonder how long the convention circuit, as I know it, will last. Only a few weeks ago, in May 2023, the Science Fiction and Fantasy Writers Association warned its membership, via mass email, that this year's in-person Nebula Conference in Los Angeles may be the final one anywhere because capitalism is basically pricing non-profits like ours out of the convention industry. Beginning pre-pandemic and accelerating since, our annual get-together is going from being a cash cow for the organization's many other activities to being such a drain on the budget that nothing is left over *for* any other activities.

I hear the same thing from other organizations in the humanities. Online conferences have much to recommend them: cheaper, more accessible, more diverse. Poe may not have recognized those as goals, but we certainly do. By *we*, I mean *I*. Those in-person conventions, after all, were for many years minefields for aspiring writers less privileged than myself—who were women or Black or queer or otherwise didn't fit the dominant paradigm or just lacked a patron with deep pockets or someone at home to mind the kids.

We'll see what happens. In the meantime, I keep trying: to write, to research, to teach; to publish my weird Duncanesque stories; to help other creators realize their own visions and laud them when they do; and, like everyone else in the 21st-century United States, to keep my head above the rank miasma of the tarn just a little bit longer.

> And now whole nations hear the scratch of bloody fingernails wanting Out, about to bring their houses down around the haunted palaces of their skulls.

John M. Ford wrote the above in his reflection on Poe's relevance to the year 1988. He continued:

> Edgar told us what horror was, and where it comes from, and in terms that will carry the message as long as horror and its source exist: which is to say, as long as we are human.[10]

It's a holy and wholesome thought, reacting to the past. It's also a complex legacy, being one of Poe's children. As I type this, I feel the raven's presence behind me, perched, poised. Waiting. Watching. Waiting.

---

[10] Ford, 31, 32.

17

ECHOES OF POE'S DETECTIVE FICTION IN MODERN MEDIA: ENGAGING HIGH SCHOOL STUDENTS

Jessica L. Osnoe

I first encountered Edgar Allan Poe's fiction in my ninth-grade high school classroom. On a rainy, soporific afternoon in October, we opened our books and followed along with the deep, grave voice that scratched out "The Cask of Amontillado" from a record player in the corner. We must have been what Poe would consider an ideal audience, perfectly situated by time and setting to experience the full intended effect of his work. Despite not being a fan of suspense or horror, I was an avid student, so I committed to the story as a requirement until its own merit proved that it was worth my time. I remember feeling simultaneously enthralled and horrified as the story progressed and subtly foreshadowed its conclusion. As students beside me fell asleep, zoned out, or disappeared into their own experiences, I began to feel strangely isolated as if the story had singled me out, and despite the twenty-odd other people in the room, the narrator on the record player was confessing solely to me.

The whole experience conveyed such a chilling impression of calculated malice that I was unsettled by it for days afterward. This effect kept me from voluntarily reading Poe's work for some time thereafter. After the mournful sadness I discovered earlier in his poetry, I suppose I expected something similar from his prose. The loss of a loved one, as described in "Annabel Lee" and "Lenore," was familiar and unfrightening, but I found such a visceral depiction of vengeful murder in "The Cask of Amontillado" to be terrifying, a reaction which I now think would have delighted Poe. My experience testifies to the success of his story in creating a lingering effect, a goal professed in his essay "The Philosophy of Composition."[1] The opportunity for such a reading experience is an increasing rarity in a world which prioritizes accessibility and on-demand options but is therefore all the more necessary, especially in classrooms.

Based on his own claims in "The Philosophy of Composition," Poe anticipated the demands of a twenty-first century audience. His insistence on prioritizing extent as a consideration to achieve his desired effect in writing echoes the struggle of every teacher in planning content and tasks for the classroom: how long can I expect students to focus on something? Teachers must contend not only with interruptions from "the affairs of the world" as Poe calls them but also with internal attention spans which have adapted to seek fresh stimulation every few seconds.[2] Accordingly, part of the classroom challenge becomes curating or adapting historical content like Poe's work for an audience unused to consuming complex syntax or piecing together figurative elements of language, skills specifically required by Common Core standards for English Language Arts (ELA) as well as College Board's Advanced Placement (AP) English courses at a more nuanced level.[3] While I have taught Poe's work to high school freshmen and juniors, I most consistently include it in my AP Language & Composition course, which often

---

[1] Edgar Allan Poe, "The Philosophy of Composition," in *The Complete Works of Edgar Allan Poe, Vol. XIV: Essays and Miscellanies*, ed. James A. Harrison (New York: T.Y. Crowell, 1902), 196.

[2] Ibid.

[3] "Common Core State Standards for English Language Arts & Literacy in History/Social Studies, Science, and Technical Subjects." Council of Chief State School Officers, Accessed February 15, 2023, https://learning.ccsso.org/wp-content/uploads/2022/11/ELA_Standards1.pdf.

incorporates elements of the standard third-year ELA course focused on American literature. I focus the class on a discussion of American identity, covering a variety of texts which help define the nation, its people, and ideas. Poe, among many authors, represents how writers help to reflect and shape our country.

I began teaching Poe more extensively in a year of firsts: my first year of AP Language was also my first in a new school. An essential element of course construction involved discovering texts not yet "claimed" by teachers at other levels. I stumbled gratefully into the suitability of Poe's detective fiction and his aforementioned essay, "The Philosophy of Composition." As a student of primarily English literature, I was delighted to discover that one of my favorite genres had an American origin and was so well suited to cover the unique demands of the course. Poe's essay became the starting point for a unit on rhetorical analysis in the same way it acted as a thesis for his writing. Students generally read the essay immediately followed by "The Murders in the Rue Morgue" and often "The Purloined Letter." (In the way of so many trilogies, the middle text, "The Mystery of Marie Rogêt," lacks appeal.) AP Language focuses primarily on nonfiction writing, and the essay and story together function as a hypothesis and experiment by which students can test the efficacy of Poe's claims about writing in his own practice.

Most of my teaching experiences with Poe take place in two North Carolina high school settings: one private, one public. Both are in the same city, where the United States military is the largest employer. The first is a private school with a typical class size of eight to fourteen pupils who are well-rounded in academics, arts, and athletics. The second is a small public school with a liberal arts focus and a comparable class size for my courses. As a public school with a high military-connected population, the student body is more diverse, and more students concentrate on music and theater rather than athletics. In both schools, I generally taught Poe's work to juniors, ages 16–17. I found that by the start of high school students were generally familiar with Poe's poems and more popular short stories such as "The Tell-Tale Heart," "The Cask of Amontillado," or

"The Fall of the House of Usher." Roughly one student in a dozen claims to admire or enjoy his work while the others are generally indifferent. To most that I encounter, Poe is an eccentric course requirement or an overly descriptive hurdle in their reading. Each year, I have roughly one student in a group of forty who reads beyond the required Poe works, indulging a sense of curiosity and learning more about Poe or his writing.

AP Language students, most of whom are high school juniors, reach me with ideas of Poe founded primarily upon his poetry and biography. Students consistently describe him and his writing as "creepy," "weird," "depression-riddled," "melancholy," "troubled," and even "tortured." While these descriptors endear him to a few students, the majority find him disconcerting or even unhealthy. There are also the dedicated scholars who view Poe as an important member of the literary canon, who should be studied at least on principle. As a student, I initially identified with the latter perspective, viewing Poe as something of a strange but necessary study. As a teacher, I now delight in subverting student expectations (including those of my former self) by reviewing Poe's broader cultural contributions.

I usually begin the unit on Poe by asking students what they know of him, including both works and biography. Given their prior knowledge, I avoid any further discussion of his biography. Instead, I supply cultural context for the time period designed to help them situate his writing within a historical framework. Since Poe alludes to Charles Dickens and William Godwin in the opening sentences of "The Philosophy of Composition," I focus on the figures of the Romantic period, including Godwin and his wife, Mary Wollstonecraft, their daughter, Mary W. Shelley, and the ideas of the time as expressed in works by Percy Shelley, William Wordsworth, and their contemporary circles. I also include a selective timeline of inventions and developments in science and technology to illustrate the shift between the Romantic and Victorian periods. Poe creates his detective in the midst of this transition period, a perfect blend of mathematician and poet, a figure both creative and analytical.[4] Since students often view Poe himself as all poetry and emotion, this step proves essential to introducing new perspectives.

As students read "The Philosophy of Composition," I ask them to focus their annotations and analysis on details of tone and structure. We begin discussing the essay's tone in particular. Almost invariably, the first words which students apply to Poe are "arrogant" and "pretentious." A former student memorably compared him to the self-important Gilderoy Lockhart from *Harry Potter and the Chamber of Secrets*. Many students are genuinely surprised by what they label as a "self-righteous" approach from a man they previously saw as weak-willed or self-doubting; they struggle to reconcile the confidence which boasts of casual correspondence with Charles Dickens (an established literary bastion for most students) with their preconceptions of Poe. Those who also call him "pretentious" or "arrogant" must weigh such claims against the proof of his method: his example from "The Raven" within the essay. I thoroughly enjoy the variety of student responses as they process Poe's argument that one of the moodiest, emotionally driven poems in their memory was written with the calculation and method of a science experiment. This conversation compels students to blend art and literature with math and science, subjects which they often view as mutually exclusive.

As we transition into "The Murders in the Rue Morgue," I encourage students to dispense with their modern expectations and examine the story as the first of its kind. The opening analysis of the draughts game proves challenging for many readers, though it makes more sense in light of the thesis provided by "The Philosophy of Composition." The facts of the case are easily accessible to most students, particularly those familiar with the works of Agatha Christie, though the description of the murders disconcerts a few of them. For

---

[4] Edgar Allan Poe, "The Purloined Letter," in *Ten Great Mysteries by Edgar Allan Poe*, ed. Groff Conklin (New York: Scholastic, 1960), 69.

others, something about the historical nature of the crime lulls them into a sense of safety, as if older murders are less grisly than those on modern TV shows. They also connect the Parisian setting with a veneer of sophistication which sets them up to expect more elegant, or at least genteel, deaths for the ladies of the house instead of brutal mutilation. One student described his surprise at the descriptions of the bodies by saying, "I was fine until the head almost came off."

The horror of the murders is generally the only commonality students find between the Poe of detective fiction and his other work. They expect emotional descriptions rather than the cool detachment of case file details. Students also express surprise (and some disappointment) at the unwittingly guilty ourang-outang. After the thrilling chase of a villain in more modern locked-room mysteries, the resolution feels somehow inadequate. The ourang-outang also elicits expressions of defense and sympathy from many students, including comparisons with Harambe, the gorilla killed for dragging around a three-year-old boy who fell into his zoo enclosure.[5] Students see the ourang-outang as more of a victim than a villain, but they also refuse to blame its owner, the sailor, for the deaths. They tend to view the sailor as a permissive or neglectful parent, whose behavior creates the method and opportunity for the murders. For those students familiar with *Frankenstein*, which some read in a previous course, the thematic similarities between the texts establish a clearer connection with the Gothic tradition as well as the broader cultural context. The inclusion of a seemingly "unnatural" element in an intelligent but unwitting animal villain "seems more like Poe," according to one student.

We finish the unit with a cursory review of "The Purloined Letter," primarily to discuss the creation of the archnemesis, the

---

[5] See Merrit Kennedy, "Gorilla Killed to Save Boy at Cincinnati Zoo," *NPR*, May 29, 2016, https://www.npr.org/sections/thetwo-way/2016/05/29/479919582/gorilla-killed-to-save-boy-at-cincinnati-zoo.

"Unprincipled man of genius, as a foil for the detective."[6] I introduce students to an episode of *Wishbone* based on the story. This PBS show follows the adventures of a Jack Russell Terrier named Wishbone whose family circumstances parallel those of classic literary works. Wishbone himself acts the role of the hero in retelling the stories, complete with relevant costumes and supporting casts. The few seasons of the show cover a variety of works, including *The Odyssey, The Time Machine, Pride and Prejudice,* "Rip Van Winkle," and "The Purloined Letter." The show was a hallmark of my childhood, and it instilled a desire to read the full stories after seeing them on screen. Despite aging out of the target audience by high school, I still remember watching reruns in the afternoons once I got off the bus. It is with this blend of nostalgia and genuine admiration for the show's work that I introduce students to the episode on "The Purloined Letter," or "The Pawloined Paper" as the show renames it.[7] The show situates Poe's story within the framework of two modern contexts: Wishbone's search for a favorite toy newspaper hidden in plain sight and a similar problem for Wishbone's owner, Joe. Both modern situations offer varying levels of accessibility for viewers to grasp the elements of the story. Joe faces an unprincipled bully at school who threatens to publicize an embarrassing acrostic poem written in adoration to Joe's crush, his history teacher. Joe plays both victim and detective to retrieve his paper, walking through the deductive process with the help of Wishbone and two friends to retrieve his letter and preserve his reputation from middle school infamy. Within the historical half of the narrative, Wishbone himself plays Dupin as an armchair detective, complete with miniature cravat and smoking jacket to look the part. The episode illustrates the story with surprising totality within its thirty minutes, depicting the

---

[6] Edgar Allan Poe, "The Purloined Letter," in *Ten Great Mysteries by Edgar Allan Poe*, ed. Groff Conklin (New York: Scholastic, 1960), 75.

[7] *Wishbone*, season 1, episode 22, "The Pawloined Paper," directed by Ken Harrison, featuring Larry Brantley, Jordan Wall, and Christie Abbott, aired November 6, 1995, PBS.

procedure-bound frustration of the police, Dupin's coolly assured competence, and the theme that analytical creativity may work for evil as well as good. Given the show's age, most students are unfamiliar with it, so they experience its full 1990s glory for the first time in class. While a cute dog in period costume charms most students, the adaptation also impresses them with its proficiency. They find the idea of a student's crush on a teacher to be cringeworthy or even creepy, but the rest of the parallel story is relatable and engaging. Aside from its vintage delight, *Wishbone* appeals to students for its simple effectiveness in telling the story. One student remarked, "This is better than SparkNotes!" Beyond the compliment, this comment betrays the prevalence of an increasing preference for visual storytelling among students. They now watch summary videos instead of reading SparkNotes as a textual substitute as if reading itself has become a chore.

I recently had a high school junior tell me that the reason she dislikes reading is because of poetry in general and "The Raven" in particular. She seemed to be frustrated by what she described as a repetitive circuit of feelings in the poem; she wondered why Poe could not be more direct and added that the bird was creepy. An increasing number of students declare this perspective, both about poetry and about writers like Poe whom they would classify as "overly descriptive." While students might enjoy macabre or thrilling content, they prefer to stream it in episodes rather than mine for it through intricate syntax.

I seized upon this preference in creating a project for the detective unit. Throughout our discussion of "The Murders in the Rue Morgue," we outline the essential traits of the detective archetype as derived from Poe's C. Auguste Dupin. With some variation, we generally conclude that the archetypal detective meets the following traits: this person is a reclusive genius or societal outsider from a noble family but now in reduced circumstances; the detective operates within a dark, often gloomy or Gothic setting; and this person applies deductive reasoning, or as Poe terms it, ratiocination, the process of exact thinking, to allay irrational fears and subdue what

Edmund Burke describes as "the sublime." The detective also happens upon a companion who, though not as sharp, operates as the detective's link to the real world. One trait which emerges more clearly in "The Purloined Letter" is the detective's possible sympathy with a criminal's mind, more notably explored by later writers, perhaps most famously by Sir Arthur Conan Doyle.

With this understanding, I ask students to apply this archetype to a later iteration of the detective. As part of their analysis, students explore how elements of Poe's original archetype may have shifted to reflect cultural change or how other genres may include detectives in atypical contexts. Students are generally familiar with Sherlock Holmes and Scooby-Doo, so both become models for class discussion as part of the project. While Sherlock Holmes and Dr. Watson clearly compare with Poe's Dupin and his companion, Scooby-Doo and the Mystery Machine gang pose a more creative challenge as characteristics of the detective and companion develop among five characters rather than the traditional two. The very idea of an animated talking dog and an Edgar Allan Poe character having anything in common helps to excite their imaginations, which may be ironic considering Poe's use of a talking bird in his most famous poem. Given those examples, students choose a detective in any form to present to the class as an adaptation of Poe's archetype. Most examples come from film, including classics such as Inspector Jacques Clouseau of *The Pink Panther* series as well as the more recent Benoit Blanc in *Knives Out* and the animated Judy Hopps from *Zootopia*. While students meet a number of course objectives through the project, they become thoroughly convinced of Poe's relevance and worthiness in a canon of classics which they might have considered historically important but not interesting. The ability to trace the influence of Poe, or any historical writer, across genres and time periods helps students not only find their own voices as scholars but also grants them a sense of personal ownership with a piece of literary history.

Two students recently used this project to demonstrate the extent of Poe's influence on emerging culture. Both are avid fans of

Japanese and Korean storytelling, so they looked for their detectives within these mediums. One pupil chose to explore how the detective archetype applied to the protagonist in a multi-ending horror adventure game called *Your Turn to Die*. The game follows two teenagers, Sara and Joe, who find themselves trapped in an escape room scenario with nine other people, all of whom work together to solve puzzles or challenges in the hope of surviving the round. The game invites players to invest in its visual narrative through various plot choices such as deciding a character's death by majority vote. Framing a detective story as a game suits the nature of Poe's own comparisons between deduction and the game of draughts while also allowing players to experience greater tension and catharsis as characters discover someone's "turn to die" throughout the various levels. In comparing the game to Poe's detective work, my student emphasized the necessity of social observation and deduction for survival, traits which Poe celebrates repeatedly in his characterization of Dupin.

Further similarities include a companion (Joe), with whom the detective (Sara) processes her findings, and the "otherness" of the detective created by the need to survive. My student also mentioned the increasing sense of doom throughout the game, as if the players have been marked for death like so many of Poe's subjects. The main difference between Dupin and Sara, as my student argued, was the need to foster relationships with other characters. While Dupin and his friend are content to "exist within [them]selves," Sara's continued existence in the game depends on a majority vote, so she cultivates useful relationships while subtly protecting her own interests.[8] Notwithstanding the fact that these relationships lack trust, the argument suggested that social interaction, even of a forced nature, makes a detective more accessible and, therefore, more appealing to an audience. While the requisite genius of a detective establishes that individual beyond the reach of a common audience, it also creates distance from the audience, which frustrates the goal of a more immersive, game-based experience. Following the presentation,

---

[8] Poe, "The Murders in the Rue Morgue," 9.

several students (one of whom also played the game) talked about the uncertainty and the interactive storytelling that made the game so compelling. Whereas a detective story generally loses some of its appeal once its novelty wears off, the varied possibilities draw in return players. Someone also compared it to a high stakes escape room, which they thought Poe would probably enjoy.

A second student made a similar point by exploring Poe's archetype through a Korean web novel, *Omniscient Reader's Viewpoint*, serialized in over 100 episodes.[9] The student seemed almost embarrassed to confess that she voraciously read more than 6,000 pages of text to finish the novel, but everyone else in the room simply marveled at such a level of dedication. The experience of reading, moreover, mirrors that of the protagonist, who dedicates a substantial amount of time to a book. The protagonist and narrator, Kim Dokja, lives as a social outsider, a victim of school bullying with a substandard post-graduation success rate. Rather like a Poe character absorbed in his own world, the narrator becomes the sole audience for an apocalypse-themed online novel and assiduously reads each installment over a ten-year period. The day after the novel finishes, the events of the novel become reality, leaving Kim in a unique position of narrative power. As my student argued, Kim's sole readership makes him both detective and hero as he navigates the intersection of fiction and reality. Like Dupin, he employs logic and deduction to calculate and resolve conflicts, many of which his knowledge of the novel allows him to anticipate. Kim also recruits the protagonist of the novel as a companion with whom he works to avoid the worst consequences of the apocalypse. The detachment from reality suggested by the title of the novel and by the detective archetype enables Kim to view events as elements of fiction. However, my student pointed out that he also exhibits extraordinary compassion demonstrated by his wish to create an arguably "unrealistic" outcome

---

[9] Singshong, *Omniscient Reader's Viewpoint*, Omniscient Reader Manga Online, accessed February 21, 2023, https://omniscientreadersviewpoint-manga.com/manga/omniscient-reader-chapter-143-2/.

without massive casualties.

Of all the student choices, these two caught my interest not only for their novelty but also for their connection between Poe and these experiential mediums. As an avid fan of live theater, I love when characters and stories come to life beyond their original pages. As escape rooms, immersive theater, and gaming experiences reimagine classic stories, it delights me that students make such connections across cultures and genres. Ultimately, these students saw how elements of Poe's work could achieve power and influence beyond his imagined scope by blurring the lines between fiction and reality.

Throughout these and other presentations, I also noticed that students with more modern detectives noted archetypal divergence in the detective's social capacity or in the nature of the companion. During our discussion of "The Murders in the Rue Morgue" and "The Purloined Letter," a student argued that the narrator must be obscure in order to be a vehicle for the detective's thoughts and stories. As he argued, Dupin's companion supplies practical needs by covering the bulk of their expenses and chronicling Dupin's genius; almost anyone, including the reader, could imagine themselves in that nameless role. The student went on to compare Dupin and his companion with Benoit Blanc, from *Glass Onion*, and his companion/partner Philip, as played by Hugh Grant.[10] The first cameo we see of Hugh Grant's character features him answering the door, dusted with flour and wearing an apron, while Blanc lies moodily ensconced in the bath. While the companion still functions as an amanuensis, the depiction conveys a domestic relationship more relatable to modern audiences. We concluded that this suggests a cultural need for the detective to be more accessible or outgoing, particularly in a world where reclusive or solitary people are perceived as "weird," "creepy," or even "dangerous," according to my students. As I reminded them that they used many of the same words to describe Edgar Allan Poe, some smiled, laughed, or looked mildly

---

[10] *Glass Onion: A Knives Out Mystery*, directed by Rian Johnson (2022; Los Gatos, CA: Netflix).

embarrassed, as if in transgression of an unspoken classroom law requiring them not to insult an acclaimed author. One student, however, immediately defended their actions by claiming that perceived loners might be "creepy" or could be misunderstood, like Poe himself. This response suggests a tendency toward either compassion or judgment on their parts, without a clear indication as to which might be the default. Another student suggested a compromise which downgraded the label of "weird" to "interesting," making those thusly classified into a curiosity instead of a threat.

At the end of our study on Poe, some students are content to leave him with that assessment: a curious person whose writing reflects the same idiosyncrasies. Others choose to reflect on the influence of the detective archetype and the usefulness of "knowing where things come from." Some consider him a master manipulator who knows how to use emotions and tension throughout a story to "mess with the reader." Like-minded students claim that they "enjoy how dark [Poe] can make his [stories]" or that the "mournful," "creepy," and "sorrowful" nature of his work appeals to them. Some students prefer to think of him as a sympathetic figure, traumatized by loss and drug or alcohol dependence, or cursed by extreme bad luck and fated to suffer repeated tragedies. However, some students look beyond his biography and discover a deeper admiration for the diversity of his work. They conclude that the traditional diet of Gothic poetry limits their perspective on Poe to an "inherently melancholy" figure, characterized by personal tragedy and depression. Students are likewise surprised by the versatile craftsmanship of "The Murders in the Rue Morgue," which they would hesitate to attribute to their previously conceived idea of Poe. The mathematical precision and self-righteous tone of "The Philosophy of Composition" banishes their image of Poe as a reclusive artist, unwilling to accept either praise or criticism, leaving them with a complicated and thoroughly human figure. Through these newly discovered characteristics, Poe transcends the confines of eccentricity to become more widely knowable and admirable. This last perspective most closely resembles my own journey with Poe, as both a student and a teacher. The more time I spend with Poe and his work the more I appreciate the craftsmanship behind the characters and stories, which not only endure but also evolve. Poe's influence and adaptability, particularly with his detective stories, make him integral to the ongoing development of both American literary identity and of cultures around the world, including those represented by my teenage students.

18

THE GREEN LIGHT: PERMISSION FOR DARK HEARTS + ARTISTIC IDENTITIES

MILITIA VOX

In loving memory of Mary, aka Mom

My name is MILITIA. I earned this name in the New York rock/metal scene in the early 2000s for being a badass performer and taking my career and creative expression into my own hands. I have managed to make a name for myself, on my own terms, but our story goes back way before then. When I was simply…Stephanie.

Madeline

I was a girl, maybe seven years old, when I found the only graphic novel in our house. It was called *Poe: Tales of Terror*. It has been missing since my parents moved. I continue to hunt for it to this day and still have yet to find copies of it anywhere. I remember flipping through its pages and seeing striking images depicting beautiful melancholy and somehow elegant horror. The story that struck me most at the time was "The Fall of the House of Usher." The drawings and plot twist of Madeline coming back from the dead like some sort of glamour zombie is still burned into my brain. I remember studying the drawing of when she threw open her bedchamber door to scare Roderick. Her hair was wild, gown shredded, her teeth bared, and she shook everyone to their core. She was mesmerizing to me. I thought to myself, "Damn—I want to be that powerful," which perhaps is not the first thing that most children may think…and my enduring fascination with Poe began.

The Green Light

Frankly, the dates and details mentioned are somewhat askew because my memories are messy. Like blots of ink, they are runny, gradient, and shapeless. That, and I do my damndest to live in the present and keep it moving. I have no real concept of time, which is perhaps what has kept me young! Time is "a construct," as the kids say. I am often running late. I can get hyper-fixated on things and hammer at them for hours. For example, I can obsessively work on music all through the night, past the sunrise. And I have seen a lot of sunrises, at the *end* of my day. Initially, I sit down to get an idea out, suddenly hours have passed, and I have lost myself in it—no weed required. I call it "my lunacy"; I am moon powered. It has gotten worse—*over time (ha!)*—and exacerbated from modern-life oversaturation, low bandwidth, and dissociation due to grief from the death of my mother, brain fog from having had COVID twice, and likely some damage from the drugs I did in high school and college. Suffice to say, that all my memories congeal like layers of psychic paper mâché—constantly collaging. How I envy those who can scan through their memories like a timeline. I don't always recall the verbiage of things, but I somehow remember details like people's faces, music, and song lyrics exceptionally well, and I always remember the vibe.

All this explanation is to make this point: because of Edgar Allan Poe I first became self-aware of my intrinsic affection for the beauty in darkness. He was the one who, by example, first gave me the green light to acknowledge that part of myself. At a young and impressionable age, he was the first artist I found who romanticized the dark and creatively expressed it. Like I wanted to. Like I knew I had to. Like I do. For that, I feel eternally linked to Poe—this stranger, this madman, this Romantic, this drunk, this wordsmith, this deceased legend, this human. This connection has been a consistent through-line in my life. He is fuel to me.

Love That Red

I was the flower girl at my cousin's wedding. I wore a white, flowing gown with loose ruffles down to my feet. After the wedding, when we got that dress home, I thought that it kind of resembled Madeline's in that graphic novel. Early on a Saturday morning, when I should have been watching cartoons, I grabbed my mother's brightest red Revlon lipstick—a classic 80s shade called "Love That Red." I smeared it on my face, lips, hands and streaked it up and down that poor doomed dress. I shredded the dress and took Polaroids of myself looking ragey in my bathroom mirror. I felt like a horror goddess, supervillain, and final girl all rolled into one. It felt like something that I needed to do. An important experiment. A calling.

My folks weren't exactly thrilled to see those pictures. Mom was annoyed that I ruined her lipstick and equally aggravated that I raked that pristine little white dress, that I was rapidly outgrowing, into tatters. I remember my father being most ticked off about the abhorrent waste of Polaroids because the film was considered expensive back then. Interestingly enough, they chose not to harp on my weird bloody zombie reenactment fantasy for some reason. At least, not to my face.

Identity

God, Jesus, nuns, uniforms....My mother was Methodist, my father is Jewish, and they sent me to Catholic schools—go figure. For private schools in my home state of Maryland, the Catholic schools ran the roost. Not sure how the vibe is these days with all the negative attention—check out the infamous docu-series *The Keepers* on Netflix for a glimpse of my high school alma mater, Seton Keough, formerly known as Archbishop Keough, in Poe's death city of Baltimore. Their not-so-flattering and very public claim-to-fame was bad enough that the Archdiocese abruptly closed the school and bulldozed it to the ground with a "nothing-to-see-here" epitaph. I wonder—does it still look good on my resume?

I attended The Trinity School from fourth to eighth grade in Ilchester, Maryland, a Tudor-style collection of buildings set on sprawling, scenic acreage surrounded by a serene forest and huge grassy fields. Trinity housed some of their most pious faculty in a convent on the property. When the nuns passed away, they graduated to a small graveyard behind the convent with an imposingly large wooden cross with a three-dimensional figure of Jesus immortalized on it. During parent/teacher nights and afterschool events, my friends and I would stalk the graveyard in the dark, telling ghost stories and imagining what lay underneath the surface, who they were, and where their spirits could be.

In fifth grade, we began a new unit in English class—the works of Edgar Allan Poe. I remember so vividly the classroom and my excitement. I knew I was tapping into a part of my true self—nothing force-fed, imposed, societal, or inherited. Something I innately understood but could not yet put into words. My own identity was forming deeper, thanks to Poe's imagination.

Carnations

During this unit, we were told that we would be going on a field trip to visit Poe's grave and Baltimore home. I was so stoked! The night before, I had to prepare. I was anxious—like "butterflies" as people say—but more kinetic—I call it my "dragonflies." I asked my mother to take me to the grocery store to buy flowers for my beloved idol. I remember mom and I, in the flower section at Safeway, bickering over roses versus carnations. I wanted the best; she wanted the best for her wallet. Cannot say I blame her since they were being left on a grave. Carnations or not, I meant business. I grabbed two child fistfuls of blood red carnations. Turns out, upon a present-day quick Google search while writing this, the red carnations were fortuitous. These flowers are known for representing love and affection for those who have passed away: love, commitment, and devotion.

The Caretaker

The next day, the students in my English class, some nuns, parent chaperones, and I went to King Edgar's humble home. A slender brick building at 203 N. Amity Street in a not-so-tidy part of Baltimore. This is where I first met the legendary Jeff Jerome—the reigning caretaker at the time. Jeff had all the attributes of the picture-perfect caretaker—thick glasses, brown tweed jacket, focused and steady eyes, and a mind like a library. He also has four fingers on his left hand, which I never asked him about but always thought made him ideal for the job.

Jeff led us through Poe's tight-quartered "B-more" home then across MLK Boulevard to the gravesite at Westminster Hall. I proudly laid the flowers at Poe's final resting place along with some "pennies for Poe," which is a customary tradition. (The penny coins at his monument are used for any upgrades or maintenance.) Jeff escorted my class through the burial grounds, the church, and even the catacombs underneath the Church, which is no longer recommended for children under 12. Perhaps that is due to the rows and rows of skulls and bones shelved in them. Little me took pictures of these remains because they blew my little mind. It was like something out of a horror movie, and it was the most intense viewing of death I had witnessed in my little life so far. I am sure whoever developed those images at CVS probably threw up in their mouth a little. As for me, I hung the shots up on my desk in my bedroom. Wednesday Addams, over here.

A Mouthful of Metal

The next fall, Trinity School received a phone call. Mr. Jeff Jerome himself asked for me to come and participate in the anniversary ceremony to honor Edgar Allan Poe's death! He mentioned that out of all the school field trips and all the kids who have come to Poe's grave over all these years *I was the only one to ever bring flowers.*

That day, I was beaming. My folks bought a video camera to capture the event. In black wide-leg pants, paisley vest, polka-dot headband, and with a mouthful of metal, I was in my glory. I am amazed my braces did not burst from all my smiling. There was a crowd of about 50–60 people: some press, my caretaker hero Jeff, and a bagpiper to represent Poe's Scots-Irish descent. I placed gifts upon the grave along with another student that I—full transparency—hated to share this epic spotlight with. We posed for photos and videos, holding Poe's brand-new bronze grave marker. I felt so fucking cool.

Visits and Tchotchkes

In 1999, after being expelled from music conservatory (another story for another time, I have since been given my BFA—Google it, if you must), I moved from Boston to New York City to pursue my dreams of being a music and visual artist, actress, and more. Both cities are Poe home cities as well. Over the next years, I continued to adore and honor Edgar, read his work, and better understand and respect his struggles. He has always been a muse to me and a recurring source of inspiration. I am now a member of the Poe Society of Baltimore that works to keep Poe's memory alive as well as raise awareness about his works and contributions to dark storytelling. Fun fact: Poe coined the term "short story."[1] I have visited his home in Philly, his statue in Boston, his cottage in the Bronx, and the High Bridge in New York City where he is rumored to have gotten the inspo to write "The Bells." I have been to Sullivan's Island, South Carolina, where he was stationed as a young man in the Army. I have dined at the mighty Poe's Tavern there, which has delectable burgers. As well as Edgar's Café on the Upper West Side of Manhattan, home of Edgar's Favorite Omelette.

I have also become a bit of a collector of Poe tchotchkes—scarves, pins, shirts, magnets, stamps, a bobblehead, candles, and various book editions. Anytime I am in Baltimore, I try to visit Edgar at the cemetery. I have even dragged my bands there before and/or after our Baltimore-area concerts.

---

[1] Martin Greenup, "Poe and the First Use of the Term 'Short Story,'" *Notes and Queries* 60 (2013): 251–254.

In August 2017, Judas Priestess visited Westminster Hall and Burying Ground to remember Edgar Allan Poe. Left to Right: Tara McLeod, Josette, MILITIA VOX, Gyda Gash, and Hillary Blaze.

Courtesy Edward Chimera

The Villainess

I wrote my first solo full-length album and released it in 2018—in an era when people seem to care only about singles and no longer really buy or commit to albums. When Instagram and TikTok trim the essence of songs down to mere seconds and billion-dollar streaming services pay artists a pittance of royalties. Regardless, I envisioned it, made it, had to remake it, refined it, mixed it, remixed it, released it, promoted it, and made music videos for it. It basically bankrupted me.

And I would do it again.

Because I had to express myself and what I felt was missing from the world: a genre-bending, avant-dark, future sound that is polarized—dark and light, soft and hard, a scope of musicality that splays styles for boundaryless fun and expression. It is mixed like I am mixed race. It is yin and yang with contrasting sections and vibes rooted in badass divine feminine energy. An ode to wicked women, *The Villainess* was my response to the pop-princesses of the day.[2] I knew I was not one of them (you know who they are, you are force-fed them regularly). I wanted to offer a different kind of female: a rebel who claims the scariest parts of herself with pride.

Here are some samples of my lyrics from *The Villainess*:

"BORN OUT OF DARKNESS"
BORN OUT OF DARKNESS
But I saw the light
Turned my back on reason
And the reasons why
A lone wolf, wild and wandering
A rebel soul
Queen without an empire
Will take her throne
Just off the grid enough
An outlaw of life

---

[2] MILITIA VOX, *The Villainess*, recorded 2018, MILITIA VOX.

No choice but to embrace it
Now I'm addicted to the fight
BORN OUT OF DARKNESS
But I'll make it right
I'm the great American outcast
With hell on my side

Call me jaded, baby
Talkin' so tough
One thing's for certain now
You can't get enough
I'm the new black sheep
But not the whore
I want it bad
And I want it more
'Cause I'm
BORN OUT OF DARKNESS
Born to be bad
You can't control me
And I can't be had
'Cause I'm
BORN OUT OF DARKNESS
Born to be bad
You can't control me
Does that make you mad?...[3]

The "outsider artist" theme is a constant presence in my work and why I feel simpatico with Edgar. He had a contrarian idea of how to write and what to write about that sparked horror and passion in so many people. For decades since his death, his words and ideas have caught fire and spread to so many. He knew what he was doing at the time was a must. Even though he deserved it, he was not positively reinforced through money or major fame in his lifetime...and he created his art anyway. Shame he did not get to enjoy

---

[3] MILITIA VOX, "BORN OUT OF DARKNESS," YouTube, https://www.youtube.com/watch?v=x-lU18jtBe0.

the fruits of his genius. But I believe people love that about him too—he lived his dark tragedies.

"NYCTOPHILIA"
Comfort in shadows
Under veil of night
Swaddled in starry darkness
A sea of fright
Amethyst lips
Tease like storm clouds
Rolling in like
Impending sins now

I am night
I am dreams
Death in the light
NYCTOPHILIA
Breath that melts into moonlit charms
Buried deep in velvet arms

I am night
I am dreams
Death in the light
NYCTOPHILIA...[4]

Nyctophilia is the love of night and finding comfort in darkness. I used to go on late night walks often in New York City, typically after a whiskey or two. I know that Poe had a similar habit. I imagine some of our best work was written just before twilight.

"THIS IS SHE"
This leather heart
Has been hardened
A patchwork of art

---

[4] MILITIA VOX, "NYCTOPHILIA," YouTube, https://www.youtube.com/watch?v=GvkTrk1ixwg.

Stitched with pride
A woman's design
Is ripe with secrets
So don't deny
What you can't refuse

Close to the flame
No room for sorrow
The sins of today
You'll forget tomorrow
A promise made
But not for free
Your flesh and bone
Offer it to me

Drunk with power intoxicating
Speak the words for she is waiting
Close your eyes 'cause she is lying
In the dark for you she's dying small…[5]

Poe's effect on my own work is deeply subconscious. He is embedded in my fabric because I identify with his energy deeply—dark heart, being misunderstood and undervalued in a space we have had to define as we go. Like Poe, myself, and many other artists who have had to carve their own niche, we stand alone in that we are the architects of our own genres. There are no blueprints. We walk on new terrains, alone, while many others follow proof of concepts. We are creators that dare and sacrifice their lives for their art.

The Raven

During the lockdown in 2020, I built up my home studio and began one-stop-shop writing, recording, producing, mixing, and mastering my musical creations from my living room. I decided to praise Poe

---

[5] MILITIA VOX, "THIS IS SHE," YouTube, https://www.youtube.com/watch?v=3sRafGT4asU.

by recording "The Raven" and setting it to original music.[6] I composed, produced, mixed, and mastered it—the first time I ever did it all. It was nominated for a *Saturday Visiter* Award in 2022. Even during a lockdown, New York City still must have held the title as the noise capital of the world. The sounds of the city that I could not extricate are embedded deep into that track. At one point, my neighbor and his dog shaking his leash and tags can be heard. I added delay and reverb to these environmental sounds, and I believe it adds to the spooky ambience of the track. Also, I do not know if you have ever heard real-life raven sounds, but they are somewhat underwhelming. Not so fear-inducing. I had to blend and pitch shift multiple bird sounds that I ripped from YouTube to get what I created on the final recording.

I was so compelled to narrate this classic work and give it girth by creating a sonic landscape and effects—it was a true joy to record.

Saudade

Fall 2021. I was feeling homesick for my home state. I often miss Baltimore, my hometown of Columbia (I am truly lucky to have grown up there; there are actual Facebook support groups for people who grew up there but had to leave the town!), and my old stomping grounds in Old Ellicott City, DC, and the surrounding areas. I sometimes crave a taste of my childhood and teendom and seafood prepared the "right way." Maryland is a funky, wacky, civilized, haunted, progressive, grounded, and eccentric place all at once. Just look at some of its most famous exports—the "Pope of Trash" John Waters and my October 19 birthday-mate Divine, aka Glenn Milstead. It seems fitting that the Master of the Macabre lived in and has his final resting place in the paradoxical state of Maryland.

---

[6] MILITIA VOX, "Edgar Allan Poe's The Raven," recorded 2020, single, 9:50, YouTube, https://www.youtube.com/watch?v=F2GbUpPIs6E&list=PLTe URbp-n3MxQO3AWCjltahRZL8h5bxLF. Check it out and message me your thoughts via my website: https://www.militiavox.com/contact. Let me know if you want more Poe audio recordings from me.

Since my mother's death, whenever I see signs of Maryland, my heart aches harder than ever. I often dream about the house I grew up in. I wish I could bottle it and keep that part of my family's life safe, somehow—back when our family of three was young, vibrant, and healthy. In retrospect, our life together there and our love as a trio was the ultimate luxury. #3musketeers4eva

Death Weekend

It was the Edgar Allan Poe "Death Weekend," aka Poe Fest International 2021, and I was anxious for some sweet, gothy, Charm City nostalgia. My guy, my chihuahua, and I drove down from New York City in our 1990, raven-black Cadillac hearse. Feel free to read that sentence again. The hearse deserves a moment here because it has quite a résumé. My guy, Jimmy Duff, has a thing for hearses and has had several over the years. His motivation for buying them was to promote the bar, the world-famous Duff's Brooklyn, which is a mecca for metalheads. The now iconic hearse has been featured in films, television shows, music videos, and photo shoots. It was in the Martin Scorsese movie *The Irishman*, the television show "Pose" on FX, and a posthumous Prince music video. Cardi B rented it for a Halloween photo shoot, and Depeche Mode rented it for their *Memento Mori* promo photos and album artwork. This is our day-to-day car and the vehicle we use to pick up our groceries.

We drove to The Poe House and made an impulsive decision to swing by the gravesite "to say hi" to Edgar, even though we were hangry and ready for a proper seafood feast at The Rusty Scupper in the Inner Harbor. We pulled up to the gates of Westminster Hall and Burying Ground. Who was sitting at Poe's grave as if he had been waiting there in the same spot that I had last seen him in the 90s? The legendary caretaker himself, Jeff Jerome. I exited the death mobile, screaming "JEFF!!!" as I ran over to him. He had no idea who I was. *LOL* But he was really taken with me in that moment because I had just jumped out of a hearse, so he entertained my superfandimonium. We sat graveside and talked. I confessed that I had

reached out to him on Facebook, but he did not remember me because I look a bit different since he last saw me as a tween. We caught
up, and we connected on socials. I hugged him hard. When I returned home, I sent him a clip of the video of us at the ceremony
from back in the day. He shared our crazy story on Edgar Allan Poe:
Evermore—the Poe legacy Facebook page.

213th B-Day Bash

Jeff Jerome is now Poe Curator Emeritus. He invited me to Edgar
Allan Poe's birthday party in the winter of 2022. His 213th birthday
to be exact. Like, how many people can say that they went to an
official birthday party for a dead literary icon? Welp, I can. And it
was fabulous. And freezing. Thirty-something degree weather on
January 22, 2022, at the southeast corner of West Fayette and North
Greene Street in Baltimore, outside at Poe's grave, during a global
pandemic. Black birthday cake, of course, with red icing. Ornate flo-
ral arrangements—mostly red carnations (wink!) and amontillado.
We gathered, an intimate group of five: radio personality Ron Sav-
age, Jeff, his assistant Sherri, my gothy ride-or-die Willow Waxdoll,
and me—in an exclusive private party to celebrate America's Shakespeare and King of Melancholy in front of a livestreaming international audience of more than 300,000 people.

Our dead poet's society rounded out the night at Annabel Lee,
a Poe-centric tavern in the Canton neighborhood on the eastside of
Baltimore. They are worth a visit. An outdoor fire-pit on the sidewalk corner and inside a treasure-trove of Edgar art, collectibles, rar-
ities, memorabilia, and more. The interior is appropriately mood-lit,
topped with witty Poe-centric named yummy eats and spirits such
as the "Edgar" absinthe or the classic "Jeff Jerome." If this spot were
in New York City, I would be a regular.

The Dark Gift

I guess I did not realize how influential Poe has been in my life, truly,
until writing this piece. I do not spend a whole lot of time reflecting in

this way. I have always accepted the way that I am and the things that I like without overanalyzing. Stopping and acknowledging this history, patterns, and correlations and putting it all into words is mind-blowing. Why do I cling sacredly to this man that I have never met? Why do I cherish him? Art and tragedy, perhaps. I love his story and how he devoted his life to telling stories, obsessively, at all costs. Even though he was not appropriately celebrated and compensated in his lifetime for his brilliance and impact on poetry, literature, and horror, he made his art *anyway*. I know this devotion—it is an obsession, a mental illness to some, a passion, true love, constant crisis, delicious torment, and sheer bliss. When you see the world through a unique and specific creative lens and you must communicate it no matter what. "The Dark Gift," I call it. (Thank you, Anne Rice.)

I think one of the biggest tragedies for any artist is to catch fire in the hearts of many *after* you die. This, unfortunately, is the story for many creatives. We rarely get our flowers in our lifetimes. Maybe it is easier to dismiss someone when they are always around…their presence is taken for granted. Plus, they are doing things in an unfamiliar way. What is first labeled as "disruptive" becomes "revolutionary" and then, eventually, "mainstream." Yet an alternative tragedy presents itself. Perhaps the most horrific fate in life, to me, is to die with unexpressed art inside of you.

If there is an afterlife, I hope that Edgar can see the waves in the literary ocean he has made. How he is studied, adored, resonated, knocked-off, and damn near worshipped in modern times. His work is now deemed pioneering. The mission of any artist is to create what you know is true. "Find what you love and let it kill you"—and he did.

Poe and I will never meet on this earth. He will likely never know the impact of what he has created or The Dark Gift that he has passed on to me and countless others. For whatever it is worth, I will put the energy out there—into the vast and starry darkness: Thank you, Edgar, for the green light."

MILITIA

PS: Oh look, the sun is up!

19

EDGAR ALLAN POE'S LIFE, DEATH, AND FUTURE, FROM A POE PERFORMER

Tim Beasley

The book in my mother's bookcase, *The Works of Edgar Allan Poe*, compelled me as a youngster to take it down for a read as it had an interesting raven embossed on its cover. Surprised at how entertaining this collection of his stories and poems were, I became a fan at an early age of about twelve years old. Also, I had heard of Edgar Allan Poe many times as several movies of a fun horror nature played at the drive-in during the early 1960s. They were based on his Gothic horror works "The Black Cat," "The Pit and the Pendulum," and "The Raven." Being foremost a young natural "cut up" and with an appetite for attention, I was already doing impersonation performances of popular and classic characters from TV and movies for family, friends, and school activities. I had the good fortune to carry my knowledge of Edgar Allan Poe into my adulthood and became an Edgar Allan Poe tribute performer as one of my varieties of acting impersonations in my career. Poe was easy for me to "become" as I felt a connection to him simply because his works written in the "first person" gave me an inner monologue and personality "to wear." In a similar manner, I also perform as Mark Twain and other historical characters such as General Patton, President Reagan, and Teddy "Roughrider" Roosevelt.

Tim Beasley as Edgar Allan Poe.

Courtesy Tim Beasley

Having much experience in my professional performances recreating many characters in wardrobe and makeup effects, all I had to do for Poe was to find the right dark and somber vintage clothing. Then, adding the long, disheveled black hair and mustache effects along with pale, sallow makeup gave my Poe that melancholy countenance he was recognized for in his archaic images. To breathe life into my Poe performance, my own natural voice was, I felt, suitable and probably close in timbre and tonal quality, for of course, Edgar Allan Poe grew up as a "Southern speaking" Virginian in Richmond as I had in my native Roanoke.

Performing as Edgar Allan Poe, I allow myself to interpret his works and voice them as I feel he would have. Yes, he can be portrayed as a cliché, but I prefer to embody the man's soul as I understand it, adding a real, vivid, and live connection with my audiences. In this sense, I rehearse his works closely, verbatim, and I leave the personality to be more natural and relaxed.

After my very first performance, I am pleased to say I received a standing ovation. This was for the Casemate Museum of Fort Monroe, Virginia, fundraiser. The place and time were poignant as well, for the event took place on October 30 in the Chamberlin Hotel, not far from where Poe wrote and performed his haunting "Annabel Lee" at the Hygeia Hotel of the 1800s.

Being quite active nationally in this role, I was very pleased when I was asked to be him while emceeing the first International Edgar Allan Poe Festival in Baltimore, a city of important history for all Poe fans. This was such a success that the offer was extended for five years of the event. As Poe, I welcomed the attendees and began presenting each act or special guest as though Poe himself considered them all as his guests at some surrealistic soiree from the past. In this role, I am honored to introduce entertainers who specialize in reenacting personalities from that period such as a young lady who specializes in recreating Virginia Clemm Poe, his ill-fated bride.

Edgar Allan Poe and I have an intimate connection, and I often wondered how odd it was that he died such an unusual and unsolved

267

death. Although I had read quite a few theories on his early demise, I felt there was something just a bit more bizarre in the shadows of those damp, dark nights of Baltimore in the chill of October 1849. I felt I could relate to something deadly and dangerous and so poignant to his mysterious passing.

Growing up in the 1960s in Mason's Cove, a rural area of Virginia in the Blue Ridge Mountains near Salem and Roanoke, I had the gruesome occasion of seeing our pet cat die from what I believe was a black widow spider bite. Oh yes, we had those shiny and deadly black widow beauties living in the gutter downspouts of our old house.

I once captured one very nice specimen in a glass jar and proudly took it to my elementary school for a sort of "show and tell" item. As I presented it up close to my teacher, the fear drained the blood from her face, and she turned very pale. Very slowly she took the jar from me, cautiously opened it, and poured some rubbing alcohol that was kept for children's cuts and scrapes onto it. As it convulsed and died, she let out a gasp as she had been holding her breath for fear of the eight-legged monster!

About the cat...It had come to our door scratching in vain to get into the house, and upon allowing it in, we noticed its eyes were extremely dilated. It hissed and moaned fearfully and rolled around on the floor as it scraped spiderwebs from its whiskers; it was in its death throes. It apparently had been bitten by one of those spiders as its curiosity had gotten the best of it.

In this profession, I often have occasion to wonder about different aspects of Poe's life, particularly his demise. It is generally accepted that on his last day he was discovered incoherent, lying in the street, and was involved in some voting day fraud. The speculation is that some unscrupulous men carried him from one voting location to another, in effect throwing an election. Further mysterious details emerged that he wore someone else's clothing and that he uttered outbursts of mumbled words and names before he died a few days later. However, that does not explain the mystery enough for me.

I have considered that perhaps Edgar Allan Poe had a bit too much drink on those evenings before his death and had staggered and fallen into some muddy puddle, very common on those old, rough, cobblestone streets, which led him to seek some dry clothes at a shop. Being a bit tight on pocket money, he, perhaps, would have opted for some inexpensive used clothing and a hat. In October, a hat would be very handy as the winds can be very cold in that season in Baltimore. Donning the hat, and it being typically black beaver felt, it may have been infested with, yes, a black widow spider!

Being he had a considerable amount of long black hair, a spider bite on his scalp or back of neck would have been hard to see or discover and not an immediate suspect for a doctor or nurse to have noticed. His reported moaning and irrational vocal outbursts just before his death were a delirium brought on by the spider bite's deadly poison affecting his brain directly from the close proximity of a scalp bite and, ultimately, more powerful in its lethal effect.

This is similar to what I witnessed in our cat…a poor beast that died by getting too close to the fearsome black widow spider!

In addition to immersing myself in Poe's life, I also perform in the roles of other famous figures, some who met similar tragic fates. For instance, I cannot help but notice striking coincidences between Poe and Jim Morrison. As I have often referred to the 1960s rock and roll superstar legend Jim Morrison of The Doors as the Edgar Allan Poe of rock music, I have been enjoying performing as both "Jim" and "Edgar" in tributes, now professionally for over twenty years. As a matter of fact, I have also performed them in conjunction as a "Double Dead Legend" act, a unique offering in my Dead Legends™ national performances.[1]

Recently I began backfilling my historical knowledge of Edgar Allan Poe, as I was approached for my fifth year as Master of Ceremonies for the annual International Edgar Allan Poe Festival. This program of events focused on the bicentennial of the birth of Poe's wife, Virginia Clemm Poe.

---

[1] For more information, see "The Dead Legends," *Vegas Tributes*, 2023, http://www.vegastributes.com/Dead-Legends-Rock-Show.html.

Doing my research on her life, I came upon a letter that Edgar sent to his aunt (and subsequent mother-in-law), Maria Poe Clemm, about his wife Virginia and their trip to New York. There I found this odd coincidence of name:

> Then I went up Greenwich St. and soon found a boarding-house. It is just before you get to Cedar St. on the west side going up—the left-hand side. It has brown stone steps, with a porch with brown pillars. "Morrison" is the name on the door.[2]

Immediately The Doors's famous musical LP *Morrison Hotel* came to mind!

That was a strange story, as the group's next LP, their fifth, needed an unusual and compelling photo cover and title. It is one of the most famous stories in rock and roll history. The Doors, along with photographer Henry Diltz, were knocking around downtown Los Angeles on a photo shoot for this album. They were headed for the Morrison Hotel, a low-rent SRO (single-room occupancy) hotel on Hope Street that keyboardist Ray Manzarek had spotted a few days before. Its front window, with the band members gazing from behind it, became the LP cover and, subsequently, the location became the LP's title. Several strange coincidences and juxtapositions are evident when it comes to Edgar Allan Poe and Jim Morrison!

Like Poe, Morrison had his personal demons to deal with. Facing a possible 1970 jail term conviction for a controversial immoral act while performing in Miami, Morrison was in an apparent exile in France to escape the penalty. He often found his refuge in the bottom of a whiskey bottle, a dead-end solution for quite a few notables in the world of literature and performing arts (Ernest Hemingway and Dylan Thomas come to mind). Perhaps the strangest parallel between them both is they died under mysterious circumstances. Morrison's untimely death, like Poe's, is shrouded in

---

[2] Edgar Allan Poe to Maria Clemm, April 7, 1844, in *The Collected Letters of Edgar Allan Poe*, ed. J. W. Ostrom, B. R. Pollin, and J. A. Savoye (Cambridge: Harvard University Press, 2008), 437.

questions such as why he was quickly and unceremoniously buried in the historic Père Lachaise Cemetery in Paris, a very popular tourist attraction where Irish playwright Oscar Wilde, French cabaret singer Édith Piaf, and many other notable performers and authors are buried.

It is another compelling coincidence that Edgar, the father of the detective story, should die in the manner of an unsolved mystery. As the years progress, I often think of the extended greatness he probably would have achieved. I do believe his genius in painting his works with vivid word imagery will keep him as popular in the future as ever. His prose is eternal in the hearts and minds of many millions of fans. As a performing artist, I feel my interpretations of Edgar and his vast works bring my audiences an enjoyable "Poe experience" for the senses.

As each new year extends the reach of the media with regard to the popularity of works by Edgar Allan Poe, I am always pleasantly surprised to see and meet many new young Poe fans at the Poe Fests. I have seen this popularity of his works continue to expand. When the extremely popular movie series *A Night at the Museum* came out in 2006, museums wanted to get into the fun and featured their own Night at the Museum events. One place where I really enjoyed performing was the prestigious Walters Art Museum in Baltimore, coincidentally not far from the final resting places of Edgar, his wife Virginia, and mother-in-law Maria Clemm at the Westminster Hall and Burying Ground. These appearances led to being recruited to emcee the Private Eye Writers of America's Shamus Awards banquet held in 2008 at the same Westminster Hall. This celebration honored attendees and featured the authors who were recognized for their top-selling mysteries, including Reed Farrel Coleman, Sean Chercover, Richard Aleas, Cornelia Read, and Bill Pronzini.

When the National Endowment for the Arts chose select Poe

tales and poems for its Big Read Project, I became Poe again.[3] One of the organizers contacted me to make personal appearances as Poe and to conduct readings of his works as entertainment in local theaters and schools coast to coast. It was always so enjoyable to see the smaller towns such as Vincennes, Indiana, and Hartland, Michigan, get into the spirit of those Big Read programs; they decorated the libraries with artwork created by students as well as other salutations to Poe and his works. These events also led other communities to seek out my Edgar appearances such as my invitation to the Lewisburg Literary Festival in West Virginia.

Edgar Allan Poe and his works have been a favorite personality and subject of mine, and I hope to continue sharing my knowledge and understanding of him with others for many years to come!

[3] In May 2008, the NEA announced a volume by Edgar Allan Poe would be added to its book list. The edition titled *Edgar Allan Poe: Great Tales and Poems* was issued in 2009 by Vintage Classics.

20

POSTHUMOUSLY, POE

MaryBeth Schade

"While I nodded, nearly napping, suddenly there came a tapping."

"The Raven" by E. A. Poe[1]

"As no thought can perish, so no act is without infinite result. Since every vibration once set in motion is eternal, the power of the word once spoken is also everlasting."

Edgar Allan Poe,
"The Power of Words"[2]

With all the confidence of somebody who had not yet experienced failure, I would swing for hours on my childhood swing set. Little legs pumping forward and backward, scooping air until I was almost parallel to the ground, I aimed three feet in front of my swing and let go. Only hours before, I had buried a handful of charcoal barbecue briquets and was intent on packing the dirt over them. My plan was that, sometime in the future, when I was *really old*, I would return to my spot, dig up, and retrieve what would surely have turned

---

[1] Edgar Allan Poe, "The Raven," in *The Collected Works of Edgar Allan Poe*, ed. T. O. Mabbott, vol. 1 (Cambridge: Belknap Press of Harvard University Press, 1969), 364.
[2] Edgar Allan Poe, "The Power of Words," in *The Collected Works of Edgar Allan Poe*, ed. T. O. Mabbott, vol. 3 (Cambridge: Belknap Press of Harvard University Press, 1978), 1210.

into the most beautiful diamonds. Somewhere I had learned that carbon plus pressure on the earth's surface produced diamonds! Aside from the waiting billions of years part, I figured I could do it. Daydreaming and worlds away, I focused on my task; wispy clouds moving across the blue sky melted away, autumn air blew on my cheeks, gentle movements timed by creaking sounds from the ungreased chains held my weight, and time stood still. I was meditating and did not even know it.

My Poe connection is the surprising result as well as a reward for years of daily meditation. I learned ways to distract my conscious and critical mind; the process became as effortless as those days so long ago, swinging and imagining my precious charcoal turned into diamonds.

My first introduction to Poe was a cursory reading of "The Raven" by the nuns at my Catholic high school. Years later, on my honeymoon, I visited his Amity Street home in Baltimore, but I recall very little other than my 5'7" frame struggling to climb the narrow, steep, winding staircase to the upper-floor bedrooms.

More than thirty years passed before I gave Poe another thought. As dustings of the first snowfall often melt away barely noticed, I might as easily have ignored his first whispers. Despite the pain of a headache from hell, I had fallen asleep that afternoon. When I woke, I was momentarily confused by a blinking computer cursor halted at an unfinished stanza, and pages surrounded me in handwriting similar to my own. These pages comprised a short but forceful letter, unlike anything I would have written. This nap was the start of a decades-long relationship with Edgar Allan Poe.

Here is a transcription of the channeled letter from Poe that started it all:

Harper's Magazine
Lewis H. Lapham, Editor

Dear Sir:

At the risk of digging my grave even deeper, I submit sincere congratulations following 150 successful years of your literary publication. I am aghast that I was granted a mere passing reference, yet coinciding with my death's anniversary creates deep concern. As a man of many past-submitted letters to your predecessors, good brothers Harper, I submit, as I did so often before, one more request to be fully recognized for my talents though now, perhaps, too late. I expect this submission (the object of my visit) afford me solace in no uncertainty of terms.

Your Obedient Servant,
Edgar Allan Poe, Esq.

Then I heard a voice whisper:

For those yet trapped in physical form, there be an addendum to my life. Gather, yea hear, the timely fashioning of yet another fanciful escape. My burden is lifted. I leave with you a burden perhaps, cause to find me good at my very word—there is an Al Aaraaf.[3]

True enough, I remain very much dead. Now centuries after my death, I'm back. Having found a way to speak from the Other Side, I hope to cause a little commotion and exact my long overdue "literary revenge."

A few days later, I found myself at a bookstore, wandering the magazine aisle. One periodical seemed to jump off the shelf. Rather than a *People* or *Architectural Digest*, a dark blue cover of *Harper's Magazine*, Special Anniversary Collector's Edition, caught my attention. I cannot say that I thought much about it at the time, but I began thumbing through it. It caught my eye that this particular issue declared that it was celebrating 150 years of literature and covered 1850-2000!

---

[3] Poe refers to "Al Aaraaf," one of his early poems in which he described a medium between Heaven and Hell, a sort of purgatory, where men suffer no punishment but are stuck, neither peaceful nor happy. By saying "there is an Al Aaraaf," Poe means that he has experienced being stuck in this in-between place and comes to us now finally unburdened, finally at peace and happy. T. O. Mabbott's headnote to the work delves into the nuances of this reference. See Edgar Allan Poe, "Al Aaraaf," in *The Collected Works of Edgar Allan Poe*, ed. T. O. Mabbott, vol. 1 (Cambridge: Belknap Press of Harvard University Press, 1969), 92–94.

Flipping through the pages, I discovered the single notation: "Poe had died in 1849."[4] Rather than extolling Poe's genius, the magazine gave him one line, and he was angry.

His motive for the letter finally began to make sense.

Though Poe died on October 7, 1849, prior to *Harper's* first magazine issue, Poe expressed great fury at being relegated to what amounted to a footnote. Never short in the ego department, I can imagine his rationale; they might have offered some wiggle room with the dates and included him! After all, his exit, too soon, was a mere three months before the celebratory cut-off dates. Poe had no intention of cutting the publishers any slack. Poe dictated that forceful letter to Lewis Lapham, the editor of *Harper's Magazine* in 2000, in those first moments of my nap writing; bent on redeeming his reputation, he had been long ready to call out his detractors. This slight opened the floodgates. Poe was loaded for bear.

Poe had whispered an additional message during that momentous nap, but I did not understand it. After he had finished dictating his letter, barely pausing, he spit a name in my ear: "Griswold." Unfamiliar with the name and unsure if I had spelled it correctly, I searched the Web and found that Reverend Rufus Wilmot Griswold had lived between 1815–1857. The two men shared a professional relationship and mutual dislike. Yet shortly before his death, surprisingly, Poe instructed his Aunt Maria Clemm that Griswold should be engaged as his literary executor in the event of his death. This appointment would prove to be the greatest of Poe's mistakes. Griswold's libelous "Poe-bituary" ensured Poe's reputation as a penniless, derelict, drunken, drug addict. My discovery of this relationship confirmed that they knew each other.

Days after the experience with the magazine, hoping he would share my enthusiasm, I cautiously read the messages to my now ex-husband. I should have known better. He replied, "Are you drinking?" I was not. To have had to explain the writing-during-the-nap

---

[4] Lewis H. Lapham, "Then and Now," *Harper's Magazine: Celebrating 150 Years of Literature, 1850–2000*, June 2000, 59.

thing would have taken away the magic of the moment. To have had to make some rational sense, at least at that moment, of what I had written was like trying to explain why I had not balanced the checkbook when we were married; it was simply impossible. So my "nap writing," or automatic writing, became my secret.

Fascinated by all things psychic, this seemed, at least I thought, believable. Until that day, I had never written in the style of the language that appeared on the pages in front of me. Had the headache opened me up to contact with intelligence from another unseen world? Was I, as they say in the metaphysical world, being spoken to from the Other Side of the veil? Many years before Poe's message, I realized this gift of mediumship had been developing. Whatever was taking place piqued my curiosity.

Anyone who knows me now would be surprised to discover that I was once somewhat of a skeptic. Following a move to California in the late 1970s, I dipped my toes into metaphysics and the self-awareness trend. Until then, other than the occasional psychic palm reading at a swap meet, metaphysics was a mystery to me. I became fascinated with everything metaphysical. As the years went on, I received precognitive intuitive information in dreams and waking states, day in and day out, most of which were validated. I began to pay serious attention. A spontaneous trip to a metaphysical store in a strip mall changed everything. The experience of a Past Life demonstration by the presenter, Madeleine Gough, altered the course of my life. Until she reached the age of one month shy of ninety-nine, Madeleine mentored me in all aspects of metaphysics and continues to do so from the Other Side, guiding and editing my POEtry.

Aware of my interest in writing, she taught me a practice called automatic hypnotic writing, or inspirational automatic writing (also referred to as psychography writing without conscious intention). It appeared that I had quite an affinity for it. With this new skill, my report writing as a medical speech, language, and hearing specialist improved dramatically. Working for so many years with people who could not communicate somehow resulted in my ability to pull information out of the ethers to help them regain their speech and language skills. Unaware of what was happening, my claircognizant (clear knowing) intuitive skills developed in the background.

Prior to Poe, my earliest forays into automatic writing came as doodles or circles across the top of my paper. Then came the short story "Sock Baby" and its numerous sequels: "Petey's Pocket Surprise" along with my son's favorite "Cow Pies." After my daily meditations, I would anxiously review the notebook in my lap, hoping for otherworldly suggestions. One day upon coming out of my meditation, to my amazement, I had written specific details about an abducted child. I shared the information with the FBI and local police, and as the years passed, I continued to share cold case information with victim's rights attorneys. I can still hear the initial restrained sarcasm in their voices and almost felt their eyes roll as they listened but replied, "Uh, OK lady, if you have any more 'visions,' give us a call." When they got results from my tips, they became serious and asked for more.

Some may wonder how authorship is determined when employing automatic hypnotic writing. Must it come from paranormal communication, a discarnate personality, or as insights from one's own past lives? The simple answer is no. When in a meditative state to quiet the conscious mind, what comes through the writing, typing, or recorded dictation can take many forms such as an improved report or letter writing, solutions to problematic events of the day, or recovery of life memories and events stored in the subconscious mind. In my case, in the beginning, I wrote inspirational or silly children's stories to entertain my toddler. At first, information might begin to come as disconnected fragments, phrases, and drawings before evolving into cohesive prose or poetry. Energy cannot be destroyed. When Poe came to me, I did not "become Poe." Rather, I was "mediumistically" tuned into that which remains vibrationally of the poet Edgar Allan Poe long after his untimely passing.

My dreams became more vivid, and I remembered many more details from that initial visit from Poe. As he started to "come through," I was frozen, yet I felt as if I was greeting an old friend who approached from a distance. I could make out a silhouette—its fine lines—a feathered creature. Surely, I was seeing wings. I saw a raven—the Raven! Unmistakable! It was the very image that I pictured so long ago the first time I read Edgar Allan Poe's poem. My dream raven seemed to be floating mid-air, hovering; the dream began to focus. Oh, I saw it clearly. Then a man, Poe, came into focus. It was that voice; I knew immediately who had spoken. Even in death, Poe was instantly recognizable. I wondered "Why me?" and heard him answer:

We, you and I, had a bond; there was a certain familiarity.

Poe whispered that I was his amanuensis. I had to look up the word—a person employed to write what another dictates. I wondered if this was supposed to be a compliment. His monologue continued for days when he was sure he had my attention. He confided in me:

When I left the physical, there was so much more that I had to say, but I never, at least until now, got the chance. If I were to share my secret, could you possibly think less of me? I think not! Look at what the last centuries of rumors and gossip have done to my reputation.

To be clear, I swear I heard him whisper. I strained a bit as if to bring him closer as I listened for that voice that came from inside my head. At times, it seemed to be right next to me; it felt like a hug from a friend.

Here, in his very words, is how he remembers that afternoon when he came to me:

Having been released of my earthly restrictions, it was during an inauspicious afternoon, a Thursday at 1:30, to be exact, that I made good on my promise. What is true is that the vast majority of this text was dictated or whispered to her during her semi-waking dream state. She, my earthly scribe, was arguing with herself about how to get rid of a nagging headache. I recognized what I thought might be my last chance, and not being one to pass up an obvious opportunity, I saw my way to get even with a few enemies. I spoke through her as she napped.

Except for the fact I found the words staring at me from the blinking computer screen, I would not have believed it. It came so unexpectedly. With a halfhearted attempt to meditate, I had fallen asleep. Poe needed hands to put a pen to paper; he chose mine. There was something about the physicality of pen to paper that connected Poe and me, so I stopped using the computer to transcribe his messages.

For years I wondered why Poe selected me. Then it hit me. When Poe was upset, he sought the comfort of a woman. Perhaps he had found me a good listener, someone willing and able to interpret his latest heavenly self-reflections. Our affinity might have also had something to do with our shared Scots-Irish heritage. Could the similarities have drawn his attention? One of his University of Virginia professors was George Long, which also happens to be my father's, grandfather's, and great-grandfather's name.[5] Moreover, Poe favorably reviewed "Jack Long; or, The Shot in the Eye"; the titular character shares my brother's name.[6] Poe visited, roamed, and wrote about Albany, New York, where I was born and raised. For a time, Poe's "frenemy," Griswold, called Albany his home. My dad graduated from Rensselaer Polytechnic Institute to which Griswold applied but failed to gain admission. I spent much of my college years near Syracuse where Griswold lived and started a newspaper. Lastly, all three of us—Poe, Griswold, and I—lived and worked in New York City and Boston. Did Poe's wayward spirit, trapped between Heaven and Hell, latch onto me during my honeymoon visit to his Baltimore Amity home?

He did not ask permission. Over the following months, his visits continued until he had dictated over sixty-plus poems and a short story. He came to visit without warning and disappeared as suddenly

---

[5] For more on the connection between Poe and George Long, see Mary E. Phillips, *Edgar Allan Poe: The Man* (Chicago: The John C. Winston Co., 1926), 238.

[6] T. O. Mabbott believes that Poe wrote the anonymous column that positively reviewed this story by Charles Wilkins Webber. See Edgar Allan Poe, "Literary," *Evening Mirror,* February 7, 1845, 2, https://www.eapoe.org/works/criticsm/em450204.htm.

as he appeared. I came to understand more and more about his life as I researched what I had written in the dream state. His vocabulary was not my vocabulary; the vernacular was of an earlier age and made little sense. A couple of times, I almost gave up. I struggled with translations and spellings since his messages didn't come with footnotes; I needed an 1828 *Webster's Dictionary*.

On one visit, he offered his motive for visiting me: "Why now, you ask, and why bother? Better to leave Poe dead and buried! His writing is already world-renowned. What more could he want?" He paused, then continued:

> I'm back to clear up a few mistaken facts and attempt to remove a bit of tarnish from my reputation. Now centuries after my death, it's my turn again. I've found a way to speak from the Other Side. I hope to cause a little commotion and exact my long-overdue literary revenge. Minds far greater than mine suggest there is more to understand. Read and listen as this long-dead poet takes over the mind of a sleeping woman.

Poe's intentions were crystal clear; he intended to dictate a book. He chose his topics. His style was serious and irreverent, sharp-tongued, witty, and funny. At times, he spoke in trochaic meter as well as with internal and end rhymes, covering everything from impotence to how potatoes could have killed him! He remarked upon Shakespeare, Dante, and his contemporaries.

Once it became apparent that neither he nor I had a clue about putting the chapters together for the book we would publish, I became exasperated and kept asking him what to do next. He suggested, "Ask George for a little help; he's a bit more current. George Plimpton and I have a lot in common." I discovered that George Ames Plimpton was an American writer, founder, and literary editor of *The Paris Review*. While Poe and I settled into our regularly scheduled 1:30 meditations, we also attempted contact with Editor Plimpton using a process called remote viewing, a branch of parapsychology involving mental telepathy to view targeted objects; it would be like giving George an energetic tap on the shoulder to get his attention—nothing creepy. Our attempts were met with silence.

Though I had found that, at times, I was able to get inspiration from the ethers and tap into what I like to call a "collective consciousness" of present-day or otherworldly experts, I did not meet George Plimpton in the flesh until 2002 at the annual *Los Angeles Times* Festival of Books. Walking through the crowd, Mr. Plimpton passed me, but he stopped and asked, "So, what are you writing about, friend?" He was genuinely interested when I told him I was a medium and I was writing a book with messages I had received from the deceased Edgar Allan Poe. He responded, "Oh, can you recite a bit to me?" He listened intently and shared that he always felt Poe was a sincere but troubled fellow, adding, "His tales were so creepy." When I finished reciting a few lines from my book, Mr. Plimpton, in his gentle, enthusiastic way, said, "Now THAT is true participatory journalism. I would like to write you a blurb for your jacket. Please stay in touch and call me." Plimpton passed on to his next adventure in 2003; he never got to read my finished product. I will always fondly remember our chance encounter. I heard his voice once more as he now holds his literary salon on the Other Side. I am confident that Poe is in attendance.

I think about how death must have been a complete shock to Poe when he left so suddenly. Making a strong case for life after death, he offered himself as a prime example:

> Wondering, are you? What evidence would you accept that would convince you that there is more to me? There is an afterlife, and we are all still connected. What evidence would it take for you to accept from me or all the others who continually try to prove it to you? Will you suspend disbelief and allow me to demonstrate that there is more that follows life? Let my message carry through this vast universe and across infinite space. There is more beyond what you presently understand of life and death and communication between the two.

> In summoning my courage and passion for reconciling science and reason with faith, my goal is truth, not deception. In coming here, I hope to finally rest in the peaceful sleep of angels.

Before I do, let me just say: This isn't the half of it!

He would return to his theme of literary revenge at times, admitting

I have yet to completely free myself from a lingering contempt toward my literary peers. Heaven knows I've tried to let it go and forgive them. Great restraint, never my strong suit, I'd vowed payback. Admittedly, it surprises me that I can finally speak my piece, though uncharacteristically for me, a heavenly-tempered version.

While others thought the visits were creepy, I enjoyed myself tremendously. When his messages ended up on the pages in front of me, I was thrilled. I suddenly became pretty full of myself and could not resist doing a Web search to see if anyone else had done what I had done. I was shocked, upset, and a little bit jealous that a woman by the name of Lizzie Doten, a Spiritualist, beat me to it about twelve years after Poe died. I fumed, realizing I was in love with a dead man and jealous of a dead woman. Admittedly, Poe laughed at Spiritualist beliefs during his life, yet his Gothic inclinations made him a magnet for those who believe that the spirits of those who have passed can communicate with the living.

The messages eventually stopped. Met with silence, I finally asked, "Why me, and why now?" I heard one final whisper. Ever the jokester, he whispered, "It's just a bit of mind medicine for being in the 'write' place! Selfish or selfless? Simply, I did it for me, not for you. Lighten up!"

When I share my Poe experiences with others, people often ask me what it was like when these occurred. For me, it was like a dream, and instead of having conversations, I was trapped, listening to a lengthy monologue! Seriously, he never let me get a word in edgewise. In addition, people want to know about the topics Poe chose to discuss, which included exacting revenge against his foster father (John Allan) and Griswold; wistful reminiscences of loves; and a few nagging misunderstandings. He eulogized some women writers, lambasted others, and crucified Elizabeth Ellet with a few well-articulated stanzas for instigating the scandal that permanently tarnished his literary and personal reputations. Most astounding were his poems addressing how he had died, focusing on his stay in Washington Medical College and revealing to me the mystery of his last words.

Recently, while working as a medical speech pathologist at a local hospital, my Poe story took an even more bizarre turn. One morning, my assignment on the med-surg floor involved checking admissions with doctors' orders for language and swallow evaluations. Patient chart in hand, I walked into Room 304, glancing at the name: Edgar Allan Poe! An attempt at hiding my shock and delight did not work. Noticing my reaction, Mr. Poe just smiled and nodded knowingly. I would love to have questioned him about his connection to our poet. Was he related? How did he receive this infamous name? Unfortunately, having suffered a recent stroke, he was bedbound and experiencing cognitive, swallowing, and language impairments; therefore, he could not talk. Medically stable that afternoon, he was transferred to a rehabilitation center for therapy, ending what might have made for a more dramatic conclusion to my Poe story.

Do thoughts continue when we die? Is there some eternal connection that binds all souls? I did not know Poe before his visits during my meditations, but I do now. Our conversations explored the secrets of his muse that made him a great poet and mesmerizing storyteller. I can say with certainty that those creative juices flowing through his every fiber remain today as vibrational energies he longs to share. The poem that follows is part of a series of channeled works from the late Edgar Allan Poe, through the medium of automatic writing. Poe's attention to detail was unequaled. When I reread this poem recently, I noticed Poe had chosen the title "Then and Now." This title just happened to be the name of the *Harper's* article that provoked his ire enough to speak to me in the first place.

Then and Now

"Ye who read are still among the living; but I who write shall
have long since gone my way into the region of shadows. For
indeed strange things shall happen"
　　　　"Shadow—A Parable," E.A. Poe[7]

True to theory of once I spoke a little more of me
A course that might set some to trembling

From where I sit, no mortal now
The thoughts so easily pared
From human emotions un-pure
I struggle no longer with a painful soul

Understand, I struggle less
From images that made me known
All of you, with eyes yet left to read
See, there is a fairer more

Some dozing deacons, I suppose, give comfort
And speak of sweet repose
A more they should be shouting
There is much, much more in forever
While even I spoke and believed it so
A death, more aptly, passing
Is grander than ever I allowed

Pen and ink, the practical tools
Are my encumbrances no longer
If it seems to some a form is broken
Then let us set to pondering
This rather serves a seaming between life once lived
And that which celebrates my now
Literary urges are never stilled

---

[7] Edgar Allan Poe, "Shadow—A Parable," in *The Collected Works of Edgar
Allan Poe*, ed. T. O. Mabbott, vol. 2 (Cambridge: Belknap Press of Harvard University Press, 1978), 188–189.

Though the chapters closed by one's mere passing

So, summarize complaints and questions
Mere mortals might compose
Line up, as once my words would do
Throw cautions to the wind and follow
That which comes in the aftermath of death
Is simply a pause, inhale, exhale
Then a continuation or going on
Forevermore.

CONTRIBUTORS

JOSÉ ALEJANDRO ACOSTA earned his BA in English Literature at the University of Maryland and a Master of Communication degree in Film and Television at Georgia State University. He has worked as an Emmy award-winning filmmaker in the Atlanta, Georgia, area for over twenty years. He is currently a full-time Lecturer in Entertainment Business at Kennesaw State University.

TIM BEASLEY is an accomplished live stage, multi-media, and film actor coast to coast in a career spanning 35 years. He is well known nationally for his "supernatural" knack of portraying over 100+ famous identities from history, music, movies, film, and literature. See them all on his website, www.VegasTributes.com.

AMY BRANAM ARMIENTO is professor of English at Frostburg State University, and she is immediate past president of the Poe Studies Association. Many of her publications and invited lectures focus on the treatment of women in nineteenth-century short stories and poems, including her co-edited book *Poe and Women: Recognition and Revision* (Lehigh, 2023).

MARK DAWIDZIAK is the author or editor of 25 books, including Edgar Award-nominated *A Mystery of Mysteries: The Death and Life of Edgar Allan Poe* and three studies of landmark television series: *The Columbo Phile: A Casebook*, *The Night Stalker Companion*, and *Everything I Need to Know I Learned in The Twilight Zone*, his lighthearted 2017 tribute to Rod Serling's classic anthology series. He also is an internationally recognized Mark Twain scholar, and five of his books are about the iconic American writer. He spent 43 years as a television, film, and theater critic at such newspapers as the *Akron Beacon Journal* and the *Cleveland Plain Dealer*. His work on the horror side of the street also includes the novel *Grave Secrets, The Bedside, Bathtub & Armchair Companion to Dracula*, short stories, and comic book scripts. He lives in Ohio.

THOMAS DEVANEY is a Pew Fellow in the Arts and the author of five books, including *Getting to Philadelphia: New and Selected Poems* (Hanging Loose Press, 2019). He is also the writer and co-director of the film *Bicentennial City* (2020), which explores the legacy of Philadelphia's 1976 Bicentennial celebration. In 2024, he earned his master's degree in Urban Design from Drexel University with a thesis titled "Reimagining Urban Parks: Philadelphia's Hidden Olmsted Park." He teaches creative writing at Haverford College and works at the Lindy Institute for Urban Innovation at Drexel University.

ANDY DUNCAN'S honors for science fiction and fantasy include a Nebula Award, a Theodore Sturgeon Memorial Award, and three World Fantasy Awards. His latest collection is *An Agent of Utopia: New and Selected Stories* from Small Beer Press and Recorded Books. He lives in the Maryland mountains, where he is a professor of writing at Frostburg State University.

ENRICA JANG is Executive Director at Poe Baltimore / The Edgar Allan Poe House & Museum in Baltimore. She is director of the International Edgar Allan Poe Festival & Awards, featuring the *Saturday Visiter* Awards, a new honor recognizing outstanding creative works adapting or inspired by the life and writing of Edgar Allan Poe. An enthusiast long before she joined Poe House, Enrica has both written and edited books, graphic novels, and anthologies inspired by Poe's works.

DEAN KNIGHT is a regional stage actor and Standardized Patient in Richmond, Virginia. He was in charge of group tours and programs at the Poe Museum for seven years.

LEVI LELAND is a Rhode Island-based Edgar Allan Poe enthusiast with a special focus on Sarah Helen Whitman and her relationship with Poe. He created "A Walking Tour of Poe's Providence," which he guides annually. For more information, visit his website at edgarallanpoeri.com.

LU ANN YOUNG MARSHALL serves as Tour Director for Westminster Graveyard & Catacombs in Baltimore, Maryland. She is Special Events Coordinator at the University of Maryland Francis King Carey School of Law.

ROGER MCCORMACK, Director of Education at The Bronx County Historical Society, is a writer, farmer, lecturer, and tour leader. He is a graduate of Merrimack College and has a master's degree in American history from Monmouth University, where his thesis focused on the antebellum United States and the Civil War. Above all, he is a dutiful steward of Edgar Allan Poe's legacy.

EMILY MICHAEL earned Bachelor of Science in English and Master of Arts in Teaching degrees from Frostburg State University. She currently teaches and resides in Cumberland, Maryland.

IAN MUNESHWAR is a Nebula-, Locus-, and Shirley Jackson Award-nominated horror writer and 2022 recipient of the Horror Writers Association's Diversity Grant. He has taught writing through Brandeis University, Tufts University, and the Clarion West Writers' Workshop. He currently resides in Boston.

CHRISTINE NEULIEB is the editorial director of Lanternfish Press, an independent publisher of gothic and speculative fiction based in Philadelphia. She lives in South Philly with her husband, their dog, and a black cat who is definitely not undead and seeking revenge.

JAMISON ODONE is an accomplished author and artist residing in Maryland. As an Associate Professor of Illustration at Frostburg State University, he shares his expertise with budding talents. Odone's imaginative creations have graced the pages of numerous publications and exhibitions, captivating audiences with their unique storytelling. His recent contributions include the graphic novels *The Man in the Painter's Room* (Black Panel Press, 2021) and *My First Pandemic* (Black Panel Press, 2022), as well as the evocative collection of illustrated poems titled *Mill Town Sonnets* (Bottlecap Press, 2023).

JESSICA L. OSNOE still prefers to read Poe's stories in broad daylight, despite having taught his work in high school and college classrooms for the past fourteen years. She is a proud alumna of Campbell University (BA) and North Carolina State University (MA) and currently shares her love of language and literature with students in her hometown of Fayetteville.

DEBORAH T. PHILLIPS grew up just outside Richmond, Virginia, which she still calls home. She completed her history degree at Salem College in Winston-Salem, North Carolina, and has worked for over fifteen years in the field of public history. She is the owner and operator of History Lives, LLC, specializing in living history programming and tours.

STEFANIE ROCKNAK is a sculptor and philosopher. She is the author of *Imagined Causes: Hume's Conception of Objects* and the creator of the bronze statue of Edgar Allan Poe in Boston, MA. She is also Chair and Professor of Philosophy at Hartwick College, where she teaches courses on philosophy of mind, philosophy of art, and David Hume.

MARYBETH "MB" SCHADE, N.D., M.A., is an Intuitive Evidential Medium and Holistic Wellness Practitioner. She incorporates a doctorate and a master's degree with her forty years of experience as a Medical Speech/Language/Hearing Specialist in the Western medical field and the Complimentary Alternative Healing Arts of Homeopathy, Naturopathy, Hypnosis, and Human Design. Her channeled "POE-try" was awarded an honorable mention by James River

Writers and the Poe Museum, 2018 Poe Museum's Birthday Bash. She has a particular interest in Automatic Writing.

CHRISTOPHER P. SEMTNER is the curator of the Edgar Allan Poe Museum in Richmond, Virginia, and has written several books and articles about Poe, visual art, cryptography, puzzles, and history with his work appearing in Crime Writers' Chronicle, Biography.com, and Cat Fancy. He has presented on exhibit design for the Virginia Association of Museums and curated exhibits for institutions across the United States.

JASON STRUTZ is a writer and illustrator currently working on *Returned*, a medieval family action horror with zombies, at Patreon.com/strutzart. His 2023 finalist Ten for All stage play, *The Night Porter*, is currently serialized in his newsletter, with signup at Strutzart.com. Along with *The House of Montresor*, he has also illustrated comics with Red Stylo Media, Full Moon Comix, Action Lab, and more. He is also an illustrator of monsters for various Role Playing Game publishers.

MILITIA VOX is an award-winning music + visual artist, actress, and producer who has recorded/performed with Cyndi Lauper, Twisted Sister, Rob Halford (Judas Priest), Living Colour, Nancy Sinatra, John Petrucci (Dream Theater), L7, Paul Shaffer, and more. M is a host and former VJ for FUSE, MTV2, VH1 and Much Music USA. This Alt. Rock/Metal badass is a trailblazing singer, songwriter, composer, and musician. Dubbed "one of the greatest rock voices," she performs all over the world—from Carnegie Hall to the world's largest festivals. MV lives in NYC.

INDEX

Jerome, Jeff, 167, 177, 254, 255, 262, 263
John Hay Library, *See* Brown University
John H. Watson, Dr., *See* Doyle, Arthur Conan
Jones, James Earl, 74
Judy Hopps, 244

Kafer, Peter, 121, 122, 122n7, 122n8, 122n9; *Charles Brockden Brown's Revolution and the Birth of American Gothic*, 121, 122n7, 122n8, 122n9
Karloff, Boris, 208
Kaufelt, Keith, 50
Kaufman, Charlie, 27; *Adaptation*, 27
Keepers, 252
Keitel, Harvey, 25
Kelly, Grace, 25
Kelly, James Patrick, 231
Kelly Writers House, 125, 125n16, 127n21
Kessel, John, 231, 232
Kidd, William, Captain, 224, 227
Kim Dokja, 246
King, Ana Ines, 52
King Lear, *See* Shakespeare, William
King, Stephen, 67, 67n9, 210, 217, 217n6; "Jaunt," 67, 67n9
Knives Out, 244, 247n10

La Bohème, *See* Giacomo Puccini
Lafayette, Marquis de (Gilbert du Motier), 13
Lanternfish Press, 113, 114, 118
La Pasion de Poe, *See* Latin Ballet of Virginia
Lapham, Lewis, 274, 276, 276n3
Largely Literary Theater Company, *See* Dawidziak, Mark
Larson, Jonathan, 111, 111n3
Latin Ballet of Virginia, 52; *La Pasion de Poe*, 52; *Poemas*, 52
Lee, Robert E., 59
Lee, Spike, 23
Les Miserables, *See* Hugo, Victor

Lewisburg Literary Festival, 272
Lewis, Paul, 101
Lewton, Val, 225, 228
Library of Virginia, 51
Light in August, *See* Faulkner, William
Lisella, Maria, 190
London (England), 185, 229
Londonderry (Ireland), 13
Long Island (NY), 179, 180, 207
Lorca, Frederico García, 52
Los Angeles (CA), 234, 270
Los Angeles Times Festival of Books, 282
Loudon Park Cemetery, 7
Loving, Kelly, 94
Lowell (MA), 174
Lowell, James Russell, 98
Lucas, George, 22, 25; *Star Wars*, 22
Lynch, Anne Charlotte, 163

Macko, Stephen, 46
Magritte, René, 182
Mailer, Norman, 186
Mammoth Book of Secret Codes and Cryptograms, *See* Dunin, Elonka
Manhattan (NY), 57, 179, 180, 183, 255
Man in the Painter's Room, *See* Odone, Jamison
Manson Family, 223
Manzarek, Ray, 270
Marshall, John, Supreme Court Chief Justice, 51
Maryland Historical Society, 9, 16
Maryland Institute College of Art (MICA), 81
Mason's Cove (VA), 268
Masque of the Red Death (film), *See* Corman, Roger
McClain, B. Paul, 37
McDaniel, Lurlene, 108
Mean Streets, *See* Scorsese, Martin
Méliès, George, 24, 24n2; *Trip to the Moon*, 24, 24n2
Melling, Harry, 27
Memento Mori, *See* Depeche Mode
Miami (FL), 270

University of Virginia, 46, 158, 280
USA Today, 50

Valentine Cottage, 14, *See also* Edgar
  Allan Poe Cottage
Valentine Vault, 14
Vance, Raymond Green, 94
van Gogh, Theodore, 76
van Gogh, Vincent, 74-76, 76n3, 79
Verne, Jules, 24, 24n2; *From the Earth to
  the Moon*, 24, 24n2
Verona (Italy), 32
Vertigo, See Hitchcock, Alfred
Vidal, Gore, 186, 187n6
Villainess, See VOX, MILITIA
Vincennes (IN), 272
  "Vincent" (short film), *See* Burton,
  Tim
Virginia Commonwealth University,
  60, 64; School of Medicine, 60, 64;
  School of Nursing, 66
Virginia Museum of Fine Arts, 56
VOX, MILITIA, "BORN OUT OF
  DARKNESS," 257-258, 258n3;
  "NYCTOPHILIA," 259, 259n4;
  "Raven," 260-261, 261n6; "THIS
  IS SHE," 259-260, 260n5; *Villain-
  ess*, 257, 257n2

Walking Dead, 29
Walking Tour of Poe's Providence, 171-
  175, 177
Wallace, William Ross, 216
Wall Street Journal, 222, 222n1
Walters Art Museum, Baltimore, 271
Washington, DC, *See* District of Co-
  lumbia
Washington, George, 13, 153
Washington Medical College, 14, 284
Waters, John, 261
Waxdoll, Willow, 263
Wednesday (Netflix series), 1
Wednesday Addams, 254
Weird Tales, 224
Welles, Orson, 183

Westminster Hall, *See* Westminster
  Hall and Burying Ground
Westminster Hall and Burying
  Ground, 7, 8, 9, 11, 13, 15, 82, 218,
  254, 262, 271
Westminster Presbyterian Church and
  Graveyard, *See* Westminster Hall
  and Burying Ground
Westminster Preservation Trust, 7, 8,
  16
West Point (NY), 17, 28, 188
White, Eliza, 157
White, Thomas Willis, 42, 42n1
Whitman, John Winslow, 170
Whitman, Sarah Helen, 49, 169, 170-
  175, 171n5, 176, 177; *Edgar Poe
  and His Critics*, 176
Whitman, Walt, 49
Whitney Biennial, 133, 133n30
Wiene, Robert, 199; *Cabinet of Dr. Ca-
  ligari*, 198
Wilde, Oscar, 271
Williamsburg (VA), 41
Williams, Roger, 170
Williams, William Carlos, 121, 121n4
Wilson, Gahan, 232-234
Wishbone, 242, 242n7, 243
Wolf Man, 207
Wollstonecraft, Mary, 239
"Woman in Crowd" (sculpture), *See*
  Rocknak, Stefanie
"Woman on a Train" (sculpture), *See*
  Rocknak, Stefanie
Wonderful Wizard of Oz, See Baum, L.
  Frank
Woodard, Isaac, 223
Wordsworth, William, 239
World Fantasy Award, 228
Wright Brothers, 125
Wright, Richard, 152

Yale University Library, 124, 125n14
Your Turn To Die (game), 245

Zootopia, 244